MY LIFE AND THOUGHT

BY ALBERT SCHWEITZER

FROM MY AFRICAN NOTEBOOK
MEMOIRS OF CHILDHOOD AND YOUTH
CHRISTIANITY AND THE RELIGIONS OF THE WORLD
George Allen & Unwin

ON THE EDGE OF THE PRIMEVAL FOREST
MORE FROM THE PRIMEVAL FOREST
THE MYSTERY OF THE KINGDOM OF GOD
THE QUEST OF THE HISTORICAL JESUS
PAUL AND HIS INTERPRETERS
THE MYSTICISM OF PAUL THE APOSTLE
THE DECAY AND THE RESTORATION OF CIVILIZATION
CIVILIZATION AND ETHICS
J. S. BACH
A. & C. Black

GUILD BOOKS No. 478

ALBERT SCHWEITZER

MY LIFE
AND THOUGHT

AN AUTOBIOGRAPHY

TRANSLATED BY C. T. CAMPION, M.A.

Guild Books

Published for
THE BRITISH PUBLISHERS GUILD LIMITED
by George Allen & Unwin Ltd. Museum Street, London

The German original, "Aus Meinem Leben und Denken,"
was published by the Felix Meiner Verlag, Leipzig, in
1931

FIRST PUBLISHED IN ENGLISH FEBRUARY 1933
SECOND IMPRESSION APRIL 1933
THIRD IMPRESSION JULY 1933
FOURTH IMPRESSION 1934
FIFTH IMPRESSION 1935
SIXTH IMPRESSION 1946
SEVENTH IMPRESSION 1948
SECOND EDITION WITH A NEW CHAPTER   EIGHTH IMPRESSION 1954
FIRST PUBLISHED IN *Guild Books* 1955

Made and printed in Great Britain by C. Tinling & Co. Ltd.
Liverpool, London and Prescot

CONTENTS

CHAPTER   PAGE

I.   CHILDHOOD, SCHOOL, AND UNIVERSITY   9

II.   PARIS AND BERLIN, 1898-1899   21

III.   THE FIRST YEARS OF ACTIVITY IN STRASSBURG   28

IV.   STUDY OF THE LAST SUPPER AND THE LIFE OF JESUS, 1900-1902   35

V.   TEACHING ACTIVITIES AT THE UNIVERSITY. THE QUEST OF THE HISTORICAL JESUS   44

VI.   THE HISTORICAL JESUS AND THE CHRISTIANITY OF TO-DAY   52

VII.   THE BACH BOOK—FRENCH AND GERMAN EDITIONS   60

VIII.   ON ORGANS AND ORGAN-BUILDING   68

IX.   I RESOLVE TO BECOME A JUNGLE DOCTOR   80

X.   MY MEDICAL STUDIES, 1905-1912   92

XI.   PREPARATIONS FOR AFRICA   103

XII.   LITERARY WORK DURING MY MEDICAL COURSE   108

XIII.   FIRST ACTIVITIES IN AFRICA, 1913-1917   125

XIV.   GARAISON AND S. RÉMY   147

XV.   BACK IN ALSACE   157

XVI.   PHYSICIAN AND PREACHER IN STRASSBURG   162

XVII.   THE BOOK OF AFRICAN REMINISCENCES   167

XVIII.   GÜNSBACH AND JOURNEYS ABROAD   174

XIX.   THE SECOND PERIOD IN AFRICA, 1924-1927   181

XX.   TWO YEARS IN EUROPE. THIRD TIME IN AFRICA   188

XXI.   EPILOGUE   194

   POSTSCRIPT, 1932-1949   215

CHAPTER I

CHILDHOOD, SCHOOL, AND UNIVERSITY

I WAS born on January 14th, 1875, at Kaysersberg in Upper Alsace, the second child of Louis Schweitzer who was shepherding just then the little flock of evangelical believers in that Catholic place. My paternal grandfather was schoolmaster and organist at Pfaffenhofen in Lower Alsace, and three of his brothers occupied similar posts. My mother Adele, (*née* Schillinger) was a daughter of the Pastor of Mühlbach in the Münster Valley, Upper Alsace.

A few weeks after my birth my father moved to Günsbach in the Münster Valley, where with my three sisters and one brother I lived through a very happy childhood and youth, unclouded but for the frequent illnesses of my father. His health improved, however, later on, and as a sturdy septuagenarian he looked after his parish during the war under the fire of the French guns which swept the valley from the heights of the Vosges mountains, making victims of many a house and many an inhabitant of Günsbach. He died in ripe old age in 1925. My mother was knocked down and killed in 1916 by cavalry horses on the road between Günsbach and Weier-im-Tal.

When I was five years old my father began giving me music lessons on the old square piano which we had inherited from grandfather Schillinger. He had no great technical skill, but improvised charmingly. When I was seven I surprised our schoolmistress by playing hymntunes on the harmonium with harmonies which I supplied myself. At eight, when my legs were hardly long enough to reach the pedals, I began to play the organ. My passion for that instrument was inherited from my grandfather Schillinger, who had been much interested in organs and organ-building, and, as my mother told me had the reputation of improvising magnificently. In any town that he visited, the first thing he did was to get to know its organs, and when the famous organ was placed in the Stiftskirche

A*

at Lucerne he made a journey thither in order to see its builder at work.

I was nine years old when for the first time I took the place of the organist for a service at Günsbach.

Till the autumn of 1884 I went to the Günsbach village school. After that I was for a year at the 'Realschule' (which is a secondary school giving no instruction in the dead languages) at Münster, and there I had private lessons in Latin to prepare me for entering the Fifth Form in the Gymnasium. In the autumn of 1885 I entered the Gymnasium at Mülhausen in Alsace. My godfather, Louis Schweitzer, my grandfather's half-brother, who was Director of the primary schools in that town, was kind enough to take me to live with him. Otherwise my father, who had nothing beyond his slender stipend on which to bring up his large family, could hardly have afforded to send me to a Gymnasium.

The strict discipline under which I came in the house of my great-uncle and his wife, who had no children of their own, was very good for me. It is with deep gratitude that I constantly think of all the kindness I received from them.

Although it had cost me some trouble to learn to read and write, I had got on fairly well in school at Günsbach and Münster. At the Gymnasium, however, I was at first a poor scholar. This was not due solely to my being slack and dreamy, but partly also to the fact that my private lessons in Latin had not prepared me sufficiently for the Fifth Form, in which I entered the school. It was only when my form-master in the Fourth, Dr. Wehmann, showed me how to work properly and gave me some self-confidence, that things went better. But Dr. Wehmann's influence over me was due above all to the fact, of which I became aware during my first days in his form, that he most carefully prepared beforehand every lesson that he gave. He became to me a model of fulfilment of duty. I visited him many times in later life. When, towards the end of the war, I went to Strassburg, where he lived for the latter part of his life, I at once enquired for him. I learnt, however, that privation had ruined his nervous system and that he had taken his own life.

For music-master at Mülhausen I had Eugène Münch, the young organist at the Reformed Church of S. Stephen. This was his first post on leaving the High School of Music at Berlin where he had been seized by the then awakening enthusiasm for Bach. I owe it to him that I became acquainted in my early years with the works of the Cantor of S. Thomas's and from my fifteenth year onwards enjoyed the privilege of sound instruction on the organ. When in the autumn of 1898 he died of typhoid fever in the flower of his age, I perpetuated his memory in a small booklet written in French. It was published in Mülhausen, and was the first product of my pen to appear in print.[1]

At the Gymnasium I was chiefly interested in history and natural science. Our history teacher was Dr. Kaufmann, brother of the Breslau historian. Natural science we were taught splendidly by Dr. Förster.

In languages and mathematics it cost me an effort to accomplish anything. But after a time I felt a certain fascination in mastering subjects for which I had no special talent. So in the upper forms I was reckoned one of the better scholars, though not one of the best. With essays, however, if I remember right, I was usually the top boy.

In the 'Prima' we were taken in Latin and Greek by the distinguished Director of the Gymnasium, Wilhelm Deecke of Lübeck. His lessons were not the dry instruction of a mere linguist, but they introduced us to ancient philosophy, and he was thereby enabled to give us glimpses of the thought of modern times. He was an enthusiastic follower of Schopenhauer.

On June 18th, 1893 I passed the leaving examination. In the written papers I did not cut a brilliant figure, not even in the essay. In the *viva voce*, however, I attracted the notice of the president of the board of examiners. Dr. Albrecht of Strassburg, by my knowledge of history and my historical judgment. My otherwise rather mediocre leaving-certificate was, at his instance, adorned with an 'Excellent' in history, substantiated by the reasons for this high praise.

In October of this year, the generosity of my father's

[1] *Eugène Münch*, 1898, 28 pages. (Brinkman, Mülhausen, Alsace.)

elder brother, who was in business in Paris, secured for me the privilege of instruction on the organ from the Parisian organist, Charles Marie Widor. My teacher at Mülhausen had brought me on so well, that after hearing me play Widor took me as a pupil, although he normally confined his instruction to the members of the Organ Class at the Conservatoire. This instruction was for me an event of decisive importance. Widor led me on to a fundamental improvement of my technique, and made me strive to attain to perfect plasticity in playing. At the same time there dawned on me, thanks to him, the meaning of the architectonic in music.

My first lesson from Widor happened to be on the sunny October day on which the Russian sailors under Admiral Avellan entered Paris for the visit which was the first manifestation of the Franco-Russian friendship that was then beginning. I was delayed by the closely packed, expectant crowds which filled the Boulevards and the central streets, and was very late in reaching the master's house.

At the end of October 1893 I became a student at Strassburg University. I lived in the theological College of S. Thomas (the Collegium Wilhelmitanum), the Principal of which was the learned Rev. Alfred Erichson. Just at that time he was occupied in completing his great edition of the works of Calvin.

Strassburg University was then at the height of its reputation. Unhampered by tradition, teachers and students alike strove to realize the ideal of a modern University. There were hardly any professors of advanced age on the teaching staff. A fresh breeze of youthfulness penetrated everywhere.

I took up the two subjects of Theology and Philosophy together. As I had learnt in the Gymnasium only the elements of Hebrew, my first term was spoilt by the work for the 'Hebraicum' (the preliminary examination in Hebrew), which I passed with much effort on February 17th, 1894. Later, spurred on again by the endeavour to master what did not come easily to me, I acquired a sound knowledge of that language.

Anxiety about the 'Hebraicum' did not prevent me from zealous attendance at a course of lectures by Heinrich Julius Holtzmann on the Synoptists—that is to say the three first Gospels—and others by Wilhelm Windelband and Theobald Ziegler on the History of Philosophy.

On April 1st, 1894, I began my year of military service, but the kindness of my captain, Krull by name, made it possible for me, during the periods of regular routine, to be at the University by eleven o'clock almost every day, and so to attend Windelband's lectures.

When in the autumn we went on manœuvres in the neighbourhood of Hochfelden (Lower Alsace), I put my Greek Testament in my haversack. I may explain that at the beginning of the winter term those theological students who wished to compete for a scholarship had to pass an examination in three subjects. Those, however, who were then doing their military service had only to take one. I chose the Synoptic Gospels.

It was to avoid disgracing myself in the eyes of a teacher whom I respected so much as I did Holtzmann by my performance in his subject, that I took my Greek Testament with me to the manœuvres, and being then so robust that I did not know what fatigue was, I was able to get through some real work in the evenings and on the rest-days. During the summer I had gone through Holtzmann's commentary. Now I wanted to get a knowledge of the text, and see how much I remembered of his commentary and his lectures. This had for me a remarkable result. Holtzmann had gained recognition in scientific circles for the Marcan hypothesis, that is, the theory that Mark's Gospel is the oldest, and that its plan underlies those of Matthew and Luke. That seemed to justify the conclusion that the activities of Jesus can be understood from Mark's Gospel only. By this conclusion I felt, to my astonishment, sorely puzzled when on a certain rest-day which we spent in the village of Guggenheim, I concentrated on the tenth and eleventh chapters of Matthew, and became conscious of the significance of what is narrated in these two chapters by him alone, and not by Mark as well.

In Matthew x the mission of the Twelve is narrated. In the discourse with which He sends them out Jesus tells them that they will almost immediately have to undergo severe persecution. But they suffer nothing of the kind.

He tells them also that the appearance of the Son of Man will take place before they have gone through the cities of Israel, which can only mean that the celestial, Messianic Kingdom will be revealed while they are thus engaged. He has, therefore, no expectation of seeing them return.

How comes it that Jesus leads His disciples to expect events about which the remaining portion of the narrative is silent?

I was dissatisfied with Holtzmann's explanation that we are dealing not with an historical discourse of Jesus, but with one made up at a later period, after His death, out of various "Sayings of Jesus." A later generation would never have gone so far as to put into His mouth words which were belied by the subsequent course of events.

The bare text compelled me to assume that Jesus really announced persecutions for the disciples and, as a sequel to them, the immediate appearance of the celestial Son of Man, and that His announcement was shown by subsequent events to be wrong. But how came He to entertain such an expectation, and what must His feelings have been when events turned out otherwise than He had assumed they would?

Matthew xi records the Baptist's question to Jesus, and the answer which Jesus sent back to him. Here too it seemed to me that Holtzmann and the commentators in general do not sufficiently appreciate the riddles of the text. Whom does the Baptist mean when he asks Jesus whether He is the "one who is to come?" (ὁ ἐρχόμενος). Is it then quite certain, I asked myself, that by the Coming One no one can be meant except the Messiah? According to late-Jewish Messianic beliefs the coming of the Messiah is to be preceded by that of his Forerunner, Elijah, risen from the dead, and to this previously-expected Elijah Jesus applies the expression the Coming One, when He tells the disciples (Matt. xi. 14) that the Baptist himself is Elijah who is to come. Therefore, so I concluded, the Baptist in his question used the expression with that same meaning. He did not send his disciples to Jesus with the question whether He was the Messiah; he wanted to learn from Him, strange as this may seem to us, whether he was the expected Forerunner of the Messiah, Elijah.

But why does Jesus not give him a plain answer to his question? To say that He gave the evasive answer He did give in order to test the Baptist's faith is only an outcome of the embarrassment of commentators, and has opened the way for many bad sermons. It is much simpler to assume that Jesus avoided saying either Yes or No because He was not yet ready to make public Whom He believed Himself to be. From every point of view the account of the Baptist's question proves that at that time none of those who believed in Jesus held Him to be the Messiah. Had He already been accepted in any way as the Messiah, the Baptist would have so framed his question as to imply that fact.

I was also driven into new paths of interpretation by Jesus saying to the disciples after the departure of the Baptist's messengers, that of all born of women John was the greatest, but that the least in the Kingdom of Heaven was greater than he (Matt. xi. 11).

The usual explanation, that Jesus expressed in these words a criticism of the Baptist and placed him at a lower level than the believers in His teaching who were assembled round Him as adherents of the Kingdom of God, seemed to me both unsatisfying and crude, for these believers were also born of women. By giving up this explanation I was driven to the assumption that in contrasting the Baptist with members of the Kingdom of God Jesus was taking into account the difference between the natural world and the supernatural, Messianic world. As a man in the condition into which all men enter at birth the Baptist is the greatest of all who have ever lived. But members of the Kingdom of Heaven are no longer natural men; through the dawn of the Messianic Kingdom they have experienced a change which has raised them to a supernatural condition akin to that of the angels. Because they are now supernatural beings the least among them is greater than the greatest man who has ever appeared in the natural world of the age which is now passing away. John the Baptist does, indeed, belong to this Kingdom either as a great or a humble member of it. But a unique greatness, surpassing that of all other human beings, is his only in his natural mode of existence.

Thus was I, at the end of my first year at the University, landed in perplexity about the explanation then accepted as historically correct of the words and actions of Jesus when He sent out the disciples on their mission, and as a consequence of this about the wider question of the conception of the whole life of Jesus which was then regarded as history. When I reached home after the manœuvres entirely new horizons had opened themselves to me. Of this I was certain: that Jesus had announced no kingdom that was to be founded and realized in the natural world by Himself and the believers, but one that was to be expected as coming with the almost immediate dawn of a supernatural age.

I should of course have held it an impertinence to hint to Holtzmann in my examination which came on shortly afterwards that I distrusted the conception of the life of Jesus which he maintained, and which was universally accepted by the critical school of that time. But, indeed, I had no opportunity of doing so. With his well-known good nature he treated me so gently, as being a young student and hindered also from hard work by my military service, that in the interview of twenty minutes he demanded from me nothing beyond a summary comparison of the contents of the first three Gospels.

During my remaining years at the University I occupied myself, often to the neglect of my other subjects, with independent research into the Synoptic question and the problems of the life of Jesus, coming ever more and more confidently to the conviction that the key to the puzzles that are awaiting solution is to be looked for in the explanation of the words of Jesus when He sent out the disciples on their mission, in the question sent by the Baptist from his prison, and, further, in the way Jesus acts on the return of the disciples.

What a matter for thankfulness I felt it that the German University does not keep the student so completely in leading strings in his studies, nor so much on the strain by constant examination as is the case in other countries, but offers him opportunity for independent scientific work!

The Strassburg theological faculty of that day had a distinctly liberal character. Associated with Holtzmann was Karl Budde, the Old Testament specialist, who had recently come to Strassburg and was my favourite theological teacher. What specially pleased me in him was his simple yet thorough method of expounding scientific results. His lectures were to me an artistic delight.

Wilhelm Nowack, too, Budde's older colleague, was an excellent scholar. Church History and the History of Dogma were represented with oustanding skill by Johannes Ficker and Ernst Lucius. My interest was centred principally on the early history of Dogma. Dogmatics were taught by Paul Lobstein, one of the Ritschlian school. In Emil Mayer, the young professor of Ethics and Dogmatics, we students valued especially the fresh vitality of his method of lecturing. Practical theology was taught by Friedrich Spitta, who also lectured on the New Testament, and Julius Smend.

I attended philosophical lectures regularly as well as those in theology.

Musical theory I studied under Jacobsthal, a pupil of Bellermann's, who in his one-sidedness refused to acknowledge as art any music later than Beethoven's. Pure counterpoint, however, one could learn thoroughly from him, and I have much to thank him for.

It meant a considerable help to my musical studies that Ernest Münch, a brother of my Mülhausen teacher, who was himself organist of S. William's in Strassburg and conductor at the Bach concerts started by himself and given by the choir of S. Wilhelm's, entrusted to me the organ accompaniment of the Cantatas and the Passion music which were performed at them. At first indeed this was only at the rehearsals, in place of his Mülhausen brother who then took my place at the actual performances. Before long, however, I played also at the performances, if the brother had been prevented from coming. Thus while I was still a young student I became familiar with Bach's creations, and had an opportunity of dealing practically with the problems of the production to-day of the Master's Cantatas and Passion music.

S. William's Church in Strassburg ranked at that time as one of the most important nurseries of the Bach cult which was coming into existence at the end of last century. Ernest Münch had an extraordinary knowledge of the works of the Cantor of S. Thomas's. He was one of the first who abandoned the modernized rendering of the Cantatas and the Passion music which at the end of the nineteenth century was almost universal, and he strove for really artistic performances with his small choir accompanied by the famous Strassburg orchestra. Many an evening did we sit over the scores of the Cantatas and the Passion music and discuss the right method of rendering them. Ernest Münch's successor as conductor of these concerts is his son Fritz Münch, the Director of the Strassburg Conservatoire.

Together with my veneration for Bach went the same feeling for Richard Wagner. When I was a schoolboy at Mülhausen at the age of sixteen, I was allowed for the first time to go to the theatre, and I heard there Wagner's *Tannhäuser*. This music overpowered me to such an extent that it was days before I was capable of giving proper attention to the lessons in school.

In Strassburg, where the operatic performances conducted by Otto Lohse were of outstanding excellence, I had the opportunity of becoming thoroughly familiar with the whole of Wagner's works, except, of course, *Parsifal*, which at that time could only be performed at Bayreuth. It was a great experience for me to be present in Bayreuth in 1896, at the memorable first repetition of the Tetralogy since the original performances in 1876. Parisian friends had given me the tickets. To balance the cost of the journey I had to content myself with one meal a day.

To-day, if I go through a Wagner performance with all sorts of stage effects claiming attention alongside the music, as though it were a film-show, I cannot help thinking with melancholy regret of the earlier *mise-en-scène* of the Tetralogy at Bayreuth, the very simplicity of which made it so marvellously effective. But not the staging alone was in the spirit of the departed master; the whole performance was the same.

The orchestra was led, as in 1876, by Hans Richter. Loge was played by Heinrich Vogl, and Brünhilda by Lilli Lehmann. Both of them had taken part in the original performance: Vogl as Loge, and Lilli Lehmann as one of the Rhine Maidens.

It was Vogl who, as Loge, made on me, both as singer and actor, the deepest impression. From the moment of his appearance he dominated the stage without perceptibly having to do anything to draw attention to himself. He did not wear the harlequin-dress of modern players of the character. Nor did he dance round the stage to the rhythm of the Loge motive, as the fashion is to-day. The only thing about him that was striking was his red cloak. The only movements that he executed to the rhythm of the music were those with which, as though acting under some compulsion, he threw his cloak now over one shoulder, now over the other, his gaze fixed on what was happening around him, yet himself quite independent of it all. Thus he stood plainly for the restless force of destruction among the gods who were marching forward, all unsuspecting, to their fatal sunset.

My student years at Strassburg passed quickly. At the end of the summer of 1897 I presented myself for the first theological examination. As subject of the so-called 'Thesis' we were given: "Schleiermacher's teaching about the Last Supper compared with the conceptions of it embodied in the New Testament and the Confessions of faith drawn up by the Reformers." The thesis was an exercise imposed upon all candidates alike, and had to be finished within eight weeks. It decided whether one could be allowed to take the examination.

This task led me back again to the problem of the Gospels and the life of Jesus. From my study of all the historical and doctrinal views about the Last Supper to which I was compelled by this examination task I came to realize how exceedingly unsatisfactory were the current explanations of the significance of the historical ceremony which Jesus celebrated with His disciples, and of the origin of the primitive Christian ceremony of the Supper. I was set thinking hard by a remark of Schleiermacher's in the section of his famous *Dogmatics* in which he treats of the Last Supper. He draws attention to the fact that according to the accounts of the Supper in Matthew and Mark Jesus did not charge the disciples to repeat the meal, so that we must familiarize ourselves as well as we can with the thought that the repetition of the festal meal in the primitive community goes back only to the disciples and not to Jesus Himseslf. This thought, which is thrown out by Schleiermacher in a brilliant piece of reasoning, but is not followed up by him to the limit of its possible historical bearing, went on working in me even when I had completed the thesis for my candidature.

If, I said to myself, the command to repeat the meal is absent from the two oldest Gospels, that means that the disciples did in fact repeat it, with the body of believers, on their own initiative and authority. That, however, they could only do if there was something in the essence of this last meal which made it significant apart from the words and actions of Jesus. But, since no explanation of the Last Supper which has been current hitherto makes it intelligible, how it could be so adopted in the primitive community without a command from Jesus to that effect, they all alike, so I had to conclude, leave the problem unsolved. Hence I went on to investigate the question whether the significance which the meal had for Jesus and His disciples were not connected with the expectation of the Messianic feast to be celebrated in the Kingdom of God, which was to appear almost immediately.

CHAPTER II

PARIS AND BERLIN

1898-1899

ON May 6th, 1898, I passed the first theological examination, the so-called Government test, and then spent the whole of the summer in Strassburg, to devote myself entirely to philosophy. During this time I lived in the house in the Old Fish Market (No. 36) in which Goethe had lived while he was a student at Strassburg. Windelband and Ziegler were outstanding men in their subject, and supplemented each other splendidly. Windelband's strength lay in ancient philosophy, and his tutorial work with us on Plato and Aristotle is, in truth, the finest of the memories of my student days. Ziegler's domain was especially ethics and the philosophy of religion. For the latter he had a special advantage in the knowledge he had acquired as a former theologian. He had been through the Theological College at Tübingen.

As a result of my examination, supported by Holtzmann's application, I was given the Goll scholarship which was administered by the S. Thomas's Chapter and the Theological Faculty jointly. Its value was £60 (1,200 marks) a year and it was awarded each time for six years. The scholar was under an obligation either to take, within six years at the longest, the degree of Licentiate in Theology at Strassburg, or to repay the money he had received.

By the advice of Theobald Ziegler, I determined that I would take in hand next the dissertation for the degree of Doctor in Philosophy. At the end of the term he suggested to me, in a conversation held on the steps of the University building under his umbrella, that my subject should be the Religious Philosophy of Kant, a suggestion which greatly attracted me. Towards the end of October 1898 I went to Paris to study philosophy at the Sorbonne, and to improve my organ-playing under Widor.

I did not attend many lectures in Paris. To begin with, the unceremonious way in which the matriculation ceremony was conducted, put me out of tune. Then the antiquated method of instruction, which made it impossible for the teaching power, that was, much of it, of such outstanding quality, to give out its best, contributed its share towards making the Sorbonne distasteful to me. There were here no comprehensive courses of four or five lectures, such as I had been accustomed to at Strassburg. Either the professors gave lectures which bore solely on the examination syllabus, or they lectured on special subjects.

At the Protestant Theological Faculty (in the Boulevard Arago) I sometimes heard lectures on doctrine by Louis Auguste Sabatier, and others by the New Testament scholar, Louis Eugène Ménégoz. I felt great esteem for them both.

But on the whole this winter in Paris was devoted to music and to my dissertation for the Doctorate.

Under Widor—who now gave me lessons gratuitously— I worked at the organ, and under J. Philipp, who a little later became a teacher at the Conservatoire, at the piano. At the same time I was a pupil of Franz Liszt's talented pupil and friend, Marie Jaëll-Trautmann, an Alsatian by birth. She had already retired from the concert-hall life in which she had for a short time shone as a star of the first magnitude, and she now lived for the study of Touch in piano-playing, to which she was trying to give a physiological foundation. I was the 'corpus' on which she tried her experiments, which were made in conjunction with the physiologist, Féré, so I shared in them. How much do I owe to this gifted woman!

The finger—that is her theory—must be as fully conscious as possible of its relation to the keys. The player must be alive to and able to control all tensing or relaxing of the muscles from the shoulder down to the finger-tips. He must learn to prevent all involuntary and all unconscious movements. Finger exercises which aim merely at rapidity must be renounced. The finger must always form for itself an idea not only of the movement intended, but of the kind of tone it desires. A resonant touch is realized by the quickest and lightest possible depression of the keys. But the finger must also be conscious of the way in which it lets the depressed key rise again. In the depression and releasing of the keys the finger finds itself in an imperceptibly rolling movement, either inwards (towards the thumb) or outwards (towards the little finger). When several keys are depressed one after another with movements rolling in the same direction the corresponding tones and chords are organically united.

Thus mere succession rises into inward relationship. Tones produced by movements which roll in different directions keep apart according to their nature. It is, then, from consciously differentiated movements of the fingers and the hand that there come at the same time tonal light and shade, and suitable phrasing.

To secure an ever more conscious and ever closer relation with the keys the finger must cultivate to the utmost its sensitiveness to their touch, and with the perfecting of this sensitiveness the player will become at the same time more sensitive both to tone-colour and to colour in general.

This theory of the hand that learns to feel and to know, a theory containing so much that is correct, Marie Jaëll developed to its limit, maintaining that by correct training of the hand unmusical people could become musical. Starting from the physiology of the piano touch, she wanted to rise to a theory about the nature of art in general. She thus wrapped up her very correct and forcible observations on the nature of artistic touch with considerations about the relations ruling between nature and art which were often thoughtful and profound, but sometimes odd and repellent, and she failed consequently to get the recognition which her researches deserved.

Under Marie Jaëll's guidance I completely altered my hand. I owe it to her that by well-directed practice taking but little time I became more and more completely master of my fingers with great benefit to my organ playing.[1]

The instruction I got from Philipp, which moved more along the traditional paths of piano pedagogy, was also extraordinarily valuable, and protected me from what was one-sided in the Jaëll method. As my two teachers had a poor opinion of each other, I had to keep each from

[1] The fundamental ideas of her method Marie Jaëll has best developed in the first volume of her work, *Touch*, which she wrote in French. In the publication by Breitkopf and Härtel of the German edition I had a share as the anonymous translator.

knowing that I was a pupil of the other. What trouble it cost me to play with Marie Jaëll in the morning *à la* Jaëll and with Philipp in the afternoon *à la* Philipp!

With Philipp I am still—Marie Jaëll died in 1925—united in a firm bond of friendship, as I am also with Widor, and the latter I have to thank for my introduction to a number of interesting and important personages in the Paris of that day. He was also concerned for my material welfare. Many a time, if he got the impression that owing to concern about the slenderness of my purse I had not allowed myself enough to eat, he took me with him after my lesson to his regular haunt, the Restaurant Foyot near the Luxembourg, that I might once more, at any rate, eat my fill!

My father's two brothers who had settled in Paris, and their wives, were also very good to me. Through the younger one, Charles, who as a linguist had made a name for himself by his efforts to improve the teaching of modern languages, I got into touch with people of the University and of the educational world. And thus I was able to feel myself quite at home in Paris.

My thesis for the Doctorate suffered in no way through the demands made on me, either by my art or by society, for my good health allowed me to be prodigal with night work. It happened sometimes that I played to Widor in the morning without having been to bed at all.

To investigate the literature about Kant's philosophy of religion in the 'Bibliothèque Nationale' proved to be impracticable on account of the cumbersome regulations of the Reading Room. I therefore resolved without more ado to write the thesis without troubling about the literature, and to see what results I could get by burying myself in the Kantian writings themselves.

Studying them thus I was struck by variations in the use of words; that, for example, in many sections of the *Critique of Pure Reason*, which dealt with religious philosophy, the word *intelligibel* ('intelligible'), which alone corresponded to the Kantian criticism, disappeared and was replaced by the simpler *übersinnlich* ('supersensible'). I thereupon tracked through the whole series of his writings the words which play a part in the expression of his religious philosophy to find out how often each is used, and any variation there might be in the meanings assigned to them. This enabled me to establish it as a fact that the long section on the "Canon of Pure Reason," as shown by its diction and its thought alike, is no real part of the *Critique of Pure Reason*, but an earlier work of the philosopher, which he adopted for a religio-philosophical Introduction to the *Critique of Pure Reason*, although it is not really in harmony with it. This earlier, pre-critical work I designated "A Sketch of the Philosophy of Religion."

A further discovery was that Kant never carried out at all the religio-philosophical scheme of transcendental dialectic as given in the *Critique of Pure Reason*. The religious philosophy which is developed in the *Critique of Practical Reason* with its three postulates of God, Freedom, and Immortality is not at all the same as we are led to expect in the *Critique of Pure Reason*. In the *Critique of the Power of Judgement* and in *Religion within the Bounds of Mere Reason* the religious philosophy of the three postulates is again abandoned. The lines of thought which appear in these later works lead one back once more to the path taken in the Sketch of the Philosophy of Religion.

Kant's Philosophy of Religion, then, which everybody made out to be identical with that of the three postulates, is in a state of constant flux. This must be referred to the fact that the pre-suppositions of his critical idealism and the religio-philosophical claims of the moral law stand in antagonism to each other. Kant gives us side by side a critical religious philosophy and an ethical, which he seeks to reconcile and to work into a unity. In the transcendental dialectic of the *Critique of Pure Reason* he believes himself able to unify them without difficulty. But the scheme he makes for doing this proves incapable of execution because he does not keep to the idea of the moral law which is pre-supposed in the transcendental dialectic of the *Critique of Pure Reason*, but continually deepens it. This deepened conception of the moral law, however, raises religious demands which go beyond what can be conceded by critical idealism according to Kant's conception of it. At the same time the religious philosophy of the deepened moral law loses its interest in claims which for critical idealism occupy the foremost place. It is significant in this connexion that in those of Kant's religious lines of thought which are dominated by the deepest ethic the postulate of Immortality plays no part.

Instead, then, of keeping to the philosophy of religion established by critical idealism, Kant allows himself to be led further by the religious philosophy of the ever deepening moral law. Becoming in this way deeper, he is unable to remain consistent.

In the middle of March 1899 I returned to Strassburg and read my finished work aloud to Theobald Ziegler. He expressed himself as being strongly in agreement with it. It was settled that I should take my degree at the end of July.

The summer of 1899 I spent in Berlin, mostly occupied in reading philosophy. It was my ambition to have read the chief works of ancient and modern philosophy. At the same time I attended lectures by Harnack, Pfleiderer, Kaftan, Paulsen, and Simmel. At Simmel's lectures I was at first an occasional, but afterwards a regular attendant.

It was only later that I became really in sympathy with Harnack, whose History of Dogma had already in Strassburg occupied me and roused my enthusiasm, although I had been introduced to him by friends, and used to visit his house. I was so overawed by his knowledge and the universality of his interests that embarrassment used to prevent me from answering his questions when he spoke to me. Later in life I received from him many friendly postcards, full of information—for the postcard was the missive which he used more than any other for his correspondence. Two very full ones which I received at Lambarene about my just published book, *The Mysticism of Paul the Apostle*, belong to the year 1930 and must be among the last that he ever wrote.

I spent a great deal of time in those days with Karl Stumpf. The psychological studies on the feeling for tone with which he was then occupied, I found very interesting. I joined regularly in the experiments which he and his assistants made, and was his *corpus vile* too, as I had been for Marie Jaëll.

The Berlin organists, with the exception of Egidi, disappointed me somewhat, because they aimed more at outward virtuosity than at the true plasticity of style to which Widor attached so much importance. And how dull and dry was the sound of the new Berlin organs compared with that of Cavaillé-Coll's instruments in S. Sulpice and Notre Dame.

Professor Heinrich Reimann, the organist of the Kaiser Wilhelm Memorial Church, to whom I had brought a letter of introduction from Widor, allowed me to play regularly upon his organ, and engaged me as his deputy when he went away on holiday. Through him I made the acquaintance of some of the musicians, painters, and sculptors of Berlin.

The academic world I got to know at the house of the widow of Ernst Curtius, the well-known Hellenist, who received me with great friendliness as an acquaintance of her step-son, the District Superintendent of Colmar. There I often met Hermann Grimm, who did all he possibly could to convert me from the heresy that the representation given by the Fourth Gospel is not reconcilable with that of the first three. I still to-day look back upon it as a great piece of good fortune, that I could at that house come into direct contact with the leaders of the intellectual life of the Berlin of that day.

The intellectual life of Berlin made a much greater impression on me than did that of Paris. In Paris, the world-city, the intellectual life was split up. One had to get thoroughly acclimatized before it was possible to reckon up the values existing in it. The intellectual life of Berlin, on the other hand, had a rallying-point in its grandly organized University, which in itself formed a living organism. Moreover, the town at that time was not yet a world-city but gave the impression of being a biggish provincial town which was developing happily in every respect. Altogether it had an air of healthy self-consciousness and of confident faith in the leaders of its destinies, such as were not to be found in contemporary Paris, which was then torn by the Dreyfus Case. Thus I came to know Berlin at the finest period of its existence, and to love it. I was specially impressed by the simple mode of life of Berlin society, and the ease with which one got admittance to its family life.

CHAPTER III

THE FIRST YEARS OF ACTIVITY IN STRASSBURG

AT the end of July 1899 I returned to Strassburg and took my degree in philosophy. In the *viva voce* I fell, as Ziegler and Windelband agreed, below the level of what my dissertation had led them to expect from me. The time I had spent with Stumpf in experiments was lost so far as preparation for this examination was concerned. Moreover, in order to read the original works I had neglected the text-books far too much.

The dissertation appeared as a book before the end of 1899 under the title *The Religious Philosophy of Kant from the "Critique of Pure Reason" to "Religion within the Bounds of Mere Reason."*[1]

Theobald Ziegler urged me to qualify as a *Privat-dozent* in the Faculty of Philosophy, but I decided for the theological. Ziegler, I must add, hinted to me that if I were a *Privat-dozent* in Philosophy people would not be pleased at seeing me active as a preacher as well. But to me preaching was a necessity of my being. I felt it as something wonderful that I was allowed to address a congregation every Sunday about the deepest questions of life.

From this time onwards I remained in Strassburg. Although I was no longer a student, I was allowed to live in the Collegium Wilhelmitanum (the College of S. Thomas), which I loved so well, as a paying guest among its ordinary inmates. The room looking on the quiet garden with its big trees—the room in which I had passed so many happy hours as a student—seemed to me the fittest place for the work which now lay before me.

The moment I had finished correcting the proofs of my Doctor's dissertation, I set to work to get my theological Licentiate. I meant to get that degree as quickly as possible

[1] *Die Religionsphilosophie Kants.* 325 pages. (Mohr und Siebeck, Tübingen.) That this well-known publishing-house accepted such a lengthy first work of a new author I owed to a warm recommendation of it from Holtzmann.

that the Goll scholarship might be vacant for another student who seemed to be thrown upon that for the continuation of his studies. The one for whose sake I hurried so much—my contemporary, Jäger, the gifted student of Oriental languages, afterwards Director of the Protestant Gymnasium at Strassburg—made later on no use of it. Had I know this I should have travelled longer before settling down, and should then have studied also in an English University. That I lost this opportunity through a misplaced consideration for others, has been a matter of regret to me ever since.

On December 1st, 1899, I obtained a post as Preacher at the Church of S. Nicholas in Strassburg, first as a Deacon, later, when I had passed the second theological examination, as a Curate.

This second examination, usually conducted by elderly clerics, I passed, but only just passed, on July 15th, 1900. Being fully occupied with the dissertation for the Licentiate I had omitted to refresh my memory as I should have done in the various branches of theology which this examination demanded. It was only through the energetic intervention of old Pfarrer Will, whom I had delighted by my knowledge of the history of dogma, that I did not get ploughed. It told especially against me that I did not know enough about the hymn writers and their lives. My many misfortunes came to a head when I tried to excuse my ignorance as to the authorship of one particular hymn— it was by Spitta, the famous poet of *Psalter and Harp*— by saying I thought the hymn too insignificant for me to notice who had composed it. I was really an admirer of Spitta's, but proffered this excuse, to the horror of all, in the presence of Professor Friedrich Spitta, the poet's son, who was sitting among the examiners as representative of the Faculty of Theology.

The staff at S. Nicholas' consisted of two elderly, but still vigorous ministers, Mr. Knittel, one of the predecessors of my father at Günsbach, and Mr. Gerold, an intimate friend of one of my mother's brothers, who had been incumbent of S. Nicholas', but had died young. To these two men I was given as an assistant, chiefly that I might relieve them of the afternoon service, the Sunday children's service, and the Confirmation classes. The activities thus allotted to me were a constant source of joy. At the afternoon service with only a small group of worshippers present I could use the intimate style of preaching which I had inherited from my father and express myself better than I could at the morning service. Even to-day I am never quite free from shyness before a large audience. As the years passed the two old gentlemen had to spare themselves more and more, and it frequently fell to my lot, of course, to preach in the morning as well. I used to write my sermons out in full, often making two or three drafts before beginning the fair copy. When delivering the sermons, however, I did not tie myself to this outline which I had carefully learnt by heart, but often gave the discourse a quite different form.

My afternoon sermons, which I looked upon as simple devotional exercises rather than sermons, were so short, that on one occasion certain circles of the congregation lodged a complaint against me on the subject before Mr. Knittel, who held also the office of "Inspector in Spiritual Matters," and he had to cite me before him. But when I appeared he was as much embarrassed as I was. When he asked what he was to reply to the aggrieved members of the congregation, I replied that he might say that I was only a poor Curate who stopped speaking when he found he had nothing more to say about the text. Thereupon he dismissed me with a mild reprimand, and an admonition not to preach for less than twenty minutes.

Mr. Knittel represented orthodoxy softened by pietism; Mr. Gerold was a liberal. But they fulfilled the duties of their office together in a truly brotherly temper. Everything was carried out in a spirit of harmony. It was thus a really ideal work that went on in this unpretending church which stood opposite S. Thomas's.

Many a time during these years, whenever I had a free Sunday, did I go to Günsbach to take the service for my father.

Three times a week, from eleven to twelve, when the morning lessons were over, I had to take the Confirmation classes for boys, which in Alsace continue for two years.

I tried hard to give them as little home work to do as possible, that the lessons might be a time of pure refreshment for heart and spirit. I therefore used the last ten minutes for making them repeat after me, and so get to know by heart, Bible sayings and verses of hymns which they might take away from these classes to guide them throughout their lives. The aim of my teaching was to bring home to their hearts and thoughts the great truths of the Gospel, and to make them religious in such a way that in later life they might be able to resist the temptations to irreligion which would assail them. I tried also to awake in them a love for the Church, and a feeling of need for a solemn hour for their souls in the Sunday services. I taught them to respect traditional doctrines, but at the same time to hold fast to the saying of S. Paul that where the spirit of Christ is, there is liberty.

Of the seed which for years I was thus sowing, some has taken root and grown, as I have been privileged to learn. Men have thanked me for having then brought home to their hearts the fundamental truths of the religion of Jesus as something to be absorbed into one's thought, and having thus strengthened them against the danger of giving up all religion in later life.

In these religious lessons I first became conscious of how much schoolmaster-blood I have in me from my ancestors.

My stipend at S. Nicholas' was 100 marks (£5) a month, but it sufficed for my needs, as my board and lodging at the S. Thomas's Hostel was very cheap.

One great advantage of my position there was that it left me plenty of time for scientific work and for music. The readiness of the two pastors to meet by wishes made it possible for me in the spring and autumn holidays, when there were no Confirmation classes, to be free to go away if I provided a substitute to do my preaching—so far as they did not, in their goodness, undertake it themselves. Thus I had three months in the year free: one at Easter and two in the autumn. The spring holiday I generally spent in Paris, as the guest of my father's eldest brother, so as to continue my studies with Widor. The autumn one I spent for the most part in the old home at Günsbach.

By these frequent periods of residence in Paris I made many valuable acquaintances. Romain Rolland I met for the first time about 1905, and at first we were to each other merely musicians. Gradually, however, we both discovered that we were men too, and we became good friends.

My relations were very cordial too with Henri Lichtenberger, the delicate but appreciative critic of German literature.

I shall never forget a chance encounter which I had one delightful spring morning at the beginning of the century in the narrow Rue S. Jacques. As I had let myself get late for an appointment, I had had to take a cab. At a certain street-crossing the two rows of vehicles had to remain stationary side by side for some time, and I was struck by the head of the occupant of the open carriage alongside mine. The first thing was that the elegant tall hat—at that time the tall hat was still worn in Paris—looked remarkably odd upon the anything but elegant head. But while I continued to look—for the block lasted a considerable time—I fell under the spell of the something uncanny and the very reverse of spiritual, which characterized the face. Such indications of the untamed primitive human nature, or features expressing such reckless and remorseless will-power I had never seen in any human being. While I was staring, it suddenly dawned upon me that it was Clemenceau.

When I learnt later that after three sittings Cézanne gave up the task of painting Clemenceau because "he couldn't make a portrait of a thing like that," I thoroughly understood what he meant.

Before the "Foreign Language Society" of Paris I delivered in German during the first years of the new century a series of lectures on German Literature and Philosophy. I still remember those on Nietzsche, Schopenhauer, Gerhart Hauptmann, Sudermann, and Goethe's *Faust*. While I was at work in August 1900 on the lecture on Nietzsche came the news that death had at last released him from his sufferings.

Thus, in the simplest way, did my life pass during the years that were decisive for my creative work. I worked much and hard, with unbroken concentration, but without hurry.

I did not go about much in the world, because I had neither time nor money for travelling, but in 1900 I accompanied the wife of my father's eldest brother to Oberammergau. The wonderful landscape behind the stage made really a stronger impression on me than the Passion Play. The latter was spoilt for me by the framing of the essential action of the Passion in pictorial scenes from the Old Testament, by the excessive theatrical display, by the imperfections of the text, and by the banality of the music. But my heart was touched by the devout way in which the actors sank themselves in the parts they played.

Who can help feeling the unsatisfying result of a Passion Play, which ought to be performed by villagers for villagers after primitive methods as a religious service, but is forced out of this setting by the flood of foreign spectators and turned into a stage-piece which must satisfy the demands of those who see it. That the people of Oberammergau make every effort to perform this Passion Play, altered as it is, in the simple spirit of earlier times, everyone must admit who has preserved any feeling for the spiritual side of things.

When my savings permitted it, I made the pilgrimage to Bayreuth, if the festival was held in that particular year.

I was greatly impressed by Frau Cosima Wagner, whom I had got to know in Strassburg while working at my Bach. She took an interest in my view that Bach's music is descriptive, and when she was in Strassburg on a visit to the ecclesiastical historian, Johannes Ficker, she let me illustrate my view to her on the fine organ in the New church there, by playing to her some of his choral preludes. She told me during those days many interesting things about the religious instruction which she had enjoyed in her youth, and later, when she was preparing to change over to Protestantism. I never could get rid of a certain feeling of shyness, however often I met this woman,

B

who was so unique in her artistic ability and queenly bearing.

In Siegfried Wagner I valued the simplicity and the modesty which characterized this man, who was in many respects so outstandingly gifted. No one who saw him at work in Bayreuth could help admiring him, both for what he did and for the way in which he did it. His music too contains much that is really significant and beautiful.

CHAPTER IV

STUDY OF THE LAST SUPPER AND THE LIFE OF JESUS

1900-1902

WHEN, after finishing my work on Kant, I returned to theology, the most obvious thing to do was to put together my studies on the problems of the life of Jesus which had occupied me since my first year at the University, and to work them up into a dissertation for my Licentiate examination. But my study of the Last Supper had widened my outlook and my interest. From the field of he problems of the life of Jesus I had stepped straightaway into the problems of primitive Christianity. The problem of the Last Supper belongs to both fields. It stands at the central point in the development of the faith of Jesus into the faith of primitive Christianity. If, I said to myself, the origin and the significance of the Last Supper remain to us such an enigma, the reason is that we have never really grasped the thought-world of Jesus nor that of primitive Christianity. Similarly we never see in their proper form the problems of the life of Jesus I had stepped straightaway tive Christianity, because we never start our examination of them from the problems of the Last Supper and Baptism.

Guided by these considerations, I formed the plan of writing a history of the Last Supper in connexion with the life of Jesus and the history of primitive Christianity. A preliminary investigation was to define my attitude in regard to previous research into the question of the Last Supper, and throw light upon the problem as a whole. A second section would give a picture of the thought and activities of Jesus as a condition of understanding the Supper which He celebrated with His disciples. A third was to treat of the Supper in the Primitive Church and in the two first centuries of Christianity.

With my work on the problem of the Last Supper I

obtained on July 21st, 1900, the degree of Licentiate in Theology.[1] The second, which treated of the Secret of the Messiahship and the Passion, served to procure me in 1902 the position of *Privat-dozent* at the University.[2]

The study I had in view as a third volume on the development of the Last Supper in the primitive and later periods was indeed completed and delivered in lectures, as was also the companion study on the history of Baptism in the New Testament and in primitive Christianity. Neither work was printed, however, because *The Quest of the Historical Jesus*,[3] which was at first intended only for a supplement to the Sketch of His Life, but which grew finally into a bulky volume, came in between and prevented me from getting them ready for the press. Then came a new intermezzo, viz. the book on Bach, which also was originally conceived as merely an essay: and after that came the study of medicine. Then, when near the conclusion of my medical studies, I could once more find time for theology, it seemed to me to be plainly indicated that I should produce a history of scientific research into the thought-world of S. Paul, to be a companion volume to the *Quest of the Historical Jesus* and an introduction to an exposition of Pauline doctrine. On the strength of my newly won comprehension of the teaching of Jesus and Paul, I meant next, while I was resting after a first period of work in Africa which was intended to last for eighteen months or two years, to bring into its final form a history of the origin and early-Christian development of the Last Supper and Baptism. This plan was ruined by the war, which only let me return to

[1] *Das Abendmahlsproblem auf Grund der Wissentschaftlichen Forschung des 19 Jahrhunderts und der Historischen Berichte* ("The Problem of the Last Supper, a study based on the scientific research of the nineteenth century and the historical accounts"). 62 pages. 1901. (J. C. B. Mohr, Tübingen.) New unaltered reprint, 1929.

[2] *Das Messianitäts- und Leidensgheimniss. Eine Skizze des Lebens Jesu* ("The Secret of the Messiahship and Passion. A sketch of the Life of Jesus"). 109 pages. 1901. (J. C. B. Mohr, Tübingen.) New unaltered reprint, 1929. The English edition bears the title: *The Mystery of the Kingdom of God. The Secret of Jesus' Messiahship and Passion.* Translated by Walter Lowrie. (Dodd, New York, and A. & C. Black, London, 1925.)

[3] *The Quest of the Historical Jesus. A Critical Study of its Progress from Reimarus to Wrede.* Translated by W. Montgomery. Introduction by F. C. Burkitt (A. & C. Black, London, 1910.)

Europe after four and a half years of absence instead of two, in bad health moreover, and deprived of my means of existence.

Meanwhile, too,—a fresh intermezzo!—I had begun some work on the Philosophy of Civilization! Consequently the *History of the Last Supper and Baptism in the Early Christian Period* has remained in the condition of manuscript for lectures. Whether I shall still find time and strength to complete it for the press, I know not. The thoughts which underlie it are put forward in my book, *The Mysticism of Paul the Apostle*.

In my work on the problem of the Last Supper I go through the various solutions which have been offered by scientific theology up to the end of the nineteenth century. At the same time I attempt to reveal its essential character dialectically. The result is to show that all attempted solutions are impossible which explain the early Christian celebration as a distribution of bread and wine which, by the repetition of the words of Jesus about bread and wine as His body and His blood, had come somehow or other themselves also to signify body and blood.

The celebration as practised in early Christendom was something other than a sacramental repetition or a symbolical representation of the atoning death of Jesus. This interpretation was first given to the repetition of the last meal of Jesus with His disciples in the Catholic sacrifice of the Mass and in the Protestant celebration of the Last Supper, as a reminder of the forgiveness of sins.

The figurative words of Jesus about bread and wine as His body and blood did not, strange as the statement may seem to us, determine for the disciples and the first believers the nature of the celebration; indeed, so far as our knowledge of primitive and early Christianity goes, those words were not repeated at the community meal in the olden time. What constituted the celebration, then, was not Jesus' words of institution so-called, which spoke of bread and wine as His body and blood, but the prayers of thanksgiving over the bread and wine. These gave both to the Supper of Jesus and His disciples, as also to the solemn meal of the primitive community, a meaning which pointed forwards to the expected Messianic meal.

Thus we get also an explanation of the fact that the celebration of the Supper in the earliest period is designated a 'Eucharist,' that is, a 'Thanksgiving,' and that it was not celebrated once a year in the evening of Maundy Thursday, but in the early hours of every Sunday as the resurrection day of Jesus, on which believers looked forward to His return at the revelation of the Kingdom of God.

In the Sketch of the Life of Jesus, which appeared under the title of the *Secret of the Messiahship and the Passion*, I express clearly my opinion of that view of the course of the public activity of Jesus which at the end of the course of the nineteenth century was held to have been historically established as the true one, and which is confirmed in detail by Holtzmann in his works on the Gospels. It rests upon two fundamental ideas: that Jesus did not share the simple realistic expectation about the Messiah which was at that time widely spread among the Jewish people, and that it was by failures which He experienced after some initial successes that He was brought to His resolution to face death.

According to the scientific research of the second half of the nineteenth century Jesus tries to divert the attention of believers from the supernatural Messianic Kingdom which they expected, by proclaiming to them a purely ethical Kingdom of God which He Himself is attempting to found upon earth. Accordingly He does not hold Himself to be the Messiah of His hearers' imagination, but tries to educate them up to a belief in a spiritual, ethical Messiah, such as will in time make them capable of recognizing the Messiah in Himself.

At first success attended His preaching. Later on, however, the multitude, influenced by the Pharisees and the rulers at Jerusalem, falls away from Him. In view of this fact He wrestles His way through to the conviction that, for the cause of the Kingdom of God and the preservation of His spiritual Messiahship, it is the will of God that He shall die. So at the next Easter festival He journeys to Jerusalem to put Himself in the power of His enemies, and at their hands to suffer death on the cross.

This view of the course of Jesus' public life is untenable, because its two fundamental ideas do not correspond to facts. Nowhere in the oldest sources, the Gospels of Mark and Matthew, is there any trace at all of Jesus intending to replace by a spiritualized expectation the realistic one, so widely spread among the people, of a supernatural kingdom which would come with glory. Nor do those Gospels know anything of a successful period of activity being followed by an unsuccessful.

As shown by the sayings which Mark and Matthew ascribe

to Him, Jesus lives in the Messianic expectation, held by late Judaism, which goes back to the old prophets and to the Book of Daniel, a book which came into existence about 165 B.C. What this expectation was we know from the Book of Enoch (*circa* 100 B.C.), the Psalms of Solomon (63 B.C.), and the Apocalypses of Baruch and Ezra (*circa* A.D. 80). Like his contemporaries he identifies the Messiah with the "Son of Man," who is spoken of in the Book of Daniel, and speaks of His coming on the clouds of heaven. The Kingdom of God which he preaches is the heavenly, Messianic Kingdom, which will be set up on earth when the Son of Man comes at the end of the natural world's existence. He continually exhorts his hearers to be ready at any moment for the judgement, as a result of which some will enter into the glory of the Messianic Kingdom, while others will depart to damnation. He even offer His disciples the prospect of sitting, at this judgement, on twelve seats around His throne and judging the twelve tribes of Israel.

Jesus accepts, then, as true the late-Jewish Messianic expectation in all its externality. In no way does He attempt to spiritualize it. But He fills it with His own powerful ethical spirit, in that, passing beyond the Law and the scribes, He demands from men the practice of the absolute ethic of love as the proof that they belong to God and to the Messiah, and that they are pre-destined to membership of the coming Kingdom. Marked out for blessedness, according to Him, are the spiritually poor, the merciful, the peace-makers, the pure in heart, those who hunger and thirst after the righteousness of the Kingdom, the mourners, those who suffer persecution for the Kingdom of God's sake, those who become as little children.

The error of research hitherto is that it attributes to Jesus a spiritualizing of the late-Jewish Messianic Expectation, whereas in reality He simply fits into it the ethical religion of love. Our minds refuse at first to grasp that a religiousness and an ethic so deep and spiritual can be combined with other views, of such a naïve realism. But the combination is a fact.

To counter the assumption that there can be distinguished in the activity of Jesus a successful period and an unsuccessful the fact must be adduced that not only in Galilee, but in the Temple at Jerusalem He is surrounded by an enthusiastic multitude. In the midst of His adherents He is safe against the plots of His enemies. With their support He can even venture in His discourses in the Temple to make the most violent attacks upon the Pharisees, and to drive the traders and the money-changers out of it.

If, not long after the return of the disciples from the work on which He has sent them out, of proclaiming the nearness of the Kingdom of God, He withdraws with them to the heathen neighbourhood of Tyre and Sidon, He does not do this because he has to retire from the field before His enemies. The people do not fall away from Him, but He gives them the slip, in order to be for a time alone with His intimates, and no sooner does He appear once more in Galilee than the crowd of his adherents gathers round Him again. It is at the head of the Galilean pilgrims on their way to the Festival that He enters Jerusalem. His arrest and crucifixion are only possible because He Himself surrenders to the authorities, who condemned Him during the night, and in the early morning, almost before Jerusalem was awake, had already crucified Him.

Following the clear statements of the two oldest Gospels, I confront the untenable explanation of the life of Jesus which has hitherto held the field, with the explanation which represents Him as determined in His thought, speech, and action by His expectation of a speedy end to the world, and of the super-natural Messianic Kingdom which would thereupon be revealed. This explanation is designated the eschatological because the traditional meaning of the word eschatology (*eschatos* is a Greek word meaning 'last') is the Jewish-Christian teaching about what will happen when the world comes to an end. Conceived in this way the life of Jesus, or rather His public career and His end—for indeed these together make up absolutely all that we know of His life—may be shortly des-cribed as follows. Just as Jesus announces the Kingdom of God not as something already beginning, but as something purely future, so He does not think that He is already the Messiah; He is only convinced that at the appearance of the Messianic Kingdom, when the predestined enter upon the supernatural mode of existence intended for them, He will be manifested as the Messiah. This knowledge about His future dignity remains His secret. To the people He comes forward merely as the announcer of the approaching Kingdom of God. There is no need for His hearers to know with Whom they have to do. When the Kingdom appears they will learn it. His self-con-sciousness displays itself only so far that to those who confess Him and accept His message about the Kingdom, He promises that the Son of Man (of whom, as though He Himself were not identical with Him, He speaks in the third person) will recognize them immediately as His own.

For Himself and those who with Him look for the speedy

coming of the Kingdom of God, Jesus expects that they will first have to endure together the pre-Messianic Tribulation and prove themselves faithful under it. For according to the late-Jewish teaching about events in the Times of the End all those who are called to the Messianic Kingdom will for a certain length of time immediately before its manifestation be at the mercy of the God-opposing world-powers.

At some point of time—whether it was weeks or months after His entry on His public life, we do not know—Jesus feels certain that the hour for the manifestation of the Kingdom has come. He hastily sends out His disciples two and two into the cities of Israel that they may spread the news. In the discourse (Matt. x) with which He despatches them He warns them to expect the Messianic Tribulation which is about to dawn immediately and bring upon them and the other elect ones fierce persecution, yes, and perhaps death itself. He does not expect to see them return, but assures them that the "Coming of the Son of Man" (which is expected simultaneously with the manifestation of the Kingdom) will take place even before they have gone over the cities of Israel.

His expectation, however, is not fulfilled. The disciples return without having suffered any persecution whatever. Of the pre-Messianic Tribulation there is no sign, and the Messianic Kingdom does not appear. This fact Jesus can only explain to Himself by supposing that there is still some event which must take place first. Wrestling with the fact that the Kingdom of God still fails to appear there dawns on Him the perception that it can only come when He, as the Messiah-to-be, has by suffering and death made atonement for those who have been elected to the Kingdom, and thereby saved them from the necessity of going through the pre-Messianic Tribulation.

On the possibility that God, in His mercy, can spare the Elect the suffering of the Tribulation, Jesus has always counted. In the Lord's Prayer, which is a prayer about the Coming of the Kingdom of God, believers are bidden to pray that God will not bring them into 'temptation' ($\pi\epsilon\iota\rho\alpha\sigma\mu\delta s$) but will deliver them from the 'Evil one.' By the word 'temptation' Jesus does not mean any individual temptation to sin, but the persecution which with God's sanction will be in the Times of the End be brought upon believers by the 'Evil One,' that means, by Satan as the representative of the powers hostile to God.

The idea, then, with which Jesus meets death is that God is willing to accept His self-chosen death as an atonement made for believers, and therefore straightaway refrains from inflicting the pre-Messianic Tribulation, in which they would

B*

otherwise have to be purified by suffering and dying and show themselves worthy of the Kingdom of God.

In some way or other the resolution of Jesus to suffer an atoning death is based upon the passages in Isaiah about the Servant of Jehovah (Isa. liii) Who suffers for the sins of others without the latter being able to explain the meaning of what He endures. The original reference of these passages, which belong to the period of the Exile, was to what the people of Israel, during their banishment, suffered as the Servant of God among the surrounding nations, in order that these nations might through them come to the knowledge of God.

The need for suffering and death to be endured by Him for Whom the dignity of the Messiah-Son of Man is destined is made known by Jesus to the disciples, in the neighbourhood of Caesarea Philippi. At the same time He discloses to them that He is the same Who at the dawning of the Kingdom of God will be that personality (Mark viii. 27-33). Then at Eastertide He goes up with the festival caravan of Galileans to Jerusalem. At present no one except the disciples knows Whom He believes Himself to be. The rejoicing at His entry into Jerusalem is not for the Messiah, but for the prophet of Nazareth of the House of David. The treachery of Judas does not consist in betraying to the Sandhedrim where Jesus can be arrested, but in disclosing to that body the claim which He makes to the dignity of Messiah.

At the last meal which He takes with His disciples, He gives them to eat and to drink bread and wine which He has consecrated by prayers of thanksgiving, and declares that He will no more drink of the fruit of the vine until that day when He will drink it new in His Father's Kingdom. Thus at His last earthly meal He consecrates them to be His companions at the coming Messianic meal. From that time onwards believers, as persons who carry within them the certain assurance that they are invited to the Messianic meal, gather together, in continuation of that last supper, for ceremonial meals at which over the food and drink prayers of thanksgiving are offered up for the speedy coming of the Kingdom and the Messianic meal.

Jesus expects then, through the effect of His atoning death, to bring in the Messianic Kingdom immediately without any preliminary Tribulation. He tells His judges that they will see Him as the Son of Man seated at the right hand of God and coming on the clouds of heaven (Mark xiv. 62).

Since on the morning after the Sabbath the disciples find the grave empty, and in their enthusiastic expectation of the glory in which their Master is soon to appear, have visions of Him as risen from the grave, they are certain that He is with God in heaven, soon to appear as Messiah and bring in the Kingdom.

What the two oldest Gospels report of the public life of Jesus takes place in the course of a year. It is in the spring that with the Parable of the Sower Jesus begins to proclaim the secret of the Kingdom of God. At harvest time He is hoping that the heavenly harvest also, like the earthly, will begin (Matt. ix. 37 f.), and He sends out the disciples to make a final proclamation of the nearness of the Kingdom. Shortly after that He abandons His public activity and lingers alone with His disciples on heathen territory in the neighbourhood of Caesarea Philippi, probably till near Easter, when He starts on His journey to Jerusalem. It is possible, then, that the period of His public activity lasted at most five or six months.

CHAPTER V

TEACHING ACTIVITIES AT THE UNIVERSITY. THE QUEST OF THE HISTORICAL JESUS

ON March 1st, 1902, I delivered my inaugural lecture before the Theological Faculty at Strassburg on the Logos doctrine in the Fourth Gospel.

I learnt later that protests against my acceptance as a University Lecturer had been lodged by two members of the Faculty. They expressed disapproval of my method of historical investigation and a fear that I should confuse the students with my views. They were impotent, however, in face of the authority of Holtzmann, who took my part.

In my inaugural lecture I took as my subject my discovery that the obscure passages in the discourses of the Johannine Christ hang together, and are not intelligible till one grasps them as being preliminary hints by which He wishes to prepare His hearers to accept sacraments deriving their power from the Logos, which would enter into effect and use after His death. The earliest opportunity of developing this theory in full I found in my book : *The Mysticism of Paul the Apostle*.

In the summer term of 1902 I began my lectures with a course on the Pastoral Epistles.

Incitement to occupy myself with the history of research on the life of Jesus was given me by a conversation with students who had attended a course of lectures by Professor Spitta on the Life of Jesus, but had learnt practically nothing about previous investigations into the subject. I therefore resolved, with Professor Holtzmann's approval, to lecture for two hours weekly during the summer term of 1905 on the history of research on the life of Jesus. I attacked the work with zeal, but the material took such hold of me that when I had finished the course of lectures I became absolutely absorbed in it. Thanks to bequests from Edward Reuss and other Strassburg theologians the

University Library possessed a practically complete collection of the literature about the life of Jesus, and it had in addition to that nearly all the controversial writings which had been provoked by Strauss's and Renan's lives. There was assuredly hardly a place in the world where circumstances were so favourable for studying the history of research on the life of Jesus.

While I was engaged on this work, I was Principal of the Theological College (Collegium Wilhelmitanum). I had been appointed to this post immediately after the death of Erichson, but only provisionally, and I held it from May 1st to September 30th, 1901, till Gustav Anrich—at that time Pastor at Lingolsheim near Strassburg, and later Professor of Church History at Tübingen—could enter on his duties there. In the summer of 1903 Anrich was appointed Professor of Church History as successor to Ernst Lucius, who had suddenly died, and on October 1st, 1903, I took over the office of Principal, with the beautiful official quarters looking out on the sunny S. Thomas Embankment, and the yearly stipend of 2,000 marks (one hundred pounds). But I kept as my study the room I had occupied as a student. While Gustav Anrich was Principal, I had lived in the town.

The Quest of the Historical Jesus appeared as early as 1906, the first edition bearing the title of *From Reimarus to Wrede*.[1]

John Samuel Reimarus (1694-1768), who lived as Professor of Oriental Languages at Hamburg, was the first to attempt, in a treatise entitled *Concerning the Aims of Jesus and His Disciples*, an explanation of the life of Jesus which started from the assumption that He shared the eschatological expectations about a Messiah which were held by his contemporaries. The treatise was first published by Lessing after his death without the author's name.

[1] *Von Reimarus zu Wrede.* 418 pages. 1906. (J. C. B. Mohr, Tübingen.) *The Quest of the Historical Jesus. A Critical Study of its Progress from Reimarus to Wrede.* (A. & C. Black. 1910. 2nd ed. 1911. Reprinted 1922 and 1926. 12s. 6d.) (There is unfortunately no English translation as yet of the second German edition, which was thoroughly revised, and enlarged to 642 pages, in 1913. It was reprinted a second time (*vierte Auflage*) in 1926. It called *Geschichte der Leben-Jesu-Forschung,* i.e. *History of Research into the Life of Jesus.*—TRANSLATOR'S NOTE.)

William Wrede (1859-1907), Professor of Theology at Breslau, in his treatise *The Messianic Secret in the Gospels*, made the first thorough-going attempt on a bold scale to deny that Jesus entertained any eschatological ideas at all, and found himself thereby compelled, for the sake of consistency, to go on to the further assertion that Jesus did not regard Himself as the Messiah, but was only made that after His death by the disciples. Since these two names indicate the two poles between which the investigation moves, it was from them that I made up the title of my book.

When I had worked through the numerous Lives of Jesus, I found it very difficult to group them in chapters. After attempting in vain to do this on paper, I piled all the 'Lives' in one big heap in the middle of my room, picked out for each chapter I had planned a place of its own in a corner or between the pieces of furniture, and then, after thorough consideration, heaped up the volumes in the piles to which they belonged, pledging myself to find room for all the books belonging to each pile, and to leave each heap undisturbed in its own place, till the corresponding chapter in the Sketch should be finished. And I carried out my plan to the very end. For many a month all the people who visited me had to thread their way across the room along paths which ran between heaps of books. I had also to fight hard to ensure that the tidying zeal of the trusty Württemberg widow who kept house for me came to a halt before the piles of books.

The earliest representatives of the historical science which busied itself with research into the life of Jesus found themselves obliged to struggle for permission to undertake the task of establishing by purely historical methods the existence of Jesus, and to test by critical methods the Gospels, as those sources to which we must go back for information about Him. It was only recognized gradually that Jesus' consciousness of His divine mission could not be established as correct in face of the critical and historical treatment of the events which make up His life, and of the ideas which He preached.

The Lives of Jesus of the eighteenth and the early nineteenth centuries depict Him as the great enlightener Whose aim is to lead His people from the non-spiritual teaching of the Jewish religion to the rational belief, which is above and beyond all dogma, in a God of love and an ethical Kingdom of God to be established on earth. They make it their special endeavour to explain all the miracles of Jesus as natural events misunderstood by the multitude, and thus they try to put an end to all belief in the miraculous. The most famous of these rationalistic Lives of Jesus is that of Karl Heinrich Venturini: *A Non-supernatural History of the Great Prophet of Nazareth*, which in the years 1800-1802 appeared anonymously in German at "Bethlehem" (in reality Copenhagen) in four volumes containing 2,700 pages. Of the attempt made by Reimarus to understand the preaching of Jesus from the standpoint of the eschatological Messianic doctrine of late Judaism, no one of that period takes any notice at all.

Research first reaches a fairway of real history through the channel of a critical scrutiny of the Gospels so as to determine the historical value of their narratives. Its work, which began with the nineteenth century and was continued for several decades, brought it to the following results: that the picture given by the Gospel of John is irreconcilable with that of the other three; that these three are the older, and therefore the more credible sources; that the matter which they contain in common with one another is given in its earliest form by the Gospel of Mark; and, finally, that Luke's Gospel is considerably later than those of Mark and Matthew.

Research into the life of Jesus is brought into sore straits by David Friedrich Strauss (1808-1874), who in his Life, published in 1835, accepts as historic only a small portion of what the two oldest Gospels report about Jesus. The greater part of it he considers to be narratives of a mythical character which came into existence gradually in primitive Christendom and, in the main, go back to themes which are provided by the stories of miracles, and the passages about the Messiah, in the Old Testament. If Strauss comes finally to such a serious calling in question of the credibility of the two oldest narratives, that is not because he is by nature a sceptic, but because he is the first to realize how difficult it is really to understand the details which they give of the public life and the preaching of Jesus.

From the middle of the nineteenth century onwards there is gradually built up the modern historical view that Jesus attempted to spiritualize the realistic Messianic hopes of contemporary Judaism; that He came forward as a spiritual Messiah and founder of an ethical Kingdom of God; and that finally, when the people, failing to understand Him, deserted Him, He came to the resolution to die for His cause, and in that way to carry it to victory. Of the delineations of the life of Jesus which have this ground-plan in common, the best known are those of Ernest Renan (1863), Theodore Keim (3 vols, 1867; 1871; 1872), Karl Hase (1876), and Oscar Holtzmann (1901). The scientific establishment in detail of this interpretation is attempted by Heinrich Julius Holtzmann in his books on the three first Gospels, and in his *New Testament Theology*. The most living presentation of this modernized theory about Jesus is to be found, I think, in Harnack's *What is Christianity?* (1901).

But as early as 1860 separate investigations into the problems of the life of Jesus began to make it clear that the view which represents Him as trying to spiritualize the eschatological, Messianic expectations of His time, cannot be sustained, because in a series of passages He speaks in a quite realistic way of the coming of the Son of Man and the Messianic Kingdom when this world comes to an end. If the attempt is given up to reinterpret or to discredit these passages, there remain two alternatives: either to recognize and admit that Jesus did really live with a belief in the ideas of late-Jewish eschatology, or assert that only those sayings are genuine in which He speaks in a truly spiritual way of the Messiah and the Messianic Kingdom, the remainder having been attributed to Him by a primitive Christianity which had fallen back into the realistic views of late Judaism. Faced by these alternatives, research decides at first for the second. That Jesus should be thought to have shared the Messianic ideas of late-Judaism, which are so alien to our ideas, seems to it so incomprehensible and so offensive, that it prefers to doubt to some extent the trustworthiness of the two oldest Gospels, and to deny the genuineness of a portion of the sayings which they report, on account of their strange content. But when it goes on, as it does in the works of Timothy Colani (*Jésus Christ et les croyances messianiques de son temps*, 1864) and Gustave Volkmar (*Jesus Nazarenus*, 1882), to establish this distinction between genuine "spiritual Messianic" and spurious "eschatological Messianic" pronouncements, it becomes clear that it must go on to deny that Jesus ever believed Himself to be the Messiah at all. For the passages in which He entrusts to His disciples the secret that He is the Messiah are, one and all, "Eschatological Messianic," in that He, according to them, holds Himself to be the person who at the end of the world will appear as the Son of Man.

The question whether Jesus thought eschatologically or not resolves itself, therefore, into the one point, whether He held Himself to be the Messiah, or not. Anyone who admits that He did so must also admit that His ideas and expectations were of the eschatological type of late Judaism. Anyone who refuses to recognize this element in His thought must also refuse to attribute to Him any consciousness of being the Messiah.

That is the way in which William Wrede in his work *The Messianic Secret of the Gospels* (1901) preserves consistency. He works throughout on the assumption that Jesus appeared in public simply as a teacher, and only after His death, that is in the imagination of His followers, became Messiah. Into the original tradition about the appearance in public and the activity of "Jesus the Teacher," this later view, says Wrede, was incorporated in such a way as to represent Him as not confessing His Messiahship, but keeping it to Himself as a secret. Naturally Wrede does not succeed in making this imaginary literary procedure even faintly intelligible.

To doubt the eschatological, Messianic statements of Jesus leads, then, with inexorable logic to the conclusion that there is nothing in the two oldest Gospels which can be accepted as historical beyond a few quite general reports about the teaching activities of a certain Jesus of Nazareth. Rather than become the prey of such radicalism as that, research resigns itself after all to the necessity of recognizing eschatological Messianic ideas in Jesus. So towards the end of the century the view which sees an eschatological character in the preaching of Jesus and His Messianic self-consciousness begins to make headway, as developed by the Heidelberg theologian, Johannes Weiss (1892), in a book written with wonderful clarity, *The Preaching of Jesus concerning the Kingdom of God.* Scientific theology cherishes, nevertheless, in secret the hope that it will not, after all, have to admit everything that Weiss propounds. In reality, however, it has to go even further than he, for he comes to a stop half-way. He makes Jesus think and talk eschatologically without proceeding to the natural inference that His actions also must have been determined by eschatological ideas. The course of His activity and His resolution to die he explains by means of the usual assumption of initial success and later failure. For the historical understanding of the life of Jesus, however, it is necessary to think out all the consequences of the fact that He did actually live in the eschatological, Messianic thought-world of late Judaism, and to try to comprehend His resolutions and actions not by means of considerations drawn from ordinary psychology, but solely by motives provided by His eschatological expectations. This consistently eschatological solution of the problems of the life of Jesus I work out in detail in *The Quest of the Historical Jesus*, after having only sketched it in 1901 in *The Secret of the Passion and Messiahship of Jesus.* Because this solution is such as to make comprehensible so much in the thought, the discourses, and the actions of Jesus which has been incomprehensible hitherto, it establishes the genuineness of a number of passages which, because unintelligible, were held to be unhistorical. In this way the eschatological interpretation of the life of Jesus puts an end to all need to doubt the credibility of the Gospels of Mark and Matthew. It shows that their reports of the public activity and the death of Jesus follow a faithful tradition which is reliable even in details. If some things in this tradition are obscure or confused, the explanation is to be found chiefly in the fact that in a number of instances the disciples themselves did not understand the sayings and actions of their Master.

After the appearance of my *Quest of the Historical Jesus* a friendly exchange of letters began between William Wrede and myself. It moved me deeply to learn from him that he suffered from an incurable heart complaint and might expect death at any moment. "Subjectively I am tolerably well; objectively my condition is hopeless"; so he writes in one of the last letters I received from him. I was weighed down by the thought that I could work on without intermission, undisturbed by trouble about my health, while he had to give up work in the best period of a man's life. The recognition expressed in my work of the value of his investigations did something to compensate him for the hostility provoked by his fearless labour in the cause of truth. He died in 1907.

To my astonishment my work at once met with recognition in England. The first to make my views known there was Professor William Sanday of Oxford in lectures which he delivered on the problems of the life of Jesus. His pressing invitation to visit him I unfortunately could not accept, because I could not spare the time. I was already studying medicine, and just at that time, in addition to the preparation of my theological lectures, was at work on the German edition of my book on Bach, which had been written in French. Thus I missed a second opportunity of becoming acquainted with England.

In Cambridge Professor Francis Crawford Burkitt championed my work, and secured its appearance in English. The excellent translation was made by his pupil, Mr. W.

Montgomery. Out of my theological relations with these two men there soon sprang up a warm friendship.

While Professor Burkitt brought to bear on my views a purely scientific interest, they met with Dr. Sanday's approval because they supported the religious position for which he stood. For the Catholic trend of his mind the modernized portrait of Jesus represented by liberal Protestant research had no attractions. That it was shown to be unhistorical by criticism which actually emanated from the circles of that same liberal investigation, was a great satisfaction to him, and seemed to him to clear the road before his Catholic type of piety.

My work also had significance for George Tyrrell. Without the scientific establishment, which he found in it, of the view that the thought and the actions of Jesus were conditioned by eschatology, he would not have been able in his *Christianity at the Cross-Roads* to portray Jesus so decisively as the ethical Apocalyptist who by his very nature was not Protestant but Catholic.

CHAPTER VI

THE HISTORICAL JESUS AND THE CHRISTIANITY OF TO-DAY

As my two books on the life of Jesus gradually became known, the question was put to me from all sides, what the eschatological Jesus, who lives expecting the end of the world and a supernatural Kingdom of God, can be to us. My own thoughts were continually busy with it while at work on my books. The satisfaction which I could not help feeling at having solved so many historical riddles about the existence of Jesus was accompanied by the painful consciousness that this new knowledge in the realm of history would mean unrest and difficulty for Christian piety. I comforted myself, however, with words of S. Paul's which had been familiar to me from childhood: "We can do nothing against truth, but for the truth" (2 Cor. xiii. 8). Since the essential nature of the spiritual is truth, every new truth means ultimately something won. Truth is under all circumstances more valuable than non-truth, and this must apply to truth in the realm of history as to other kinds of truth. Even if it comes in a guise which piety finds strange and at first makes difficulties for her, the final result can never mean injury; it can only mean greater depth. Religion has, therefore, no reason for trying to avoid coming to terms with historical truth.

How strong would Christian truth now stand in the world of to-day, if its relation to the truth in history were in every respect what it should be! Instead of allowing this truth its rights, she treated it, whenever it caused her embarrassment, in various ways, conscious or unconscious, but always by either evading, or twisting, or suppressing it. Instead of admitting that new elements towards which she had to advance were new, and justifying them by present action, she proceeded with artificial and disputable arguments to force them back into the past. To-day the condition of Christianity is such that hard struggles are now required to make possible that coming to terms with historical truth which has been so often missed in the past.

In what a condition we find ourselves to-day merely because in the earliest Christian period writings were allowed to appear, bearing quite falsely the names of apostles, in order to give greater authority to the ideas put forth in them! They have been for generations of Christians a source of painful dissension. On one side stand those who in face of the abundance of material for judgement, cannot exclude the possibility of there being in the New Testament writings which, in spite of their valuable contents that we have learnt to love, are not authentic; on the other are those who, to save the reputation of the oldest Christian thought, try to show this to be not proven. And meanwhile, those on whom the whole guilt rests were scarcely conscious of doing anything wrong. They only followed the custom which was universal in antiquity and against which no further objection was raised of maintaining that writings which were said to express the ideas of any particular person were really written by him.

Because, while I was busied with the history of earlier Christianity, I had so often to deal with the results of its sins against the truth in history, I have become a keen worker for honesty in our Christianity of to-day.

The ideal would be that Jesus should have preached religious truth in a form independent of any connexion with any particular period and such that it could be taken over simply and easily by each succeeding generation of men. That, however, He did not do, and there is no doubt a reason for it.

We have, therefore, to reconcile ourselves to the fact that His religion of love appeared as part of a world-view which expected a speedy end of the world. Clothed in the ideas in which He announced it, we cannot make it our own; we must re-clothe it in those of our modern world-view.

Hitherto we have been doing this ingenuously and covertly. In defiance of what the words of the text said we managed to interpret the teaching of Jesus as if it were in agreement with our own world-view. Now, however, it must be clear to us that we can only harmonize these two things by an act, for which we claim the right of necessity.

We are obliged, that is, to admit the evident fact that religious truth varies from age to age.

How is this to be understood? So far as its essential spiritual and ethical nature is concerned, Christianity's religious truth remains the same through the centuries. The variations belong only to the outward form which it assumes in the ideas belonging to different world-views. Thus the religion of love which Jesus taught, and which made its first appearance as an element in the late-Jewish eschatological world-view, enters later on into connexion with the late-Greek, the medieval, and the modern world-views. Nevertheless, it remains through the centuries what it is essentially. Whether it is worked out in terms of one *Weltanschauung* or another is only a matter of relative importance. What is decisive is the amount of influence over mankind won by the spiritual and ethical truth which it has held from the very first.

We of to-day do not, like those who were able to hear the preaching of Jesus, expect to see a Kingdom of God realizing itself in supernatural events. Our conviction is that it can only come into existence by the power of the spirit of Jesus working in our hearts and in the world. The one important thing is that we shall be as thoroughly dominated by the idea of the Kingdom, as Jesus required His followers to be.

The mighty thought underlying the Beatitudes of the Sermon on the Mount, that we come to know God and belong to Him through love, Jesus introduces into the late-Jewish, Messianic expectation, without being in any way concerned to spiritualize those realistic ideas of the Kingdom of God and of blessedness. But the spirituality which lies in this religion of love must gradually, like a refiner's fire, seize upon all ideas which come into communication with it. Thus it is the destiny of Christianity to develop through a constant process of spiritualization.

Jesus never undertakes to expound the late-Jewish

dogmas of the Messiah and the Kingdom. His concern is, not how believers ought to picture things but that love, without which no one can belong to God, and attain to membership of the Kingdom, shall be powerful within it. The subject of all His preaching is love, and, more generally, the preparation of the heart for the Kingdom. The Messianic dogma remains in the background. If He did not happen to mention it now and then, one could forget that it is presupposed all through. That explains why it was possible to overlook for so long the fact that His religion of love was conditioned by Time.

The late-Jewish Messianic world-view is the crater from which bursts forth the flame of the eternal religion of love.

To let the historical Jesus Himself be the speaker when the Christian message is delivered to the men and women of our time does not mean that the preacher will expound again and again the meaning which the passage taken for his text had under the eschatological Messianic world-view. It suffices if they have come to accept as a matter of course the fact that Jesus lived in expectation of the end of the world and of a Kingdom of God which would be manifested supernaturally. But whoever preaches to them the Gospel of Jesus must settle for himself what the original meaning of His sayings was, and work his way up through the historical truth to the eternal. During this process he will again and again have opportunity to notice that it is with this new beginning that he first truly realizes all that Jesus has to say to us!

How many ministers of religion have confirmed my experience that the Jesus who is known historically, although He speaks to us from another thought-world than our own, makes preaching not harder but easier.

There is a deep significance in the fact that whenever we hear the sayings of Jesus we tread the ground of a world-view which is not ours. In our own world- and life-affirming world-view Christianity is in constant danger of being externalized. The Gospel of Jesus which speaks to us out of an expectation of the end of the world leads us off the highway of busy service for the Kingdom of God on to the footpath of inwardness, and urges us, in spiritual

freedom from the world to seek the true strength for working in the spirit of the Kingdom of God. The essence of
Christianity is world-affirmation which has gone through
an experience of world negation. In the eschatological
world-view of world-negation Jesus proclaims the ethic
of active love!

Even if the historical Jesus has something strange about
Him, yet His personality, as it really is, influences us
much more strongly and immediately than when He
approached us in dogma and in the results attained up to
the present by research. In dogma His personality became
less alive; recent research has been modernizing and
belittling Him.

Anyone who ventures to look the historical Jesus straight
in the face and to listen for what He may have to teach
him in His powerful sayings, soon ceases to ask what this
strange-seeming Jesus can still be to him. He learns to
know Him as One who claims authority over him.

The true understanding of Jesus is the understanding
of will acting on will. The true relation to Him is to be
taken possession of by Him. Christian piety of any and
every sort is valuable only so far as it means the surrender
of our will to His.

Jesus does not require of men to-day that they be able
to grasp either in speech or in thought Who He is. He
did not think it necessary to give those who actually heard
His sayings any insight into the secret of His personality,
or to disclose to them the fact that He was that descendant
of David who was one day to be revealed as the Messiah.
The one thing He did require of them was that they should
actively and passively prove themselves men who had been
compelled by Him to rise from being as the world to being
other than the world, and thereby partakers of His peace.

Because, while I was investigating and thinking about
Jesus, all this became a certainty to me, I let my *Quest of
the Historical Jesus* end with the words: "As one unknown
and nameless He comes to us, just as on the shore of the
lake He approached those men who knew not who He
was. His words are the same: 'Follow thou Me!' and He
puts us to the tasks which He has to carry out in our

age. He commands. And to those who obey, be they wise
or simple, He will reveal Himself through all that they are
privileged to experience in His fellowship of peace and
activity, of struggle and suffering, till they come to know,
as an inexpressible secret, Who He is. . . ."

Many people are shocked on learning that the historical
Jesus must be accepted as "capable of error" because the
supernatural Kingdom of God, the manifestation of which
He announced as imminent, did not appear.

What can we do in face of what stands clearly recorded
in the Gospels? Are we acting in the spirit of Jesus if we
attempt with hazardous and sophisticated explanations to
force the sayings into agreement with the dogmatic teaching of His absolute universal incapability of error. He Himself never made any claim to such omniscience. Just as
He pointed out to the young man who addressed Him as
"Good Master" (Mark x. 17 f.) that God alone is good, so
He would also have set His face against those who would
have liked to attribute to Him a divine infallibility. Knowledge of spiritual truth is not called upon to prove its
genuineness by showing further knowledge about the
events of world-history and matters of ordinary life. Its
province lies on a quite different level from the latter's,
and it is quite independent of it.

The historical Jesus moves us deeply by His subordination to God. In this He stands out as greater than the
Christ personality of dogma which, in compliance with
the claims of Greek metaphysics, is conceived as omnis-
cient and incapable of error.

The demonstration of the fact that the teaching of Jesus
was conditioned by eschatology was at once a heavy blow
for liberal Protestantism. For generations the latter had
busied itself investigating the life of Jesus in the conviction that all progress in the knowledge of history could
not but make more evident the undogmatic character of
the religion of Jesus. At the close of the nineteenth century it seemed to see it finally proved that our religious
thought could without further ado adopt as its own Jesus'
religion of a Kingdom of God to be founded on earth. It

was not long, however, before it had to admit that this description was true only for the teaching of Jesus as it had been unconsciously modernized by itself, and not of the really historical teaching of Jesus. I myself have suffered in this matter, by having had to join in the work of destroying the portrait of Christ on which liberal Christianity based its appeal. At the same time I was convinced that this liberal Christianity was not reduced to living on an historical illusion, but could equally appeal to the Jesus of history, and further that it carried its justification in itself.

For even if that liberal Christianity has to give up identifying its belief with the teachings of Jesus in the way it used to think possible, it still has the spirit of Jesus not against it but on its side. Jesus no doubt fits His teaching into the late-Jewish Messianic dogma. But He does not think dogmatically. He formulates no doctrine. He is far from judging any man's belief by reference to any standard of dogmatic correctness. Nowhere does He demand of His hearers that they shall sacrifice thinking to believing. Quite the contrary! He bids them meditate upon religion. In the Sermon on the Mount He lets ethics, as the essence of religion, flood their hearts, leading them to judge the value of piety by what it makes of a man from the ethical point of view. Within the Messianic hopes which His hearers carry in their hearts, He kindles the fire of an ethical faith. Thus the Sermon on the Mount becomes the incontestable charter of liberal Christianity. The truth that the ethical is the essence of religion is firmly established on the authority of Jesus.

Further than this, the religion of love taught by Jesus has been freed from any dogmatism which clung to it, by the disappearance of the late-Jewish eschatological world-view. The mould in which the casting was made has been broken. We are now at liberty to let the religion of Jesus become a living force in our thought, as its purely spiritual and ethical nature demands. We know how much that is precious exists within the ecclesiastical Christianity which has been handed down in Greek dogmas and kept alive by the piety of so many centuries, and we hold fast to the Church with love, and reverence, and thankfulness. But we belong to her as men who appeal to the saying of S. Paul: "Where the Spirit of the Lord is, there is liberty," and who believe that they serve Christianity better by the strength of their devotion to Jesus' religion of love than by acquiescence in all the articles of belief. If the Church has the spirit of Jesus, there is room in her for every form of Christian piety, even for that which claims unrestricted liberty.

I find it no light task to follow my vocation, to put pressure on the Christian Faith to reconcile itself in all sincerity with historical truth. But I have devoted myself to it with joy, because I am certain that truthfulness in all things belongs to the spirit of Jesus.

CHAPTER VII

THE BACH BOOK—FRENCH AND GERMAN EDITIONS

WHILE busy with the *Quest of the Historical Jesus* I finished a book, written in French, on J. S. Bach. Widor, with whom I used to spend several weeks in Paris every spring, and frequently in the autumn too, had complained to me that there existed in French only biographical books about him, but none that provided any introduction to his art. I had to promise him that I would spend the autumn vacation of 1902 in writing an essay on the nature of Bach's art for the students of the Paris Conservatoire.

This was a task that attracted me because it gave me an opportunity of expressing thoughts at which I had arrived in the course of the close study of Bach, both theoretical and practical, entailed on me by my post as organist to the Bach Choir at S. Wilhelm's.

At the end of the vacation I had, in spite of the most strenuous work, not got further than the preliminary studies for the treatise. It had also become clear that this would expand into a book on Bach. With good courage I resigned myself to my fate.

In 1903 and 1904 I devoted all my spare time to Bach, my work being lightened by my becoming possessed of the complete edition of his works, which was at that time very rarely in the market and then only at a very high price. I was thus no longer under the necessity of studying the scores in the University Library, a restriction which had been a great hindrance to me, since I could find hardly any time for Bach except at night. I happened to learn at a music shop in Strassburg that a lady in Paris who had been a subscriber to the complete edition in order to support the enterprise of the Bach Society, now wanted to get rid of the long row of big grey volumes which took up so much space on her bookshelves. Pleased at being able to give somebody pleasure with them, she let me have them for the ridiculously small sum of £10. This piece of good fortune I took as a good omen for the success of my work.

It was, in truth, a very rash undertaking on my part to start writing a book on Bach. Although I had, thanks to extensive reading, some knowledge of musical history and theory, I had not studied music as one studies for a profession. However, my design was not to produce new historical material about Bach and his time. As a musician I wanted to talk to other musicians about Bach's music. The main subject of my work, therefore, should be, so I resolved, what in most other books hitherto had been much too slightly treated, namely an explanation of the real nature of Bach's music, and a discussion of the correct method of rendering it. My work accordingly sets forth what is biographical and historical as introductory rather than as the main subject.

If the difficulties in such a subject made me fear that I had ventured on a task beyond my powers, I consoled myself with the thought that I was not writing for Germany, the home of Bach scholarship, but for France, where the art of the Precentor of S. Thomas's was still practically unknown.

That I wrote the book in French at a time when I was also lecturing and preaching in German was an effort for me. It is true that ever since my childhood I have spoken French as freely as German; but I never feel French to be my mother-tongue, although in my letters to my parents I always used French because that was customary in the family. German is my mother-tongue, because the Alsatian dialect, which is my native language, is Germanic.

My own experience makes me think it only self-deception if any believes that he has two mother-tongues. He may think that he is equally master of each, yet it is invariably the case that he actually thinks only in one, and is only in that one really free and creative. If anyone assures me that he has two languages, each as thoroughly familiar to him as the other, I immediately ask him in which of them he counts and reckons, in which he can best give me the names of kitchen utensils and tools used by carpenter or smith, and in which of them he dreams.

I have not yet come across anyone who, when thus tested, had not to admit that one of the languages occupied only a second place.

I profited much in my work on Bach by the remarks made to me on the style of my manuscript by Hubert Gillot, at that time a lecturer in French in Strassburg University. He tried with special emphasis to impress upon me that the French sentence needs rhythm in far stronger measure than does the German.

The difference between the two languages, as I feel it, I can best describe by saying that in French I seem to be strolling along the well-kept paths in a fine park, but in German to be wandering at will in a magnificent forest. Into literary German there flows continually new life from the dialects with which it has kept in touch. French has lost this ever-fresh contact with the soil. It is rooted in its literature, becoming thereby, in the favourable, as in the unfavourable sense of the word, something finished, while German in the same sense remains something unfinished. The perfection of French consists in being able to express a thought in the clearest and most concise way; that of German in being able to present it in its manifold aspects. As the greatest linguistic creation in French I count Rousseau's *Contrat Social*. What is nearest perfection in German I see in Luther's translation of the Bible and Nietzche's *Jenseits von Gut und Böse* ("Beyond Good and Evil").

Always accustomed in French to be careful about the rhythmical arrangement of the sentence, and to strive for simplicity of expression, these things have become equally a necessity to me in German. And now through my work on the French *Bach* it became clear to me what literary style corresponded to my nature.

Like everyone who writes about art, I had to wrestle with the difficulty of giving expression in words to artistic judgements and impressions. All utterances about art are, indeed, a kind of speaking in parables.

In the autumn of 1904 I was able to announce to Widor, who had spurred me on again and again with letters and was now at Venice, where he was spending his holiday, that the undertaking was now so far advanced that he must start upon the preface which he had promised me. This he did at once.

The book appeared in 1905, dedicated to Madame Mathilde Schweitzer, the wife of my father's eldest brother in Paris.[1] Had she not in 1893 enabled me to meet Widor, and, thanks to her hospitable house, given me again and again the opportunity of being with him, I should never have come to be writing about Bach.

I was surprised and delighted that my work met with recognition even in Germany as an enrichment of the study of Bach, whereas I had written it merely to fill a gap in French musical literature. In the *Kunstwart* ("Art Guardian") von Lüpke raised the question of a translation. Consequently in the autumn of that year, 1905, a German edition was agreed upon, to be published by Breitkopf and Härtel.

When in the summer of 1906, after the completion of the *Quest of the Historical Jesus*, I turned to work on the German edition of the *Bach*, I soon became conscious that it was impossible for me to translate myself into another language, and that if I was to produce anything satisfactory, I must plunge anew into the original materials of my book. So I shut the French *Bach* with a bang, and resolved to make a new and better German one. Out of the book of 455 pages there sprang, to the dismay of the astonished publisher, one of 844. The first pages of the new work I wrote at Bayreuth in the "Black Horse" Inn after a wonderful performance of *Tristan*. For weeks I had been trying in vain to get to work. In the mood of exaltation in which I returned from the Festival Hill, I succeeded. While the babel of voices surged up from the Bierhalle below into my stuffy room, I began to write, and it was long after sunrise that I laid down my pen. From that time onwards I felt such a joy in the work that I had it ready in two years, although my medical course, the preparation of my lectures, my preaching activities, and my concert tours prevented me from busying myself with it continuously. I often had to lay it aside for weeks.

The German edition appeared early in 1908,[2] and is the

[1] *J. S. Bach, le musicien-poète.* 455 pages. (Costallat, Paris. Breitkopf und Härtel, Leipzig. 1905.)

[2] Albert Schweitzer, *J. S. Bach.* 844 pages (Breitkopf und Härtel, Leipzig. 1908.)

text from which the English translation was made by the clever pen of Ernest Newman.[1]

In their fight against Wagner, the Anti-Wagnerites appealed to the ideal of classical music, as they had settled it to their own satisfaction. They defined it as pure music, accepting as such only music of which they believed they could say that it afforded no scope for poetical or pictorial aims, but it was only concerned to give to beautiful lines of sound the most perfect existence possible. Bach, whose works in their completeness had been gradually getting better known, thanks to the edition produced by the Bach Society in the middle of the nineteenth century, was claimed by them on these principles, and Mozart as well, for this classical art of theirs, and they played him off against Wagner. His fugues seemed to them to be incontrovertible proof that he served their ideal of pure music. He was depicted as a classic of this kind by Philip Spitta in his large, important three-volumed work in which he puts forward the biographical—and is the first to do so—on a foundation of penetrating research into the sources.[2]

As a contrast to the Bach of these Guardians of the Grail of pure music I present the Bach who is a poet and painter in sound. All that lies in the text, the emotional and the pictorial alike, he strives to reproduce in the language of music with the utmost possible vitality and clearness. Before all else he aims at rendering the pictorial lines of sound. He is even more tone-painter than tone-poet. His art is nearer to that of Berlioz than to that of Wagner. If the text speaks of drifting mists, of boisterous winds, of roaring rivers, of waves that ebb and flow, of leaves falling from the tree, of bells that ring for the dying, of the confident faith which walks with firm steps, or the weak faith that falters insecure, of the proud who will be abased, and the humble who will be exalted, of Satan rising in rebellion, of angels poised on the clouds of heaven, then one sees and hears all this in his music.

Bach has, in fact, at his disposal a language of sound. There are in his music constantly recurring rhythmical motives expressing peaceful blessedness, lively joy, intense pain, or pain sublimely borne.

The impulse to express poetic and pictorial plastic thoughts is of the essence of music. Music appeals to the creative imagination of the hearer, and endeavours to kindle into life in

[1] The English edition appeared in 1911 in two volumes, also published by the same firm. The publishing rights in England were taken over in 1923 by Messrs. A. & C. Black, London.

[2] The first volume appeared in 1873, the second in 1880.

it the emotional experiences and the visions from which it came into being itself. But this it can do only if the person who uses the language of sound possesses the mysterious faculty of rendering thoughts with a clearness and definiteness surpassing its own natural power of expression. In this respect Bach is the greatest among the great.

His music is poetic and pictorial because its themes are born of poetic and pictorial ideas. Out of these themes the composition unfolds itself, a finished piece of architecture in lines of sound. What is in its essence poetic and pictorial music displays itself as Gothic architecture transformed into sound. What is greatest in this art, so full of natural life, so wonderfully plastic, and unique in the perfection of its form, is the spirit that breathes out from it. A soul which out of the world's unrest longs for peace and has itself already tasted peace, allows in this music others to share its own experience.

It follows from the nature of Bach's art that, in order to produce its effects, it must be presented to the hearer in living and perfected plasticity. But this principle, which is fundamental for its worthy rendering, has even to-day to struggle for recognition.

To begin with, it is a crime against the style of Bach's music that we perform it with huge orchestras and massed choirs. The Cantatas and the Passion music were written for choirs of twenty-five to thirty voices, and an orchestra of about the same number. Bach's orchestra does not accompany the choir, but is a partner with equal rights, and there is no such thing as an orchestral equivalent to a choir of a hundred and fifty voices. We shall therefore come to providing for the performance of Bach's music choirs of forty to fifty voices and orchestras of fifty to sixty instrumentalists. The wonderful inter-weaving of the voice parts must stand out, clear and distinct. For alto and soprano Bach did not use women's voices but boys' voices only, even for the solos. Choirs of male voices form an homogeneous whole. At the very least, then, women's voices should be supplemented with boys', but the ideal is that even the alto and soprano solos should be sung by boys.

Since Bach's music is architecture, the crescendos and decrescendos which in Beethoven's and post-Beethoven's music are responses to emotional experiences, are not appropriate. Alternations of forte and piano are significant in it only so far as they serve to emphasize leading phrases and to leave subsidiary ones less prominent. It is only within the limits of these alternations of forte and piano that declamatory crescendos

C

and diminuendos are admissible. If they obliterate the difference between forte and piano, they ruin the architecture of the composition.

Since a Bach fugue always begins and ends with a main theme it cannot tolerate any beginning and ending in piano.

Bach is played altogether too fast. Music which presupposes a visual comprehension of lines of sound advancing side by side becomes for the listener a chaos, if a too rapid tempo makes this comprehension impossible.

Yet it is not so much by the tempo as by phrasing which makes the lines of sound stand out before the listener in a living plasticity, that it is made possible to appreciate the life which animates Bach's music.

Whereas down to the middle of the nineteenth century Bach, curiously enough, was generally played staccato, players have since that date gone to the other extreme of rendering him with a monotonous legato. That is how I learnt to play him from Widor in 1893. But as time went on, it occurred to me that Bach calls for phrasing which is full of life. He thinks as a violinist. His notes are to be connected with each other and at the same time separated from each other in the way which is natural to the bow of a violin. To play well one of Bach's piano compositions means to render it as it would be performed by a string quartette.

Correct phrasing is to be secured by correct accenting. Bach demands that the notes which are decisive for the style of the line of sound's advance shall be given their full importance by the accenting. It is characteristic of the structure of his periods that as a rule they do not start from an accent but strive to reach one. They are conceived as beginning with an upward beat. It must, further, be noticed that in Bach the accents of the lines of sound do not as a rule coincide with the natural accents of the bars, but advance side by side with these in a freedom of their own. From this tension between the accents of the line of sound and those of the bars comes the extraordinary rhythmical vitality of Bach's music.

These are the external requirements for the rendering of Bach's music. But above and beyond them that music demands of us men and women that we attain a composure and an inwardness that will enable us to rouse to life something of the deep spirit which lies hidden within it.

The ideas which I put forward about the nature of Bach's music and the appropriate way of rendering it, found recognition because they appeared just at the right time. By the interest aroused on the publication towards the end of the last century of the complete edition of his works it was brought home to the musical world that Bach was something other than the representative of an academic, and classical, music. Over the traditional method of rendering it they were similarly at a loss, and now they began to seek for a method which corresponded to the Master's style. But this new knowledge had as yet been neither formulated nor provided with a foundation. And so my book made public for the first time views which musicians specially concerned with Bach carried in their minds. Thus I gained many a friend. With emotion I think of the many delightful letters which it brought me immediately after its appearance. Felix Mottl, the conductor, whom I had admired from a distance, wrote to me from Leipzig, after reading the book right through without a break in the train and in his hotel while travelling to that town from Munich, where some friends had given him the book as reading-matter for the journey. I met him soon after, and later enjoyed some happy hours with him on several occasions.

It was through this book that I became acquainted with Siegfried Ochs, the Berlin Bach conductor, and began with him a friendship which has grown continually closer.

It was because I had made her beloved Bach still dearer to her that Carmen Sylva wrote me a long letter which was followed by a whole series of others. The latest of them, directed to Africa, were in pencil and painfully committed to paper because her hand, which was tortured with rheumatism, was no longer equal to using the pen. I could not accept the Queen's frequently repeated invitation to spend part of my holidays with her under the single obligation of playing the organ to her for two hours daily because in the last years before my departure for Africa I could not afford time for a holiday. And when I returned home she was no longer among the living.

CHAPTER VIII

ON ORGANS AND ORGAN-BUILDING

As a corollary to the book on Bach there appeared in the autumn of 1905, before I began my medical studies, an essay on Organ-building.

I inherited from my grandfather Schillinger an interest in organ-building, which impelled me, while I was still quite a boy, to get to know all about the inside of an organ.

I was curiously affected by the organs which were built towards the end of the nineteenth century. Although they were lauded as miracles of advanced technical skill, I could find no pleasure in them. In the autumn of 1896 I made my way home after my first visit to Beyreuth, via Stuttgart, in order to examine the new organ in the 'Liederhalle' of that town, about which the newspapers had published enthusiastic reports. Herr Lang, the organist of the Stiftskirche, who both as musician and as man stood in the first rank, was kind enough to show it to me. When I heard the harsh tone of the much-belauded instrument, and in the Bach fugue which Lang played to me perceived a chaos of sounds in which I could not distinguish the separate voices, my foreboding that the modern organ meant in that respect a step not forward but backward, suddenly became a certainty. In order to convince myself finally of this fact and to find the reasons for it. I used my free time in the next few years in getting to know as many organs, old and new, as possible. I also discussed the matter with all the organists and organbuilders with whom I came in contact. As a rule I met with laughter and jeers for my opinion that the old organs sounded better than the new ones. The pamphlet, too, in which I undertook to preach the gospel of the ideal organ, was understood at first by only a few people here and there. It appeared in 1906, ten years after my Damascus at Stuttgart, and bears the title: *The Art of Organ-building and Organ-playing in Germany and France.*[1] I acknowledge in it a preference for the French style of organ-building as compared with the German, because in several respects it has remained faithful to the traditions of the art.

The action of an organ and the quality of its tone are determined by four factors: the pipes, the wind-chest, the wind-pressure, and the position it occupies in the building.

As a result of the collective experience of generations, the old organ-builders had arrived at the best proportions and the best shapes for the pipes. Further, they used for them only the best materials. The organ-building of to-day constructs the pipes in accordance with theories drawn from physics, often sacrificing thereby the achievements of earlier master-builders. It is over-economical, too, with the materials in order to build as cheaply as possible. Hence the factory organs of to-day frequently contain pipes which have no resonance because their diameter is too small and their walls are too thin, or they are constructed of other material than the best wood and the best tin.

The wind-chest, i.e. the chest on which the pipes stand and from which the wind enters them, used to be in earlier times a so-called 'Schleiflade' (old-fashioned sounding-board). This has a number of technical disadvantages compared with the wind-chest employed by the builders of to-day. Moreover, it costs considerably more. But in quality of tone produced it is far superior, because its construction offers for definite reasons great acoustic advantages.

On the old wind-chest pipes produced a round and soft but full tone; on the new one they produce a harsh and dry one. The tone of an old organ laps round the hearer in a gentle flood; that of a new one rushes upon him with with the roar of surf.

In the old organs the pipes were fed with wind under moderate pressure, because the imperfect bellows of that day could not give them anything stronger. But when with a perfected apparatus, electrically driven, wind could be produced in any desired amount, it was driven into the pipes at high pressure. Then, blinded by the fact that an organ with twenty-five stops could be as powerful as one with forty stops hitherto, organists overlooked the further fact that the sound now blustered boisterously out instead of issuing in a steady stream

[1] *Deutsche und französische Orgelbaukunst und Orgelkunst.* 51 pages. 1906. (Breitkopf und Härtel, Leipzig.) This essay appeared first in the periodical *Die Musik* (Parts 13 and 14, 1906). A second edition appeared in 1927 with an historical supplement.

as befits a wind-instrument, so that what was gained in volume was lost in quality.

Then as to the playing-apparatus, that is, the way in which the keys and the pipes are connected, there was a sad want of balance between the thought bestowed on cheapness and technical perfection, and the attention paid to the artistic aim and the way to secure it.

The best method of connecting the keys and the pipes is the purely mechanical one. On an organ with such mechanism phrasing is easiest. All small and medium-sized organs should, therefore, be constructed with it. After the mechanical method comes, as second-best, the pneumatic, with which the connexion between the keys and the pipes is effected by wind-pressure. Only in exceptional cases should organs be built with electrical mechanism, because the electric system needs constant care for its maintenance, and it is not reliable. Yet, because it is in many ways simpler to build for electricity, the organ-builders of to-day are inclined, in defiance of the simplest practical and artistic considerations, to give electricity the preference over both the mechanical system and the pneumatic.

It is also very detrimental to the sound of modern organs that they contain stops which imitate in a kind of forced way the sound of stringed instruments. That a very great variety in the sound of the pipes should be aimed at, and that pipes should be installed to produce tones which remind one of the violin, the 'cello, or the double-bass, is quite natural. But one must not go too far in that direction. The violin-, or 'cello-, or double-bass-quality of tone must only be hinted at, and not be allowed to make itself conspicuous in the combined sounds of the whole instrument. The organs of to-day, however, contain too many of these pipes which imitate stringed-instruments, and these too strong, so that the organs acquire thereby the tone of an orchestrion.

Just as the strings are the foundation of an orchestra, so are the flutes the foundation of an organ. It is only when beautiful, soft, and round-toned open stops in sufficient number provide the correct foundation for the mixtures and the reeds, that an organ can produce a beautiful, rich, and round-toned forte and fortissimo.

If the old organs sound better than those which are built to-day, that is, as a rule, partly the result of their having been placed in a better position. The best place for the organ, if the nave of the church is not too long, is above the entrance, opposite the chancel. There it stands high and free, and the sound can travel in every direction, unhindered.

In the case of very long naves it is better to build the organ at a certain height on the side wall of the nave, about half-way along it, thereby escaping the echo which would spoil the clearness of the playing. There are still many European cathedrals in which the organ hangs thus, like a 'swallow's nest,' projecting into the middle of the nave. Placed like this an organ of forty stops develops the power of one with sixty!

In the effort to build organs as large as possible, and with the further object of having the organ and the choir close together, if often comes about to-day that the organ is allotted an unfavourable position.

If in the gallery above the entrance there is room, as is often the case, only for a moderate-sized organ, the instrument is placed in the chancel, an arrangement which has the practical advantage of letting the organ and the choir be close together. But an organ standing on the ground never produces the same effect as one which delivers its sound from a height. From the former position the sound is hindered in its expansion, especially if the church is full. What a number of organs, good in themselves, and especially so in England, are unable to produce their full effect just because of their position in the chancel!

The alternative method of getting organ and choir close together is to devote the western gallery to the choir and the orchestra (if there is one) and to misplace the organ behind them in a confined and vaulted space where it cannot sound properly.

With modern architects it has already become a matter of course that any corner will do for the organ.

In recent times architects and organ-builders have begun to take advantage of the abolition of the distance difficulty by electric connexion between keys and pipes, to split up an organ into parts which are fixed in separate places and sound simultaneously though played from a single keyboard. Effects made possible by this arrangement may impose on the crowd, but the work of an organ can be truly artistic and dignified only if the instrument is one single sound-personality, which sends its music down to flood the nave from its natural place above its hearers.

The only correct solution of the choir and organ problem, if it is a case of a largish church with a strong choir and an orchestra, is to let the choir and instrumentalists be placed in the chancel, and be accompanied by a small organ standing near them. In that case it is of course impossible for the organist at the large organ to be also the conductor of the choir.

The best organs were built between about 1850 and 1880, when organ-builders who were artists availed themselves of the achievements of technical skill to realize as completely as they could the ideals of Silbermann and the other great organ-builders of the eighteenth century. The most important of them is Aristide Cavaillé-Col, the creator of the organs at S. Sulpice and Notre Dame in Paris. The organ in S. Sulpice—completed in 1862—which, apart from a few deficiencies, I consider to be the finest of all the organs I know, functions as well to-day as in the first days of its existence, and if it is always kept in good condition it will do the same two centuries hence. The organ in Notre Dame has suffered by being exposed to all the inclemencies of the weather during the war, when the stained windows were removed to a place of safety. Many a time have I met the venerable Cavaillé-Col—he died in 1899—at the organ in S. Sulpice, where he used to appear for the service every Sunday. One of his favourite maxims was: "An organ sounds best when there is so much space between the pipes that a man can get round each one." Of the other representatives of the organ-building of that period I value especially Ladegast in North Germany, Walcker, in South Germany, and certain English and northern masters who, like Ladegast, were influenced by Cavaillé-Col.

About the end of the nineteenth century the master organ-builders became organ manufacturers, and those who were not willing to follow this course were ruined. Since that time people have no longer asked whether an organ has a good tone, but whether it is provided with every possible modern arrangement for altering the stops, and whether it contains the greatest possible number of stops for the smallest possible price. With an incredible blindness they tear out the beautiful old works of their organs, instead of piously restoring them with the care they deserve, and replace them with products of the factory.

Holland is the country where there is most appreciation of the beauty and value of old organs. The organists of that country did not allow the manifold technical defects of their wonderful old organs, and the consequent difficulty of playing them, to mislead them into sacrificing the advantage of their magnificent tone. Hence there are to-day in the churches of Holland numerous organs, large and small, which by appropriate restoration will in the course of time lose their technical imperfections and keep their beauty of sound. In splendid old organ-cases, too, there is scarcely any country so rich as Holland.

Little by little attention was given to the idea of reform in organ-building which I had put forward in my pamphlet. At the Congress of the International Musical Society held in Vienna in 1909 provision was made for the first time, on the suggestion of Guido Adler, for a section on Organ-building. In this section some like-minded members joined me in working out a set of "International Regulations for Organ-building," which swept away the blind admiration for purely technical achievements, and called for the production once more of carefully built instruments of fine tone.[1] In the years that followed it came to be perceived more and more clearly that the really good organ must combine the beautiful tone of the old organs with the technical advantages of the new. Twenty-two years after its first appearance it was possible for my pamphlet on Organ-building to be reprinted without alteration as the now accepted programme of reform, with an Appendix on the present state of the organ-building industry to make it a sort of jubilee edition.[2]

While to me the monumental organs of the eighteenth century, as they were perfected later by Cavaillé-Col and others, are the ideal so far as tone is concerned, music historians in Germany have been trying lately to go back to the organ of Bach's day. That, however, is not the ideal organ, but its forerunner only. It lacks the element of

[1] *Internationales Regulativ für Orgelbau.* ("International Regulations for Organ-building.") 47 pages. 1909. (Artaria, Vienna; Breiktopf und Härtel, Leipzig.)
  Règlement général international pour la facture d'orgues. 1909. (Artarai, Vienna; Breitkopf und Härtel, Leipzig.)
  Regolamento generale internazionale per la construzione degli organi. 170 pages. (Pp. 123-170 Appendix by the translator, D. Carmelo Sangiorgio.) 1914. (Brønte.)
[2] *Deutsche und französische Orgelbaukunst und Orgelkunst* ("Organ-building and Organ-playing in Germany and France.") (Leipzig, Breitkopf und Härtel.) 2nd ed. 1927. Pp. 1-48 the original text; pp. 49-73 Appendix.

C*

majesty, which is part of the organ's essential nature. Art has absolute ideals, not archaistic ones. We may say of it: "When that which is perfect is come, that which is in part shall be done away."

Although the simple truths about artistic and sound organ-building have now obtained recognition, the advance in their practical application is very slow. That is because organ-building to-day is carried on in factories on a large scale. Commercial interest obstruct artistic ones. The carefully built and really artistic organ comes out 30 per cent dearer than the factory organ which governs the market. The organ-builder, therefore, who wants to supply what is really good, stakes his existence on the venture. Very rarely indeed can the church authorities be persuaded that they are right in giving for an instrument with thirty-three stops a sum which would procure them one with forty.

I was talking once about organs and organ-building to a confectioner with musical tastes, and he said to me: "So it's just the same with organ-building as with confectionery! People to-day don't know what a good organ is, nor do they know what good confectionery is. No one has any recollection of how things taste which are made with fresh milk, fresh cream, fresh butter, fresh eggs, the best oil, and the best lard, and natural fruit-juice, and are sweetened with sugar and nothing else. They are, one and all, accustomed nowadays to find quite satisfactory what is made with tinned milk, tinned cream, tinned butter, dried white of egg and dried yoke, with the cheapest oil and the cheapest lard, with synthetic fruit-juice and any sort of sweetening, because they never get anything different offered them. Not understanding what 'quality' means, they are satisfied so long as things look nice. If I try to produce and sell the good things of former days, I lose my customers, because, like the good organ-builder, I am about 30 per cent too dear. . . ."

How far we still are from having the ideal organ I have had to realize again and again on my concert tours, which gave me opportunities of geting to know the organs of almost every country of Europe. Still, the day must come when organists will demand really sound and artistic instruments, and so put organ-builders in a position to give up the turning out of factory articles. But when will it come to pass that the idea triumphs over circumstances? The chief problem is always the wind-chest. Until someone succeeds in building a wind-chest which has the acoustic qualities of the 'Schleiflade' (sounding-board) used by the master builders of the eighteenth century and by Cavaillé-Col, but is without the technical disadvantages of the latter, organs must remain unsatisfactory as to tone. Of course organ-builders praise up the modern wind-chests, and proclaim them to be just as good as the 'Schleiflade.' But that is not really the case.

To the struggle for the true organ I have sacrificed much time and much labour. Many a night have I spent over organ designs which had been sent to me for approval or revision. Many a journey have I undertaken in order to study on the spot the question of restoring or rebuilding an organ. Letters running into hundreds have I written to bishops, deans, presidents of consistories, mayors, incumbents. church committees, church elders, organ-builders, and organists, to try to convince them, it may be, that they ought to restore their fine old organs instead of replacing them by new ones, or, it may be, to entreat them to consider the quality, not the number, of the stops, and to spend in getting the best material for the pipes the money they had ear-marked for equipping the console with such and such superflous arrangements for the alteration of the stops. And how often did these many letters, these many journeys, and these many conversations prove ultimately in vain, because the people concerned decided finally for the factory organ, the specification of which looked so fine upon paper!

The hardest struggles were for the preservation of the old organs. What eloquence I had to employ to obtain the rescinding of death sentences which had already been passed on beautiful old organs! What number of organists received the news that the organs which on account of their age and their ruinous condition they prized so little, were beautiful instruments and must be preserved, with the same incredulous laughter with which Sarah received the news that she was to have descendants! What a number of organists were changed from friends to foes because I was the obstacle to their plan of replacing their old organ by a factory one, or was guiltily responsible for their having to cut out three or four of the stops they wanted so that the rest might be of a better quality!

Even to-day I have sometimes to look on helpless while I see noble old organs rebuilt and enlarged till not a scrap of their original beauty is left, just because they are not strong enough to suit present-day ideas; yes, and see them even broken up, and replaced at heavy cost by plebeian products of the factory!

The first old organ that I rescued—and what a task it was!—was Silbermann's fine instrument at S. Thomas's, Strassburg.

"In Africa he saves old niggers, in Europe old organs," is what my friends say of me.

The building of the so-called giant organs I consider to be a modern aberration. An organ should be only so large as the body of the church requires and the place which is allotted to it allows. A really good organ with fifty or sixty stops, if it stands at a certain height and has open space all round it, can fill the largest church. When asked to name the largest and finest organ in the world, I generally answer that, from what I have heard and read, there must be 172 which are the largest, and 137 which are the finest, in the world.

It is not so much on the number of the stops as on how they are placed that the effect of an organ depends. An organ is complete if, in addition to the Pedal-board, it has a Great-, a Choir- and a Swell-organ. It is very important that the second of these be really built as a Choir Organ, which means that, as in the old organs, it stands in a case of its own in front of the Great Organ, and is thus both in position and sound distinct from the two other organs which are housed in the main case. If it is in the main case with them, it has no tonal individuality of its own, it becomes merely a supplement to the Great Organ.

Because they have no Choir Organ, modern instruments are incomplete, however many stops and keyboards they may have. They are made up of two, not of three tonal individualities.

The time will come when people will say they cannot understand how it was that three generations of organists and organbuilders failed to recognize the importance of the Choir Organ for the musical working of the instrument. Even Cavaillé-Col, strange to say, let himself be misled into depriving the second organ of its independence, and housing it in the main case. That in S. Sulpice he left the roomy Choir Organ case empty instead of using it for stops, is distinctly a mistake.

Of course a case for the Choir Organ costs so much extra that several stops must be dispensed with, but that matters little. A second organ with ten stops, placed as a Choir Organ should be, is superior in its effect to one with sixteen stops which is housed in the main case.

Another folly of modern organ-building consists in building several organs as Swell Organs. That spoils the effect of the proper swell, apart from the fact that so many sets of shutters in the case hinder the spread of the sound.

The small organs which make up the instrument as a whole are individualities if they are allowed their special requirements as to space and sound. The speciality of the Great Organ is that its stops occupy the lower part of the main case, and have a full, round tone. That of the Choir Organ is that it is an organ by itself with clear-voiced stops which sings out freely into the church under the Great Organ. That of the Swell Organ is that it is housed in the upper part of the main case, and from the highest and furthest point of the instrument sends out an intensive tone which can be modified as desired.

The organ is a trinity in which these three tonal individualities make a unity. The better the special character of each organ is secured, and the better the three combine into a unity, the finer is the organ.

The old organ is incomplete because there is no Swell Organ in it, the new because it no longer has a Choir Organ. It is by a combination of the old and the new that we produce the complete organ.

For constructional and tonal reasons it is impossible for any organ to have more than three component organs which are really tonal individualities. Hence to give an organ four or five keyboards does not supply any artistic need.

As in organ-building so in piano construction there is to-day far too much insistence on instruments which produce the largest possible volume of sound. The powerful grand pianos which give the hammer-struck strings the fullness of sound which is required in our large concert halls are, it is true, a necessity for such large spaces, but they obtain this unnatural fullness at the expense of the peculiar beauty of the real piano tone. What a difference between these dull-sounding giant grands and a fine old Erard grand in a music-room! How much better suited is the latter for accompanying the voice! How much better its warm sound blends with that of the strings! To hear a Beethoven violin sonata with the violin accompanied by a modern grand piano is almost torture! Through the whole performance I see a silver-clear and a coal-black stream of water flowing along side by side without mingling.

In concert hall organs I was unable to interest myself in the same way as in church organs. The best of organs cannot sound with full effect in a concert hall. Owing to the crowd which fills it the organ loses brilliance and fullness of tone. Moreover architects generally push the concert hall organ into any corner that is convenient, where it cannot under any circumstances sound properly. The organ demands a stone-vaulted building in which the presence of a congregation does not mean that the room feels choked. In a concert hall an organ has not so fully as in a church the character of a solo instrument; it is rather one which provides an accompaniment to supplement choir and orchestra. Composers will assuredly use the organ with the orchestra much more in future than has been done in the past. When it is so used, there results a sound which draws brilliance and flexibility from the orchestra, and fullness from the organ. The technical significance of this supplementing of the modern orchestra by the organ is that the orchestra at once secures flute-like tones for its bass, and thus for the first time it has a bass which corresponds in character to its higher notes.

I delight in letting the organ unite its music to that of the orchestra in a concert hall. But if I find myself in the position of having to play it in such a hall as a solo instrument, I avoid as well as I can treating it as a secular concert instrument. By my choice of the pieces played and my way of playing them I try to turn the concert hall into a church. But best of all I like, in a church as in a concert hall, to introduce a choir and thus change the concert into a kind of service, in which the choir responds to the choral prelude of the organ by singing the chorale itself.

By its even tone which can be maintained as long as desired the organ has in it an element, so to speak, of eternity. Even in the secular room it cannot become a secular instrument.

That I have had the joy of seeing my ideal of a church organ very largely realized in certain modern organs I owe to the artistic ability of the Alsatian organ-builder, Fritz Haerpfer, who formed his ideas from the organs built by Silbermann, and the good sense of certain Church Councils which allowed themselves to be persuaded into ordering not the largest, but the best organ that could be procured with the sum of money at their disposal.

The work and the worry that fell to my lot through the practical interest I took in organ-building made me sometimes wish that I had never troubled myself about it, but if I do not give it up, the reason is that the struggle for the good organ is to me a part of the struggle for truth. And when on Sundays I think of this or that church in which a noble organ is sounding because I saved it from an ignoble one, I feel myself richly rewarded for all the time and trouble which in the course of over thirty years I have sacrificed in the interests of organ-building.

CHAPTER IX

I RESOLVE TO BECOME A JUNGLE DOCTOR

On October 13th, 1905, a Friday, I dropped into a letter-box in the Avenue de la Grande Armée in Paris letters to my parents and to some of my most intimate acquaintances, telling them that at the beginning of the winter term I should enter myself as a medical student, in order to go later on to Equatorial Africa as a doctor. In one of them I sent in the resignation of my post as Principal of the Theological College of S. Thomas's, because of the claim on my time that my intended course of study would make.

The plan which I meant now to put into execution had been in my mind for a long time, having been conceived so long ago as my student days. It struck me as incomprehensible that I should be allowed to lead such a happy life, while I saw so many people around me wrestling with care and suffering. Even at school I had felt stirred whenever I got a glimpse of the miserable home surroundings of some of my schoolfellows and compared them with the absolutely ideal conditions in which we children of the parsonage at Günsbach lived. While at the University and enjoying the happiness of being able to study and even to produce some results in science and art, I could not help thinking continually of others who were denied that happiness by their material circumstances or their health. Then one brilliant summer morning at Günsbach, during the Whitsuntide holidays—it was in 1896—there came to me, as I awoke, the thought that I must not accept this happiness as a matter of course, but must give something in return for it. Proceeding to think the matter out at once with calm deliberation, while the birds were singing outside, I settled with myself before I got up, that I would consider myself justified in living till I was thirty for science and art, in order to devote myself from that time forward to the direct service of humanity. Many a time already I had tried to settle what meaning lay hidden for me in the saying of Jesus! "Whosoever would save his life shall lose it, and whosoever shall lose his life for My sake and the Gospel's shall save it." Now the answer was found. In addition to the outward, I now had inward happiness.

What would be the character of the activities thus planned for the future was not yet clear to me. I left it to circumstances to guide me. One thing only was certain, that it must be directly human service, however inconspicuous the sphere of it.

I naturally thought first of some activity in Europe. I formed a plan for taking charge of abandoned or neglected children and educating them, then making them pledge themselves to help later on in the same way children in similar positions. When in 1903, as Warden of the theological hostel, I moved into my roomy and sunny official quarters on the second floor of the College of S. Thomas, I was in a position to begin the experiment. I offered my help now here, now there, but always unsuccessfully. The constitutions of the organizations which looked after destitute and abandoned children made no provision for the acceptance of such voluntary co-operation. For example, when the Strassburg Orphanage was burnt down, I offered to take in a few boys, for the time being, but the Superintendent did not even allow me to finish what I had to say. Similar attempts which I made elsewhere were also failures.

For a time I thought I would some day devote myself to tramps and discharged prisoners. In some measure as a preparation for this I joined the Rev. Augustus Ernst at S. Thomas's in an undertaking which he had begun. He was at home from 1 to 2 p.m. and ready to speak to anyone who came to him asking for help or for a night's lodging. He did not, however, give the applicant a trifle in money, or let him wait till he could get information about his circumstances. He would offer to look him up in his home or at his lodging-house that very afternoon and test the statements he had volunteered about his condition. Then, and then only, would he give him help, but as much, and for as long a time, as was necessary. What a number of bicycle rides we made with this object in the town and the suburbs, and very often with the result that the applicant was not known at the address he had given. In a great many cases, however, it provided an opportunity for giving, with knowledge of the circumstances, very seasonable help. I had some friends, too, who kindly placed a portion of their wealth at my disposal.

Already, as a student, I had been active in social service as a member of the student association known as the Diaconate of S. Thomas, which held its meetings in S. Thomas's College. Each of us had a certain number of poor families assigned to him, which he was to visit every week, taking to them the help allotted to them and making a report on their condition. The money we thus distributed we collected from members of the old Strassburg families who supported this undertaking, begun by former generations and now carried on by us. Twice a year, if I remember right, each of us had to make his definite number of such begging appeals. To me, being shy and rather awkward in society, these visits were a torture. I believe that in these preparatory studies for the begging I have had to do in later years I sometimes showed myself extremely unskilful. However, I learnt through them that begging with tact and restraint is better appreciated than any sort of stand-and-deliver approach, and also that the correct method of begging includes the good-tempered acceptance of a refusal.

In our youthful inexperience we no doubt often failed, in spite of the best intentions, to use all the money entrusted to us in the wisest way, but the intentions of the givers were nevertheless fully carried out in that it pledged young men to take an interest in the poor, For that reason I think with deep gratitude of those who met with so much understanding and liberality our efforts to be wisely helpful, and hope that many students may have the privilege of working, commissioned in this way by the charitable, as recruits in the struggle against poverty.

While I was concerned with tramps and discharged prisoners it had become clear to me that they could only be effectively helped by a number of individuals who would devote themselves to them. At the same time, however, I had realized that in many cases these could only accomplish their best work in collaboration with organizations. But what I wanted was an absolutely personal and independent activity. Although I was resolved to put my services at the disposal of some organization, if it should be really necessary, I nevertheless never gave up the hope of finding a sphere of activity to which I could devote myself as an individual and as wholly free. That this longing of mine found fulfilment I have always regarded as a signal instance of the mercy which has again and again been vouchsafed to me.

One morning in the autumn of 1904 I found on my writing-table in the College one of the green-covered magazines in which the Paris Missionary Society reported every month on its activities. A certain Miss Scherdlin used to put them there knowing that I was specially interested in this Society on account of the impression made on me by the letters of one of its earliest missionaries, Casalis by name, when my father read them aloud at his missionary services during my childhood. That evening, in the very act of putting it aside that I might go on with my work, I mechanically opened this magazine, which had been laid on my table during my absence. As I did so, my eye caught the title of an article: "Les besoins de la Mission du Congo" ("The needs of the Congo Mission").[1]

It was by Alfred Boegner, the President of the Paris Missionary Society, an Alsatian, and contained a complaint that the Mission had not enough workers to carry on its work in the Gaboon, the northern province of the Congo Colony. The writer expressed his hope that his appeal would bring some of those "on whom the Master's eyes already rested" to a decision to offer themselves for this urgent work. The conclusion ran: "Men and women who can reply simply to the Master's call, 'Lord, I am coming,' those are the people whom the Church needs." The article finished, I quietly began my work. My search was over.

My thirtieth birthday a few months later I spent like the man in the parable who "desiring to build a tower, first counts the cost whether he have wherewith to complete

[1] *Journal des Missions Evangéliques.* June 1904. Pp. 389-393.

it." The result was that I resolved to realize my plan of direct human service in Equatorial Africa.

With the exception of one trustworthy friend no one knew of my intention. When it became known through the letters I had sent from Paris, I had hard battles to fight with my relations and friends. Almost more than with my contemplated new start itself they reproached me with not having shown them so much confidence as to discuss it with them first. With this side issue they tormented me beyond measure during those difficult weeks. That theological friends should outdo the others in their protest struck me as all the more preposterous, because they had, no doubt, all preached a fine sermon—perhaps a very fine one—showing how S. Paul, as he has recorded in his letter to the Galatians, "conferred not with flesh and blood" beforehand about what he meant to do for Jesus.

My relatives and my friends all joined in expostulating with me on the folly of my enterprise. I was a man, they said, who was burying the talent entrusted to him and wanted to trade with false currency. Work among savages I ought to leave to those who would not thereby be compelled to leave gifts and acquirements in science and art unused. Widor, who loved me as if I were his son, scolded me as being like a general who wanted to go into the firing-line—there was no talk about trenches at that time— with a rifle. A lady who was filled with the modern spirit proved to me that I could do much more by lecturing on behalf of medical help for natives than I could by the action I contemplated. That saying from Goethe's *Faust* ("In the beginning was the Deed"), was now out of date, she said. To-day propaganda was the mother of happenings.

In the many verbal duels which I had to fight, as a weary opponent, with people who passed for Christians, it moved me strangely to see them so far from perceiving that the effort to serve the love preached by Jesus may sweep a man into a new course of life, although they read in the New Testament that it can do so, and found it there quite in order. I had assumed as a matter of course that familiarity with the sayings of Jesus would produce a much better appreciation of what to popular logic is non-rational, than my own case allowed me to assert. Several times, indeed, it was my experience that my appeal to the act of obedience which Jesus' command of love may under special circumstances call for, brought upon me an accusation of conceit, although I had, in fact, been obliged to do violence to my feelings to employ this argument at all. In general, how much I suffered through so many people assuming a right to tear open all the doors and shutters of my inner self!

As a rule, too, it was of no use allowing them, in spite of my repugnance, to have a glimpse of the thoughts which had given birth to my resolution. They thought there must be something behind it all, and guessed at disappointment at the slow growth of my reputation. For this there was no ground at all, seeing that I had received, even as a young man, such recognition as others usually get only after a whole life of toil and struggle. Unfortunate love experiences were also alleged as the reason for my decision.

I felt as a real kindness the action of persons who made no attempt to dig their fists into my heart, but regarded me as a precocious young man, not quite right in his head, and treated me correspondingly with affectionate mockery.

I felt it to be, in itself, quite natural that relations and friends should put before me anything that told against the reasonableness of my plan. As one who demands that idealists shall be sober in their views, I was conscious that every start upon an untrodden path is a venture which only in unusual circumstances looks sensible and likely to be successful. In my own case I held the venture to be justified, because I had considered it for a long time and from every point of view, and credited myself with the possession of health, sound nerves, energy, practical common sense, toughness, prudence, very few wants, and everything else that might be found necessary by anyone wandering along the path of the idea. I believed myself, further, to wear the protective armour of a temperament quite capable of enduring an eventual failure of my plan.

As a man of individual action, I have since that time

been approached for my opinion and advice by many people who wanted to make a similar venture, but only in comparatively few cases have I taken on me the responsibility of giving them immediate encouragement. I often had to recognize that the need "to do something special" was born of a restless spirit. Such persons wanted to dedicate themselves to larger tasks because those that lay nearest did not satisfy them. Often, too, it was evident that they had been brought to their decisions by quite secondary considerations. Only a person who can find a value in every sort of activity and devote himself to each one with full consciousness of duty, has the inward right to take as his object some extraordinary activity instead of that which falls naturally to his lot. Only a person who feels his preference to be a matter of course, not something out of the ordinary, and who has no thought of heroism, but just recognizes a duty undertaken with sober enthusiasm, is capable of becoming a spiritual adventurer such as the world needs. There are no heroes of action : only heroes of renunciation and suffering. Of such there are plenty. But few of them are known, and even these not to the crowd, but to the few.

Carlyle's *Heroes and Hero Worship* is not a profound book.

Of those who feel any sort of impulse, and would prove actually fitted, to devote their lives to independent personal activity, the majority are compelled by circumstances to renounce such a course. As a rule this is because they have to provide for one or more dependents, or because they have to stick to their calling in order to earn their own living. Only one who, thanks to his own ability or the devotion of friends, is in worldly matters a free man can venture nowadays to take the path of independent activity. This was not so much the case in earlier times because anyone who gave up remunerative work could still hope to get through life somehow or other, while anyone who thought of doing the same in the difficult economic conditions of to-day would run the risk of coming to grief not only materially but spiritually as well.

I am compelled, therefore, not only by what I have observed, but by experience also, to admit that worthy and

capable persons have had to renounce a course of independent action which would have been of great value to
the world, because circumstances rendered such a course
impossible.

Those who are so favoured as to be able to embark on a
course of free personal activity must accept this good
fortune in a spirit of humility. They must often think of
those who, though willing and capable, were never in a
position to do the same. And as a rule they must temper
their own strong determination with humility. They are
almost always destined to have to seek and wait till they
find a road open for the activity they long for. Happy are
those to whom the years of work are allotted in richer
measure than those of seeking and waiting! Happy those
who in the end are able to give themselves really and completely!

These favoured persons must also be modest so as not
to fly into a passion at the opposition they encounter;
they have to meet it in the temper which says: "Ah, well,
it had to be!" Anyone who proposes to do good must not
expect people to roll stones out of his way, but must
accept his lot calmly if they even roll a few more upon
it. A strength which becomes clearer and stronger through
its experience of such obstacles is the only strength that
can conquer them. Resistance is only a waste of strength.

Of all the will for the ideal which exists in mankind
only a small part can be manifested in action. All the rest
is destined to realize itself in unseen effects, which represent, however, a value exceeding a thousandfold and more
that of the activity which attracts the notice of the world.
Its relation to the latter is like that of the deep sea to the
waves which stir its surface. The hidden forces of goodness
are embodied in those persons who carry on as a secondary
pursuit the immediate personal service which they cannot
make their life-work. The lot of the many is to have as a
profession, for the earning of their living and the satisfaction of society's claim on them, a more or less soul-
less labour in which they can give out little or nothing
of their human qualities, because in that labour they have
to be little better than human machines. Yet no one finds
himself in the position of having no possible opportunity

of giving himself to others as a human being. The problem produced by the fact of labour being to-day so thoroughly organized, specialized, and mechanized depends only in part for its solution on society's not merely removing the conditions thus produced, but doing its very best to guard the rights of human personality. What is even more important is that sufferers shall not simply bow to their fate, but shall try with all their energy to assert their human personality amid their unfavourable conditions by spiritual activity. Anyone can rescue his human life, in spite of his professional life, who seizes every opportunity of being a man by means of personal action, however unpretending, for the good of fellow-men who need the help of a fellow-man. Such a man enlists in the service of the spiritual and good. No fate can prevent a man from giving to others this direct human service side by side with his life-work. If so much of such service remains unrealized, it is because the opportunities are missed.

That everyone shall exert himself in that state of life in which he is placed, to practise true humanity towards his fellow-men, on that depends the future of mankind. Enormous values come to nothing every moment through the missing of opportunities, but the values which do get turned into will and deed mean wealth which must not be undervalued. Our humanity is by no means so materialistic as foolish talk is continually asserting it to be. Judging by what I have learnt about men and women, I am convinced that there is far more in them of idealist will-power than ever comes to the surface of the world. Just as the water of the streams we see is small in amount compared to that which flows underground, so the idealism which becomes visible is small in amount compared with what men and women bear locked in their hearts, unreleased or scarcely released. To unbind what is bound, to bring the underground waters to the surface: mankind is waiting and longing for such as can do that.

What seemed to my friends that most irrational thing in my plan was that I wanted to go to Africa, not as a missionary, but as a doctor, and thus when already thirty years of age burdened myself as a beginning with a long period of laborious study. And that this study would mean for me a tremendous effort, I had no manner of doubt. I did, in truth, look forward to the next few years with dread. But the reasons which determined me to follow the way of service I had chosen, as a doctor, weighed so heavily that other considerations were as dust in the balance.

I wanted to be a doctor that I might be able to work without having to talk. For years I had been giving myself out in words, and it was with joy that I had followed the calling of theological teacher and of preacher. But this new form of activity I could not represent to myself as being talking about the religion of love, but only as an actual putting it into practice. Medical knowledge made it possible for me to carry out my intention in the best and most complete way, wherever the path of service might lead me. In view of the plan for Equatorial Africa, the acquisition of such knowledge was especially indicated because in the district to which I thought of going a doctor was, according to the missionaries' reports, the most needed of all needed things. They were always complaining in their magazine that the natives who visited them in physical suffering could not be given the help they desired. To become one day the doctor whom these poor creatures needed, it was worth while, so I judged, to become a medical student. Whenever I was inclined to feel that the years I should have to sacrifice were too long, I reminded myself that Hamilcar and Hannibal had prepared for their march on Rome by their slow and tedious conquest of Spain.

There was still one more point of view from which I seemed directed to become a doctor. From what I knew of the Parisian Missionary Society, I could not but feel it to be very doubtful whether they would accept me as a missionary.

It was in pietistic and orthodox circles that at the beginning of the nineteenth century societies were first formed for preaching the Gospel in the heathen world. About the same time, it is true, Liberal Christendom too began to comprehend the need for carrying the teaching of Jesus to far-off lands. But when it came to action, the faith that was in the fetters of dogmatism was first in the field. With their own living and active societies outside the ecclesiastical organization they were more capable of independent action than was Liberal Christianity, which at that time was playing the leading part in the Church and was consequently wholly absorbed in ecclesiasticism. Moreover the dogmatic bodies had in their pietistic ideas about "the saving of souls" a stronger motive for mission work than Liberal Christianity, since the latter's aim was to set the Gospel working primarily as a force for the restoration of mankind and the conditions of human society in the heathen world.

When the missionary societies started by pietism and orthodoxy once got to work they found support in Liberal circles which were friendly to missions. These believed for a long time that they could dispense with missionary societies of their own, expecting that, as a result of Protestants of every shade of belief working for and with them, the existing societies would in time come to carrying on the mission-work of Protestanism as such. They were mistaken, however. The societies accepted, indeed, all the material help offered them by Liberal Protestantism—how hard my father and his Liberal colleagues in Alsace worked for the missionary societies which had a quite different doctrinal outlook!—but they sent out no missionaries who would not accept their own doctrinal requirements. As a result of going on for so long in this self-forgetting way without any missionary undertakings of its own and supporting those which were not its own, Liberal Protestantism obtained the reputation of having no appreciation of mission work and doing nothing for it. Then, but much too late, it resolved to establish missionary societies of its own, and to give up the hope of having a mission run by the Protestant Church as a whole.

It was always interesting to me to find that the missionaries themselves usually thought more liberally than the officials of their societies. They had, of course, found by experience that among outside peoples, especially among the primitive races, there is a complete absence of those pre-suppositions which compel our Christianity at home to face the alternative of doctrinal constraint or doctrinal freedom, and that the important thing out there is to preach the elements of the Gospel as given in the Sermon on the Mount, and to bring men under the lordship of the spirit of Jesus.

For the Paris Mission my father cherished a special sympathy because he thought he could detect in it a more liberal tendency than in others. He particularly appreciated the fact that Casalis and others among its leading missionaries used in their reports not the sugary language of Canaan, but that of the simple Christian heart.

But that the question of orthodoxy played the same rôle in the Committee of the Paris Society as in others I at once learnt, and very explicitly, when I offered it my services. The kindly Director of the Mission, Monsieur Boegner, was much moved at finding that someone had offered to join the Congo Mission in answer to his appeal, but at once confided to me that serious objections would be raised to my theological standpoint by members of the Committee, and that these would have to be cleared away first. My assurance that I wanted to come "merely as a doctor" lifted a heavy weight from his mind, but a little later he had to inform me that some members objected even to the acceptance of a mission-doctor, who had only correct Christian love, and did not, in their opinion, hold also the correct Christian belief. However, we both resolved not to worry about the matter too much so long beforehand, and relied on the fact that the objectors still had some years to wait during which they might be able to attain to a truly Christian reasonableness.

No doubt the more liberal Allgemeine Evangelische Missionsverein (General Union of Evangelical Missions) in Switzerland would have accepted me without hesitation either as missionary or doctor. But as I felt my call to Equatorial Africa had come to me through the article in the Paris Mission magazine, I felt I ought to try to join that Mission, if possible, in its activities in that colony. Further, I was tempted to persist in getting a decision on the question whether, face to face with the Gospel of Jesus, a missionary society could justifiably arrogate to itself the right to refuse to the suffering natives in their district the services of a doctor, because in their opinion he was not sufficiently orthodox.

But over and above all this, my daily work and daily worries, now that I was beginning my medical course, made such demands upon me, that I had neither time nor strength to concern myself about what was to happen afterwards.

CHAPTER X

MY MEDICAL STUDIES

1905-1912

WHEN I went to Professor Fehling, at that time Dean of the Medical Faculty, to give in my name as a student, he would have liked best to hand me over to his colleague in the Psychiatric Department.

On one of the closing days of October 1905 I set out in a thick fog to attend the first of a course of lectures on Anatomy.

But there was still a legal question to solve. As a member of the staff of the University I could not be enrolled as a student at the same time. Yet if I attended the medical courses only as a guest, I could not, according to existing rules, be admitted to the examinations. The governing body met the difficulty in a friendly spirit, and permitted me to enter for the examinations on the strength of the certificates which the medical Professors would give me of having attended their lectures. The Professors, on their side, resolved that, being a colleague, I might attend all the lectures without paying the fees.

My teachers in the five terms preceding the clinical were: Schwalbe, Weidenreich, and Fuchs in Anatomy; Hofmeister, Ewald, and Spiro in Physiology; Thiele in Chemistry; Braun and Cohn in Physics; Goette in Zoology; Graf Solms and Jost in Botany.

Now began years of continuous struggle with fatigue. To immediate resignation of my theological teaching, and of my office of preacher, I had not been able to bring myself. So while I studied medicine, I at the same time delivered theological lectures, and preached almost every Sunday. The lectures were especially laborious at the beginning of my medical course, as it was in them that I began dealing with the problems of the teaching of S. Paul.

The organ, too, now began to make bigger claims on me than before. For Gustave Bret, the conductor of the Paris Bach Society which had been founded in 1905 by him, Dukas, Fauré, Widor, Guilmont, d'Indy, and myself, insisted on my undertaking the organ-part in all the Society's concerts. For some years, therefore, I had to make, each winter, several journeys to Paris. Although I only had to attend the final practice, and could travel back to Strassburg during the night following each performance, every concert took at least three days of my time. Many a sermon for S. Nicholas did I sketch out in the train between Paris and Strassburg! I had also to be at the organ for the Bach Concerts of the "Orféo Català" at Barcelona. And in general I now played oftener in concerts, not only because I had during recent years become known as an organist, but also because the loss of my stipend as Principal of the Theological College compelled me to find some new source of income.

The frequent journeys to Paris afforded me a welcome opportunity of meeting friends whom in the course of time I had made in that city. Among those I knew best were the clever and musically gifted Frau Fanny Reinach, the wife of the well-known scholar, Theodor Reinach, and Countess Mélanie de Pourtalès, the friend of the Empress Eugenie, at whose side she figures in Winterhalter's famous picture. At the country house of the Countess, near Strassburg, I frequently saw her friend, Princess Metternich-Sander, the wife of the Austrian Ambassador at Paris in Napoleon III's day. It was she whom Wagner, in his day, had to thank for getting his *Tannhäuser* produced in the Grand Opera House at Paris. In the course of a conversation with Napoleon III during a ball she induced him to order that this opera should be included in the list of works for performance. Under a somewhat rude exterior she concealed much sagacity and kindness of heart. I learnt from her much that was interesting about Wagner's stay in Paris, and about the people who formed Napoleon's entourage, but how much of soul this unusually gifted woman possessed first became known to me from the letters which she wrote to me when I was in Africa.

While in Paris I also saw a good deal of Mademoiselle

Adèle Herrenschmidt, an Alsatian lady occupied in teaching.

To Luis Millet, the conductor of the "Orféo Català," I was attracted at our very first meeting as a first rate artist and a man of thought. Through him I met the famous Catalonian architect, Gaudi, who was at that time still fully occupied with his work on the peculiar Church of the Sagrada Familia (Holy Family), of which only a mighty portal, crowned with towers, had then been completed. Like architects of the Middle Ages, Gaudi began this work with the consciousness that it would take generations to finish it. I shall never forget how in the builder's shed near the church, speaking as if he embodied the spirit of his countryman, Raymond Lull, he introduced me to his mystical theory about the proportions prevailing in the lines formed by the architecture, to reveal everywhere symbols of the divine triunity. "This cannot be expressed (he said) in either French, German, or English, so I explain it to you in Catalonian, and you will comprehend it, although you do not know the language."

As I was looking at the "Flight into Egypt," carved in stone at the entrance of the big portal, and wondering at the ass, creeping along so wearily under its burden, he said to me : "You know something about art, and you have a sort of feeling that the ass here is not an invention. Not one of the figures you see here in stone is imaginary; they all stand here just as I have seen them in reality, Joseph, Mary, the infant Jesus, the priests in the Temple : I chose them all from people I met, and have carved them from plaster casts which I took at the time. With the donkey it was a difficult job. When it became known that I was looking out for an ass for the 'Flight into Egypt,' they brought me all the finest donkeys in Barcelona. But I could not use them. Mary, with the Child Jesus, was not to be mounted on a fine strong animal, but on one poor, old, and weary, and surely one which had something kindly in its face and understood what it was all about. Such was the donkey I was looking for, and I found it at last in the cart of a woman who was selling scouring sand. Its drooping head almost touched the ground. With much trouble I persuaded its owner to bring it to me. And then, as it was copied, bit by bit, in plaster of Paris, she kept crying because she thought it would not escape with its life. That is the ass of the 'Flight into Egypt,' and it has made an impression on you because it is not imagined, but is from actual life."

It was during the first months of my medical course that I wrote the essay on Organ-building and the final chapter of the *Quest of the Historical Jesus*. I resigned my post as Principal of the College in the spring of 1906. So now it seemed I had to turn out of the college building which had been my home since my student days. Leaving the big trees in the walled-in garden, trees with which for so many years I had conversed while I was working, was very hard. But, to my great joy, I found that I should be able, after all, to stay on in the big house belonging to the Chapter of S. Thomas's. Frederick Curtius, formerly District Superintendent of Colmar, and after that, nominated, at the request of the whole body of Alsatian clergy, as President of the Lutheran Church of Alsace, held, as such, possession of a large official residence in the Chapter's big house. He now placed at my disposal four small attics under its gables, and I was thus enabled to continue living under the shadow of S. Thomas's. On the rainy Shrove Tuesday of the year 1906 the students carried all my belongings out through one door of the house on the S. Thomas Embankment and brought them in through another.

That with the Curtius family I could go in and out as if I were a member of it I prized as a great piece of good fortune. Frederick Curtius, who, as already mentioned, was a son of the well-known Greek scholar of Berlin, had married Countess Louisa of Erlach, the daughter of the governess of the Grand Duchess Louisa of Baden, who was a sister of the Emperor Frederick. Thus traditions of the aristocracy of learning were in this family united with those of the aristocracy of birth. The spiritual centre of the household was the aged Countess of Erlach—by birth Countess de May from the neighbourhood of Neuchâtel. Her health now prevented her from going out of doors, so, in order to make good to some extent her loss of concerts which she felt very deeply, for she was passionately fond of music, I used to play the piano to her for an hour every evening, and so I got to know her better, although now she scarcely saw anybody. This distinguished noblewoman gradually acquired a great influence over me, and I owe it to her that I have rounded off many a hard angle in my personality.

On May 3rd, 1910, an airman named Wincziers made from the drill-ground at Strassburg-Neudorf the first flight ever made over Strassburg, and it was quite unexpected. I happened to be at the time in the Countess's room, and led her, for she could no longer move about alone, to the window. When the aeroplane, which had flown quite low down past the house had disappeared in the distance, she said to me in French! "Combien curieuse est ma vie! J'ai discuté les règles du participe passé avec Alexander von Humbolt, et voici que je suis témoin de la conquête de l'air par les hommes!"

Her two unmarried daughters, Ada and Greda von Erlach, who lived with her, had inherited from her a talent for painting, and while I was still Director of the College I had given over to Ada, who was a pupil of Henner's, a room with a northern aspect in my official residence for her to use as a studio. I also, at her mother's request, sat for her as a model, since it was hoped that she would feel herself quite restored after a severe operation which had brought her a temporary alleviation of an incurable and painful disease, if she again took up her painting. This picture of me she completed on my thirtieth birthday, without any suspicion of all that was stirring in my mind during this last sitting.

As an uncle of the old Countess von Erlach had been for years an officer in the Dutch Colonial Service without suffering from fever, and attributed this to his having never in the Tropics gone out of doors after sunset bareheaded, I was made to promise her that in memory of her I would have the same rule. So for her sake I now renounce the pleasure of letting the evening breeze play upon my head after a hot day on the Equator. The keeping of my promise, however, has agreed with me. I have never had an attack of malaria, although of course the disease does

not result from going with uncovered head in the Tropics
after sundown!

It was only from the spring of 1906 onwards, when
I had finished with the *Quest of the Historical Jesus* and
had given up the headship of the College, that I could give
to my new course of study the time it required. But then
I set to work with eagerness at the natural sciences. Now
at last I was able to devote myself to what had held
most attraction for me when I was at the Gymnasium: I
was at last in a position to acquire the knowledge I needed
in order to feel the firm ground of reality under my feet
in philosophy!

But study of the natural sciences brought me even more
than the increase of knowledge I had longed for. It was
to me a spiritual experience. I had all along felt it to be
psychically a danger that in the so-called Humanities with
which I had been concerned hitherto, there is no truth
which affirms itself as self-evident, but that a mere
opinion can, by the way in which it deals with the subject-
matter, obtain recognition as true. The search for truth in
the domains of history and philosophy is carried on in
constantly repeated endless duels between the sense of
reality of the one and the inventive imaginative power of
the other. The argument from the facts is never able to
obtain a definite victory over the skilfully produced
opinion. How often does what is reckoned as progress consist in a skilfully argued opinion putting real insight out
of action for a long time!

To have to watch this drama going on and on, and deal
in such different ways with men who had lost all feeling
for reality I had found not a little depressing. Now I was
suddenly in another country. I was concerned with truths
which embodied realities, and found myself among men
who took it as a matter of course that they had to justify
with facts every statement they made. It was an experience which I felt to be needed for my own intellectual
development.

Intoxicated as I was with the delight of dealing with
realities which could be determined with exactitude, I
was far from any inclination to undervalue the Humanities

D

as others in a similar position often did. On the contrary. Through my study of chemistry, physics, zoology, botany, and physiology I became more than ever conscious to what an extent truth in thought is justified and necessary, side by side with the truth which is merely established by facts. No doubt something subjective clings to the knowledge which results from a creative act of the mind. But at the same time such knowledge is on a higher plane than the knowledge based only on facts.

The knowledge that results from the recording of single manifestations of Being remains ever incomplete and unsatisfying so far as it is unable to give the final answer to the great question of what we are in the Universe, and to what purpose we exist in it. We can find our right place in the Being that envelops us only if we experience in our individual lives the universal life which wills and rules within it. The nature of the living Being without me I can understand only through the living Being which is within me. It is to this reflective knowledge of the Universal Being and of the relation to it of the individual human being that the Humanities seek to attain. The results they reach contain truth so far as the spirit which is creatively active in this direction possesses a sense of reality, and has passed through the stage of gaining a knowledge of facts about Being to reflection about the nature of Being.

On May 13th, 1908—on the rainy day on which the famous Hohkönigsburg in Lower Alsace was ceremonially opened after its restoration—I entered for the examination in anatomy, physiology, and the natural sciences, the so-called 'Physikum.' The acquisition of the necessary knowledge did not come easily. All my interests in the subject-matter could not help me over the fact that the memory of a man of over thirty no longer has the capacity of that of a twenty-year-old student. Moreover, I had stupidly got into my head the idea of studying pure science only right to the end, instead of preparing for the examination. It was only in the last few weeks that I let remonstrances from my fellow-students make me become a member of a cramming club (*Paukverband*), so that I got to know what sort of questions, according to the records kept by the students, the professors usually set, together with the answers they preferred to hear.

The examination went better than I ever expected, although during those days I was going through the worst crisis of fatigue that I can recall during the whole of my life.

The terms of clinical study which followed proved far less of a strain than the earlier ones, because the various subjects were more akin.

My principal teachers were: Moritz, Arnold Cahn, and Erich Meyer for Medicine; Madelung and Ledderhose for Surgery; Fehling and Freund for Gynæcology; Wollenberg, Rosenfeld, and Pfersdorff for Psychiatry; Forster and Levy for Bacteriology; Chiari for Pathological Anatomy; and Schmiedeberg for Pharmacology.

I felt a special interest in the teaching about drugs, as to which the practical instruction was given by Arnold Cahn, and the theoretical by Schmiedeberg, the well-known investigator into the derivatives of digitalis.

About Schmiedeberg and his friend Schwalbe, the anatomist, the following delightful story was current in the University. Schwalbe was due to give a lecture on Anthropology to the Adult Education Society of an Alsatian town, and would of course have to mention the Darwinian theory. He told Schmiedeberg of his fear that he might give offence, when the latter replied: "Don't spare them! Tell them all about Darwinism, only take care not to use the word 'monkey.' and they'll be quite satisfied both with Darwin and with you." Schwalbe took the advice, and had the success that was promised.

At that time people in Alsace were beginning to demand University Extension to satisfy a population that was hungering for education, and one day the Professor of Philosophy, Windelband, announced to us in the Common Room with joyful astonishment that a deputation of working-men had requested him to give some lectures on Hegel.

He could hardly speak warmly enough of the way in which ordinary people, with their healthy feeling for what is really valuable, had become alive to the importance of Hegel. Later on, however, it came out that what they wanted to hear was something about Ernst Haeckel and the materialistic popular philosophy, so akin to Socialism, that was expounded in his book *The Riddle of the Universe* which appeared in 1899. In their Alsatian pronunciation the *ä* had sounded like *e*, and the *k* like *g!*

Years later I was to find myself in a position to render a service to Schmiedeberg, whom I very much admired. In the spring of 1919 I happened to be passing the Strass-Burg-Neudorf station, from which some Germans whom the French authorities had decided to expel were about to be transported, when I saw the dear old man standing among them. To my question whether I could help him to save his furniture, which like the rest he had been obliged to leave behind, he replied by showing me a parcel wrapped in newspaper, which he had under his arm. It was his last work on Digitalin. Since everything that these expelled people had on them or with them was strictly examined by French N.C.O.s at the railway station, he was afraid that he might not be allowed to take with him his bulky parcel of manuscript. I therefore took it from him and sent it later on, when a safe opportunity offered, to Baden-Baden, where he had found a refuge with friends. He died not long after the appearance of his work in print.

While at the beginning of my medical course I had to contend with money difficulties, my position improved later on through the success of the German edition of my book on Bach, and the concert fees I earned.

In October 1911 I took the State Medical Examination. The fee for it I had earned the previous month at the French Musical Festival at Munich, by playing the organ part of Widor's recently completed *Symphonia Sacra*, he himself conducting the orchestra. When on December 17th, after my last examination, held by Madelung, the surgeon, I strode out of the hospital into the darkness of the winter evening, I could not grasp the fact that the terrible strain of the medical course was now behind me. Again and again I had to assure myself that I was really awake and not dreaming. Madelung's voice seemed to come from some distant sphere when he said more than once, as we walked along together, "It is only because you have such excellent health that you have got through a job like that."

Now I had to complete the year of practical work as a volunteer in the hospitals, and to write my thesis for the Doctorate. For this I chose as my subject the collection and examination of all that had been published from the medical side on the mental derangement of which the writers supposed Jesus to have been a victim.

In the main I was concerned with the works of De Loosten, William Hirsch, and Binet-Sanglé. In my studies in the life of Jesus I had shown that He lived in the thought-world (which seems to us such a fantastic one) of the late Jewish expectation of the end of the world and the appearance, thereupon, of a supernatural Messianic Kingdom. I was at once reproached with making Him a visionary, or even a person under the sway of delusions. My task now was to decide, from the medical standpoint, whether this peculiar Messianic consciousness of His was in any way bound up with some psychic disturbance.

De Loosten, William Hirsch, and Binet-Sanglé had assumed the existence in Jesus of some paranoiac mental disturbance, and had discovered in Him morbid ideas about His own greatness and about being persecuted. In order to put myself into a position to deal with their really quite insignificant works, it was necessary to immerse myself in the boundless problem of paranoia, and thus a treatise of forty-six pages took over a year to write. More than once I was on the point of throwing it aside, and choosing another subject for my dissertation.

The result I aimed at was to demonstrate that the only psychiatric characteristics which could be accepted as historical, and about which there could be any serious dispute—Jesus' high estimation of Himself and possible hallucinations at the time of His baptism—were far from sufficient to prove the presence of any mental disease.

The expectation of the end of the world and the coming of the Messianic Kingdom has nothing in it of a nature of a delusion, for it belongs to a world-view which was widely accepted by the Jews of that time, and was contained in their religious literature. Even the idea held by Jesus, that He was the One Who on the appearance of the Messianic Kingdom would be manifested as the Messiah, contains nothing of a morbid delusion of greatness. If on the ground of family tradition He is convinced that He is of the House of David, He may well think Himself justified in claiming for Himself one day the Messianic dignity promised to a descendant of David in the writings of the prophets. If He chooses to keep to Himself as a secret His certainty of being the coming Messiah, and nevertheless lets a glimmer of the truth break through in His discourses, His action, looked at solely from the outside, is not unlike that of persons with a morbid delusion of greatness. But it is, in reality, something quite different. The concealment of His claim has with Him a natural and logical foundation. According to Jewish doctrine the Messiah will not step out of His concealment until the revelation of the Messianic Kingdom. Jesus, therefore, cannot make Himself known to men as the coming Messiah. And if, on the other hand, in a number of His sayings there breaks through an announcement of the coming of the Kingdom of God made with all the authority of Him who is to be its King, that, too, is from the logical point of view thoroughly intelligible. Altogether, Jesus never behaves like a man wandering in a system of delusions. He reacts in absolutely normal fashion to what is said to Him, and to the events that concern Him. He is never out of touch with reality.

That these medical experts, in the face of the simplest psychiatric considerations, succeed in throwing doubt on the mental soundness of Jesus, is explicable only by the fact of their not being sufficiently familiar with the historical side of the question. Not only do they omit to use the late-Jewish world-view in explanation of the world of ideas in which Jesus lived, they fail also to distinguish the historical from the unhistorical statements which we have about Him. Instead of keeping to what is recorded in the two oldest sources, Mark and Matthew, they bring together everything which is said in the four Gospels collectively, and then sit in judgement on a personality which is in reality fictitious and consequently can be pronounced abnormal. It is significant that the chief arguments for the mental unsoundness of Jesus are drawn from S. John's Gospel.

The real Jesus is convinced of His being the coming Messiah because, amid the religious ideas then prevailing, His powerful ethical personality cannot do otherwise than arrive at consciousness of itself within the frame of this idea. By His spiritual nature He was in very fact the ethical ruler promised by the prophets.

CHAPTER XI

PREPARATIONS FOR AFRICA

WHILE occupied with the dissertation for my medical degree, I was already making preparations for my journey to Africa. In the spring of 1912 I gave up my teaching work at the university and my post at S. Nicholas'. The courses of lectures which I gave in the winter of 1911-1912 dealt with the reconciliation of the religious world-view with the results of the historical research on the world-religions and with the facts of natural science.

The text of my last sermon to the congregation of S. Nicholas' was S. Paul's words of blessing in his Epistle to the Philippians: "The peace of God which passeth all understanding, keep your hearts and minds in Christ Jesus," a text with which all through the years I had closed every service I had held.

Not to preach any more, not to lecture any more, was for me a great sacrifice, and till I left for Africa I avoided, as far as possible, going past either S. Nicholas' or the University, because the very sight of the places where I had carried on work which I could never resume was too painful for me. Even to-day I cannot bear to look at the windows of the second lecture-room to the east of the entrance of the great University building, because it was there that I most often lectured.

Last of all I left my residence on the S. Thomas Embankment, in order that with my wife—Helen Bresslau, the daughter of the Strassburg historian, whom I had married on June 18th, 1912—I might spend the last months, so far as I was not obliged to be travelling, in my father's parsonage at Günsbach. My wife, who had already before our marriage been a valuable collaborator in the completion of manuscripts and correction of proofs, was a great help again with all the literary work which had to be got through before we started for Africa.

The spring of 1912 I had spent in Paris to study tropical

medicine and begin my purchase of things needed for Africa. While I had at the beginning of my medical studies acquired scientific knowledge of my subject, now I had to work at it on practical lines. This, too, was an experience for me. Till then I had been engaged only in intellectual work. But now I had to make out from catalogues lists of things to be ordered, go shopping for days on end, stand about in the shops and seek out what I wanted, check accounts and delivery notes, fill packing-cases, prepare accurate lists for the custom-house examinations, and occupy myself with other similar jobs. What an amount of time and trouble it cost me to get together the instruments, the drugs, the bandages, and all the other articles needed for the equipment of a hospital, to say nothing of all the work we did together in preparation for housekeeping in the primeval forest! At first I felt occupation with such things to be something of a burden. Gradually, however, I came to the conclusion that even the practical struggle with material affairs is worthy of being carried on in a spirit of self-devotion. To-day I have advanced so far that the neat setting out of a list of things to be ordered gives me artistic satisfaction. The annoyance, which I do feel again and again, is only at the fact that so many catalogues, including those of chemists, are arranged as unclearly and unpractically as if the firm in question had entrusted the compilation to its porter's wife.

To obtain the necessary funds for my undertaking I undertook a round of begging visits among my acquaintances, and experienced in full measure the difficulty of winning their support for a work which had not yet justified its existence by showing something achieved, but was for the present only an intention. Most of my friends and acquaintances helped me over this embarrassment by saying that they would help my adventurous plan, because I was its author. But I must confess to having also experienced that the tone of my reception became markedly different when it came out that I was there, not as a visitor but as a beggar. Still the kindness which I experienced on these rounds outweighed a hundredfold the humiliations which I had to put up with.

That the German professors at Strassburg University

gave so liberally for an enterprise to be founded in a French colony moved me deeply. A considerable portion of the whole sum which I received came from members of my congregation at S. Nicholas'. I was supported also by Alsatian parishes, especially by those whose pastors had been fellow-students or pupils of my own. Money for the work to be founded flowed in also from a concert which the Paris Bach Society with its choir, supported by Maria Philippi and myself, gave on its behalf. A concert and a lecture, too, in Le Havre, where I was known through having helped at a Bach concert, were a financial success.

Thus the financial difficulty was for the present surmounted. I had money enough for all purchases necessary for the voyage, and for the running of the hospital for about a year. Moreover, well-to-do friends allowed me to anticipate that they would help me again, when I had exhausted my present resources.

I was given valuable help in the management of financial and business matters by Mrs. Annie Fischer, the widow of a Professor of Surgery at the Strassburg University, who had died young. Later on, when I was in Africa, she took upon herself all the work that had to be done in Europe. Later on her son also became a doctor in the Tropics.

When I was certain that I could collect funds enough for the establishment of a small hospital, I made a definite offer to the Paris Missionary Society to come at my own expense to serve its mission-field on the River Ogowe from the centrally situated station at Lambaréné.

The Mission Station at Lambaréné was established in 1876 by the American missionary and medical man, Dr. Nassau, the commencement of missionary work in the Ogowe district having been taken in hand by the American missionaries who came into the country in 1874. Somewhat later the Gaboon became a French possession, and from 1892 onwards the Paris Missionary Society replaced the American, since the Americans were not in a position to comply with the requirement of the French Government that all instruction should be given in French.

Monsieur Boegner's successor as Superintendent of Missions, Monsieur Jean Bianquis, whose piety of deeds

D*

rather than words and able management of the Society's affairs won him many friends, maintained with all the weight of his authority that they must not lose this opportunity of obtaining, free of cost, the mission doctor whom they had been so ardently longing for. But the strictly orthodox objected. It was resolved to invite me before the Committee and hold an examination into my beliefs. I could not agree to this, and based my refusal on the fact that Jesus, when He called His disciples, required from them nothing beyond the will to follow Him. I also sent a message to the Committee that, if we are to follow the saying of Jesus: "He that is not against us is on our part," a missionary society would be in the wrong if it rejected even a Mahommedan who offered his services for the treatment of their suffering natives. Not long before this the Mission had refused to accept a minister who wanted to go out and work for it, because his scientific conviction did not allow him to answer with an unqualified *Yes* the question whether he regarded the Fourth Gospel as the work of the Apostle John.

To avoid a similar fate I declined to appear before the assembled Committee and let them put theological questions to me. On the other hand, I offered to make a personal visit to each member of it, so that conversation with me might enable them to judge clearly whether my acceptance really meant such terrible danger to the souls of the negroes and to the Society's reputation. My proposal was accepted and cost me several afternoons. A few of the members gave me a chilly reception. The majority assured me that my theological standpoint made them hesitate for two chief reasons: I might be tempted to confuse the missionaries out there with my learning, and I might wish to be active again as a preacher. By my assurance that I only wanted to be a doctor, and that as to everything else I would be *muet comme une carpe* ("as mute as a fish"), their fears were dispelled, and these visits actually brought me into quite cordial relations with a number of the Committee members.

Thus on the understanding that I would avoid everything that could cause offence to the missionaries and their converts in their belief, my offer was accepted, with the result indeed that one member of the Committee sent in his resignation.

One more thing now remained to be done, namely to secure from the Colonial Department permission to practise as a doctor in the Gaboon, although I had only the German diploma. With the help of influential acquaintances this last difficulty, also, was got over. At last the road was clear!

In February 1913 the seventy packing-cases were screwed down and sent to Bordeaux by goods train in advance. Then when we were packing our hand-baggage, my wife raised objections to my insistence on taking with us 2,000 marks in gold instead of in notes. I replied that we must reckon on the possibility of war, and that, if war broke out, gold would retain its value in every country in the world, whereas the fate of paper-money was uncertain, and an embargo might be laid on bank-credit.

I took into account the danger of war because from acquaintances in Paris whose houses were visited by members of the Russian Embassy I had learnt that the latter announced war as something which would come as soon as Russian had completed her strategic railway in Poland.

I was quite convinced, indeed, that neither the French people nor the German wanted war, and that the parliamentary leaders of each nation were eager for opportunities of getting to know each other and of giving expression to their ideas. As one who had been working for years to bring about an understanding between Germany and France, I knew how much was being done at that very time for the preservation of peace, and I had some hope of success. On the other hand, I never shut my eyes to the fact that the fate of Europe had been placed by the development of events in the hands of the semi-Asiatics. . . .

It seemed to me ominous of evil that in Germany, as in France, gold was being withdrawn as far as possible from circulation, and being replaced by paper-money. From 1911 onwards the State employees of both countries had been receiving hardly any gold in the payment of their salaries. Till then German officials had been able to choose whether their salary should be paid in gold or in paper.

CHAPTER XII

LITERARY WORK DURING MY MEDICAL COURSE

DURING the last two years of my medical course and the period which I spent in the hospitals as house physician, I found time, by means of serious encroachment on my night's rest, to bring to completion a work on the history of scientific research into the thought-world of S. Paul, to revise and enlarge the *Quest of the Historical Jesus* for the second edition, and together with Widor to prepare an edition of Bach's Preludes and Fugues for the organ, giving with each piece directions for its rendering.

Immediately after completing the *Quest of the Historical Jesus* I had gone on to study the teaching of S. Paul. From the very beginning I had been left unsatisfied by the explanations of it given by scientific theology, because they represented it as something complicated and loaded with contradictions, an account of it which seemed irreconcilable with the originality and greatness of the thought revealed in it. And this view became thoroughly questionable to me from the time when I became convinced that the preaching of Jesus was entirely determined by the expectation of the end of the world and the supernatural advent of the Kingdom of God. So now I was faced by the question, which for preceding investigators had not come in sight, whether the thought-world of S. Paul as well was not rooted entirely in eschatology.

When I began examining it with this possibility in view, I arrived with astonishing rapidity at the conclusion that that was the case. As early as 1906 I had been able to expound in a course of lectures the ideas underlying the eschatological explanation of the very remarkable Pauline teaching about the being in Christ, and the having died and risen again with Him.

While engaged on the working out of this new view I was drawn to make myself acquainted with all the attempts which had up to then been made to give a scientific explanation of the Pauline teaching, and to show clearly the way in which the whole complex of questions constituting the problem had gradually made themselves felt in those attempts.

With my investigations into S. Paul's teaching I had the same experience as I had had with the Last Supper and the Life of Jesus. Instead of contenting myself with simply expounding the solution I had discovered, I took upon my shoulders each time the further work of writing the history of the problem. That I three times brought myself to follow such a laborious by-road is the fault of Aristotle. How often have I cursed the hour in which I first read the section of his *Metaphysics* in which he develops the problem of philosophy out of a criticism of previous philosophizing! Something which slumbered within me then awoke. Again and again since then have I experienced within me the urge to try to grasp the nature of a problem not only as it is in itself, but also by the way in which it unfolds itself in the course of history.

Whether the supplementary work has proved worth while, I know not. I am certain only of one thing, that I could take no other course than proceed in this Aristotelian fashion, and that it brought me scientific and artistic satisfaction.

Research into the history of the scientific exposition of the Pauline teaching had a special attraction for me because it was a task that no one had ever yet undertaken. And there were special facilities available for me, in that the Strassburg University contained a collection of books upon S. Paul almost as complete as that of its books on the life of Jesus. Moreover, the Head Librarian, Dr. Schorbach, gave me much help, for which I was most grateful, in discovering all the books bearing on the subject, as well as all the articles which had been published in periodicals.

I had thought at first that this literary-historical study could be treated so briefly that it would form just an introductory chapter to the exposition of the eschatological significance of the Pauline teaching. But as I worked, it became clear that it would expand into a complete book.

The scientific investigation of the thought-world of S. Paul begins with Hugo Grotius. In his *Annotationes in Novum Testamentum* which appeared about the middle of the seventeenth century he put forward the self-evident principle that one's aim must be to understand the epistles of S. Paul in accordance with the plain meaning of the words. Till then they had been interpreted in Catholic and Protestant theologies alike, in accordance with the Church doctrine of Justification by Faith.

That the sentences about being in Christ and having died and risen with Him conceal within them important problems never, as we can see, enters the heads of the earliest champions of historical exposition. For them the first business is to make it clear that S. Paul's teaching is not dogmatic, but "according to reason."

The first thing accomplished by Pauline research, then, was the drawing of attention to differences of thought which distinguish individual epistles from the rest, and as a corollary to that comes at once the necessity of regarding some of them as unauthentic. In 1807 Schleiermacher expresses doubts about the genuineness of the First Epistle to Timothy. Seven years later John Godfrey Eichorn proves with convincing arguments that neither of the epistles to Timothy nor that to Titus can be by S. Paul. Then Ferdinand Christian Baur goes further still in his *Paulus der Apostel Jesu Christi* ("Paul the Apostle of Jesus Christ") which appeared in 1845. As indisputably genuine he recognizes only the two Epistles to the Corinthians and those to the Romans and the Galatians. All the others appear to him, when compared with these, to be more or less open to objection.

Later research mitigates the severity of this fundamentally correct judgement in that it reveals as equally genuine the Epistles to the Philippians and to Philemon together with the first to the Thessalonians. By far the greater number, then, of the epistles which bear the name of Paul can really be attributed to him. For the critical science of to-day the epistles which pass as undoubtedly not genuine are the second to the Thessalonians, that to Titus, and the two to Timothy. About the Epistles to the Ephesians and the Colossians a final judgement is not possible. They contain thoughts which are closely allied to those of the certainly genuine epistles but differ from them markedly in details.

Baur finds the criterion for genuine or not genuine in the contrast which he discovers between the Christ-belief of S. Paul and that of the apostles at Jerusalem. He is the first who ventures to maintain that the Epistle to the Galatians is a controversial document which is really directed against the apostles at Jerusalem. He is also the first to recognize that the difference of opinion as to the binding character of the Law is based on a difference of teaching as to the significance of the death of Jesus. From this contrast, now brought to light, he concludes that the epistles in which it is mentioned come from S. Paul's own hand, while the others in which it plays no part were written by pupils of his who wanted to carry back into S. Paul's own time the reconciliation between the two parties which came about later.

With this starting-point, then, in the Pauline epistles, Baur is now the first to open up the problem of the beginnings of Christian dogma. He finds, and rightly, the way prepared for it by the fact that S. Paul's thought of freedom from the Law, and his statements about the significance of the death of Jesus, became in the course of one or two generations the common property of Christian faith, although they stand originally in contradiction to the traditional teaching represented by the apostles at Jerusalem.

The reconciliation comes about later, according to Baur, through the fact that the Gnostic-Christian teaching which arose at the turn of the first and second centuries compelled all the anti-Gnostic tendencies in the Church to unite in a common defence and therewith in a mutual reconciliation. This explanation has shown itself since then to be partly correct, but also very far from comprehensive enough.

By his recognition that the problem of the Pauline teaching forms the kernel of the problem of how Christian dogma originated, Baur first set flowing the stream of historical research into the beginning of Christianity. Before his time it had made no progress, because its task had not been definitely formulated.

Eduard Reuss, Otto Pfleiderer, Karl Holsten, Ernest Renan, H. J. Holtzmann, Karl von Weizsäcker, Adolph Harnack, and the others who in the second half of the nineteenth century continued the work of Baur, deal with the component elements of the Pauline teaching in detail. In doing so they agree in showing clearly that, side by side with the doctrine of redemption which goes back to the thought of the sin-offering, there is in S. Paul another doctrine of an entirely different character, according to which believers experience in themselves in a mysterious way the death and resurrection of Jesus, and thereby become sinless, ethical persons ruled by the spirit of Jesus. The fundamental thoughts of this mystic-ethical doctrine find expression for the first time in Herrmann Lüdemann's *Anthropology of S. Paul* which appeared in 1872.

The solution of the Pauline problem, then, means explaining why S. Paul asserts that the Law no longer has any force for believers in Christ; why, side by side with the doctrine of redemption by belief in the atoning death of Jesus, which he holds in common with the apostles, he lays down the mystical doctrine of Being in Christ and having died and risen again with Him; and, finally, how he combines these two beliefs in his system of thought.

The research of the end of the nineteenth and the beginning of the twentieth century believes itself able to make comprehensible the views in which S. Paul advances beyond the position of primitive Christianity by assuming, on the ground of his having been born and educated in Asia Minor where society was entirely under the influence of the Greek language and civilization, that he combines the Greek habit of thought with the Jewish. As a result of this combination, they maintain, he becomes an opponent of the Law. As a further result he feels himself compelled to conceive of redemption through the death of Jesus not only under the Jewish figure of the sin-offering, but also as a mystical participation in that death itself.

This solution of the problem seems the most obvious and natural in view of the fact that the mystical habit of thought is something unknown to Judaism, while it is quite common in the Greek world.

In its assumption that S. Paul's mystical teaching about redemption is Greek in character, investigation is further strengthened by the abundant supply of new material bearing on the Graeco-Oriental mystery religions collected about the end of the century by Hermann Usener, E. Rhode, François Cumont, Hugo Hepding, Richard Reitzenstein, and others from the late-Greek literature which had been as yet very scantily examined, and from newly discovered inscriptions. The information supplied by this fresh material makes clear the part which is played by sacramental action in the religiousness of the period, then beginning, of Graeco-Oriental decadence. Hence the assumption that the mysticism of S. Paul is somehow or other determined by the ideas of Greek religiousness seems best calculated to explain the fact that Baptism and the Lord's Supper actually accomplish, in the Apostle's view, the believer's participation in the death and resurrection of Jesus, not symbolizing it only, as was assumed down to the close of the nineteenth century, before anyone ventured to admit that the Apostle really thinks on sacramental lines. Since Judaism knows as little of sacraments as of mysticism it is thought necessary to bring S. Paul into connexion with Greek religiousness merely on account of his view of Baptism and the Supper.

Much as this assumption has in its favour at first, it shows itself, nevertheless, strange to say, to be insufficient to give a real explanation of the mysticism of the Being in Christ. As soon as this assumption is examined in detail it becomes evident that the ideas of S. Paul are quite different in character from those of the Graeco-Oriental mystery religions. They are in no way essentially connected with the latter; there is merely a remarkable analogy between them. Nevertheless, since research believes that the solution of the problem can be reached by no other road than that on which it has entered, it abates not a jot of its confidence, and persuades itself that the material differences between the two views, so far as they have to be admitted, are due to the fact that S. Paul took over the Greek motives unconsciously, so to say, and worked out the doctrine as a whole by a method peculiar to himself.

In spite of its difficult position, research never once ventures to admit that the documents about the Graeco-Oriental mystery religions to which it appeals depict those religions as they were in the second and third centuries A.D., when the original Greek and Oriental religions had become fused together, and through a kind of renaissance which they experienced had become repositories of the ideas of the now prevailing Graeco-Oriental religiousness in its state of decadence. They had obtained thus an importance which was not theirs in S. Paul's day.

The Mithras cult, the original home of which was Persia, needs no consideration in connexion with S. Paul, because it was only in the second century after Christ that it attained to any importance in the Greek world.

It is interesting to note how Adolph Harnack steadily refused to recognize that any deep influence was exerted on S. Paul by Greek ideas.

If S. Paul's mystical teaching about redemption and his sacramental views cannot be made comprehensible on the basis of Hellenistic ideas, the only other possible course it to attempt the to all appearance impossible task of understanding them through late-Judaism, that is through the ideas of eschatology. This plan is followed by Richard Kabisch in *The Eschatology of S. Paul in its Connexion with the Whole Idea of Paulinism* (1893), and, quite independently of him, by William Wrede in his *S. Paul* (1904), which has unfortunately remained a mere sketch. A complete explanation of the thought-world of S. Paul is not reached by either of them, nor are they able to lay bare the last secret of the logic in which the Being in Christ and the having died and risen again in Him are maintained to be not only something to be experienced spiritually, but also something natural and real. They do, however, offer with convincing force the proof that, when brought into connexion with eschatology, a number of S. Paul's ideas which at first sight do not suggest any such relation, are revealed as being not only something simpler and more living than they were under the old conception, but show themselves also, in their mutual interdependence, as belonging to a system which is a definite and consistent whole.

The investigations thus made off the beaten track are ignored by contemporary research, because the assumption of a Paul whose thought is at once Greek and Jewish passes not only with the theologians but also with the scholars occupied with late-Hellenism as something which explains itself and may be taken as a matter of course. But they fail to see the danger into which the unfortunate Apostle is brought by their assertion that the fundamental ideas of the epistles which bear his name stand in an essential connexion with those of the Graeco-Oriental religiousness as it is known to us from evidence supplied by the second and third centuries A.D.! There arises at once, of course, the question, which cannot be put on one side, whether, if that is so, these letters really belong to the fifties and sixties of the first Christian century, and did not rather originate in that later period, being attributed to the Rabbi Paul of primitive Christianity only by a literary fiction.

In the second half of the nineteenth century Bruno Bauer and certain adherents of the so-called radical Dutch School—A. D. Loman, Rudolph Steck, W. C. van Manen, and others—put forward the assertion that the Greek ideas in the letters which bear the name of Paul are much easier to explain if it is admitted that the writings themselves are actually of Greek origin than they are on the supposition that immediately after the death of Jesus a Rabbi gave a new, Greek character to the primitive Christian belief. They urge, and successfully, as their chief argument, that the struggle against the Law cannot have been undertaken by the Rabbi Paul. The demand for freedom from the Law must naturally first have been made when Greeks began to be the dominant influence in the Christian Churches, and thus rebelled against the Christianity which was still centred in Judaism. The struggle over the Law, therefore, must have been fought out, not in the middle of the first century between Paul and the apostles, but two or three generations later between the two parties which had come into existence in the intervening period. To legitimize their victory the unorthodox were supposed to have already attributed it to S. Paul in epistles written for the purpose and issued under his name. This paradoxical theory of the origin of the Pauline letters cannot, of course, be historically proved, but it throws a glaring light upon the difficulties in which research find itself when it assumes the existence of Greek thought in S. Paul.

For a conclusion to the history of scientific research into the thought-world of S. Paul I had in 1911 to establish the fact that the attempt, then universally regarded as promising success, to trace back to Greek ideas the Apostle's mystical teaching about redemption which was assumed to be non-Jewish could not be carried through, and that there could be no question of any explanation other than one provided by eschatology.

At the time when this introductory examination appeared in print my exposition of the eschatological explanation of the thought-world of S. Paul was so near completion that I could have got it ready for the press within a few weeks. But these weeks were not at my disposal, since I had at once to begin the work needed for the State medical examination. Later on so much of my time was taken up by the thesis for the Doctorate, and the revision of the *Quest of the Historical Jesus*, that I had to give up all hope of publishing this second part of my work on S. Paul before my departure for Africa.

In the autumn of 1912 when I was already busy shopping and packing I started working into the *Quest of the Historical Jesus* the new books which had appeared on that subject since its publication, and recasting sections of the work which no longer satisfied me. I was especially concerned to set forth the late-Jewish eschatology more thoroughly and better than I had been able to do before because I had ever since been constantly occupied with the subject, and besides that to analyse and discuss the works of John M. Robertson, William Benjamin Smith, James George Frazer, Arthur Drews, and others, who contested the historical existence of Jesus. Unfortunately the later English editions of my history are all based on the text of the first German one.

It is no hard matter to assert that Jesus never lived. The attempt to prove it, however, infallibly works round to produce the opposite conclusion.

In the Jewish literature of the first century the existence of Jesus is not satisfactorily attested, and in the Greek and Latin literature of the same period there is no evidence for it at all. Of the two passages in which the Jewish writer Josephus makes incidental mention of Jesus in his *Antiquities* one was undoubtedly interpolated by Christian copyists. The first pagan witness for His existence is Tacitus, who in the reign of Trajan, in the second decade of the second century A.D., reports in his *Annals* (XV, 44) that the founder of the sect of 'Christians,' which was accused by Nero of causing the great fire at Rome, was executed under the government of Tiberius by the Procurator of Judaea, Pontius Pilate. Anyone, therefore, who is dissatisfied since Roman history only takes notice of the existence of Jesus because of the continuance of a Christian movement, and that, too, for the first time some eighty years after His death, and who is, further, bent on declaring the Gospels and S. Paul's Epistles to be not genuine, can consider himself justified in refusing to recognize the historical existence of Jesus.

But that does not settle the matter. It still has to be explained when, where, and how Christianity came into existence without either Jesus or Paul; how it came, later on, to wish to trace its origins back to these invented historical personalities; and finally for what reasons it took the remarkable course of making these two founders members of the Jewish people. The Gospels and the Epistles of S. Paul can, indeed, be demonstrated to be not genuine only when it is made intelligible how they could have come into existence if they really were not genuine.

Of the difficulties of this task which has come to them the champions of the unhistorical character of Jesus take no account, and it is in an inconceivably frivolous way that they go to work. Though they differ from each other widely as to details, the method which they all apply attempts to reach a proof that there existed already in pre-Christian times, in Palestine or elsewhere in the East, a Christ-cult or Jesus-cult of a Gnostic character, the centre of which, as in the cults of Adonis, Osiris, and Tammuz, is a god or demi-god who dies and rises again. Since we have no information about any such pre-Christian Christ-cult, its existence must be made as probable as possible by a process of combination and fantasy. Thereon must follow a further act of imagination to the effect that the adherents of this assumed pre-Christian Christ-cult found at some time or other reasons for changing the object of their worship, the god who dies and rises again, into an historic human personality, and, in defiance of the facts known to the various circles of his believers, declaring his cult to have existed only from the date of this change of personality, whereas the other mystery religions show no tendency whatever to recast myths as history. As if this were not difficulty enough, the Gospels and the Pauline Epistles require from these champions of the unhistorical character of Jesus a further explanation of how their Christ-cult, instead of claiming to have originated in a long-past age of no longer verifiable events, lapsed into the mistake of dating its invented Jesus scarcely two or three generations back, and of allowing Him, moreover, to appear on the stage of history as a Jew among Jews.

As the last and hardest task of all, comes that of explaining the contents of the Gospels, in detail, as myth changed to history. If they keep to their theory, Drews, Smith, and Robertson must actually maintain that the events and the discourses reported by Matthew and Mark are only the clothing of thoughts which that earlier mystery-religion put forward. The fact that Arthur Drews and others try to establish this explanation by pressing into their service not only every myth they can discover but astronomy and astrology as well, shows what demands it makes upon the imagination.

It is clear, then, as a matter of fact, from the writings of those who dispute the historicity of Jesus that the hypothesis of His existence is a thousand times easier to prove than that of His non-existence. That does not mean that the hopeless undertaking is being abandoned. Again and again books appear about the non-existence of Jesus and find credulous readers, although they contain nothing new or going beyond Robertson, Smith, Drews, and the other classics of this literature, but have to be content with giving out as new what has already been said.

So far, indeed, as these attempts are meant to serve the cause of historical truth, they can defend themselves by claiming that such a rapid acceptance throughout the Greek world of a faith which sprang out of Judaism, as is recorded in the traditional history of the beginnings of Christianity, is incomprehensible without further confirmation, and that therefore a hearing may be claimed for the hypothesis of the derivation of Christianity from Greek thought. But the working out of this hypothesis is wrecked upon the fact that the Jesus of the two earlier Gospels has nothing whatever about Him which allows Him to be explained as a personality originating in a myth. Moreover, with His eschatological mode of thought He displays a peculiarity which a later period could not have given to a personality created by itself, for the good reason that it no longer possessed the knowledge of the late-Jewish eschatology in the generation before the destruction of Jerusalem by Titus which was needed for that purpose. Again, what interest could the assumed mystery-religion of the Christ-cult have had in attributing to the pseudo-historical Jesus, invented by itself, a belief which had obviously remained unfulfilled, in an immediate end to the world and His revelation as the Son-of-Man-Messiah? By his eschatology Jesus is so completely and firmly rooted in the period in which the two oldest Gospels place Him, that He cannot possibly be represented as anything but a personality which really appeared in that period. It is significant that those who dispute His historical existence very prudently take no account of the eschatological limitations of His thought and activities.

That before starting for Africa I was busy again with Bach was due to a request from Widor. The New York publisher, Mr. G. Schirmer, had asked him to prepare an edition of Bach's organ music with directions about the best rendering of it, and he agreed to do so on condition that I shared the work. Our collaboration took the form of my preparing rough drafts which we afterwards worked out together. What a number of times in 1911 and 1912 did I visit Paris for a day or two for this purpose! And Widor twice spent several days with me in Günsbach that we might devote ourselves to the task in undisturbed quiet.

Although as a matter of principle we both disapproved of so-called 'practical' editions which try to keep the player in tutelage, we nevertheless believed that for Bach's organ music advice was justifiable, since, with a few small exceptions, Bach has given for his organ compositions no directions at all about registration or about change of manuals, as composers for the organ have usually done since then. For the organists of his day this was indeed unnecessary. As a result of the character of their organs and of the traditional way of using them, the pieces were automatically rendered as Bach had intended. Soon after the master's death his organ compositions, which he had actually never published, were for a considerable period as good as forgotten. When, from the middle of the nineteenth century, thanks to the Peters' edition, they became known, musical taste and organs had both changed. People still knew what was the eighteenth-century tradition in playing. But they rejected this correct method of rendering the organ works of Bach as too simple and too plain, and believed they were acting in his spirit when they employed in the most generous measure possible the constant changes in volume and character of sound which could be produced on the modern organ. Thus towards the end of the nineteenth century the modern method of rendering organ music with its striving after effect had so completely supplanted the appropriate method that the latter was never thought of, if, indeed, anyone still knew what it was.

France was an exception. Widor, Guilmant, and the rest held firmly to the old German tradition which they had received from the well-known organist Adolph Friedrich Hesse (1802-1863) of Breslau. Till about the middle of the nineteenth century, indeed, there was in France no art of organ-playing at all, because the organs which had been destroyed during the great Revolution had for the most part only received a minimum amount of restoration. But when Cavaillé-Coll and others began to build good organs, and the German Peters' edition enabled organists to possess Bach's organ compositions, which had never been known in France, they did not know—I am repeating what Widor often told me—what to make of the art revealed in them, so perfect, and hitherto without parallel in France, with the further reason that the demands made on the player's pedal technique were something new to them. They had, therefore, to go abroad to learn what was required. And they all went—those who could not afford it partly at Cavaillé-Coll's expense!—to have lessons from Lemmens, the well-known Brussels organist, who had been a pupil of Hesse's.

Adolph Friedrich Hesse (1802-1863) had received the tradition of how to play Bach from his teacher, Kittel. At the inauguration of the newly built organ at S. Eustache's, in 1844, the Parisians heard for the first time, and thanks to him, Bach's organ music. In the years that followed he was also often invited to France that he might be heard at the inauguration of other organs. His playing at the International Exhibition in London in 1854 did much towards making Bach's music known in England.

To the old German tradition which they had learnt from Hesse and Lemmens the French organists continued to hold fast not merely as a matter of artistic taste, but as one of actual practical necessity. For the organs built by Cavaillé-Coll were not modern organs. They did not possess, like those of Germany, the arrangements which made possible such rich variation in the volume of the sound and its tone-colour. Hence the French organists were obliged to follow the classical method of playing which had been handed down to them. This, however, they did not feel as any drawback, because with the wonderful tone of their organs the Bach fugues could produce their full effect, as on the organs of Bach's own day, without resort to the special effects of registration.

Thus by an historical paradox the principles of the old German tradition were saved for the present age by Parisian masters of the organ, and this tradition also became known in detail when by degrees musicians again began to consult the theoretical works on their art preserved for us from the eighteenth century.

For anyone who looked out, as I did, for every possible opportunity of playing Bach on eighteenth-century organs these instruments, through what they showed to be technically possible or impossible and what to be musically effective or ineffective, proved instructors in the authentic way of rendering the master's organ music.

As to the new edition which Widor and I were to produce, we considered our task to be that of showing to organists acquainted with modern organs only and therefore strangers to the organ style of Bach, what registration and what changes of keyboard had to be considered for any particular piece on the organs with which Bach had to reckon. After that, so we thought, we might suggest experiments to discover how far beyond that use could be made without spoiling the style of the variations in the volume of sound and its tone-colours which are desirable and possible on the modern organ. We thought good taste demanded that we should not insert in the musical score itself any of our own directions or suggestions, but should rather embody what we had to say about the pieces in short articles, prefixed in a body to the musical score and serving as an introduction to the volume. Thus the organist can learn what we advise, but he alone with Bach without any cicerone as soon as he turns to the piece he is going to play. Not even fingering or phrasing does he find prescribed by us.

Bach's fingering differs from ours in that, following older fashion, he crosses any finger over another, and therefore turns the thumb under much less frequently.

In pedalling Bach could not use the heel because the pedals of his day were so short; he had to produce every note with the point of the foot. Moreover the shortness of the pedals hindered the moving of one foot over the other. He was, therefore, often obliged to let his foot glide from one pedal on to its neighbour, whereas we can manage a better legato than was possible for him by moving one foot over the other, or by using foot and heel alternatively.

When I was young I found the short pedal of the Bach

period still existing in many old village organs. In Holland many pedals are even to-day so short that to use the heel is impossible.

In matters of phrasing what Widor and I had to say is given to the player in the introduction. Since I am continually annoyed by being compelled, with almost every edition of musical works, to have before my eyes the fingering, the phrasing, the fortes and pianos, the crescendos and decrescendos, and not infrequently even the pedantic anlyses of some editor or other, even when I entirely disagree with them, I insisted on our observing the principle which, it is to be hoped, will some day be universally acted on, that the player must have before his eyes in print as part of Bach's, or Mozart's, or Beethoven's music only what was written by the composer himself.

To concessions to modern taste and modern organs we at once found ourselves driven by the fact that on modern instruments Bach's organ music cannot be played as he intended. On the instruments of his day the forte and the fortissimo were at their fullest so soft that a piece could be played through even in the latter without the hearer being fatigued thereby or feeling any need of change. Similarly, Bach could give his hearers a continual forte with his orchestra. But on modern organs, the fortissimo is usually so loud and so harsh that the listener cannot endure it for more than a few moments. He is, further, not in a position, amid all the roar, to follow the individual lines of melody, though that is necessary for the understanding of a composition of Bach's. One is obliged, therefore, with modern organs to make tolerable for the listener by changes of volume and tone-colour, long passages which Bach meant to be given in an unbroken forte or fortissimo.

But no *a priori* objection can be made to a greater variation in volume and gradations of tone than Bach could manage upon his organs, provided that the architecture of the piece is clearly perceptible, and gives no impression of unrest. Whereas Bach was satisfied to carry a fugue through with three or four variously toned degrees of loudness in alternation, we can allow ourselves six or eight. But the supreme rule must always be that in Bach's organ music sufficient prominence be given to the lines of melody, the effects may be secured by the tone-colour being treated as of secondary importance. The organist must remind himself again and again that the listener to a composition of Bach's for the organ can have it really before his mind only when the lines of melody which move along side by side pass before him in absolute distinctness. That is why Widor and I in our edition insist again and again on the player's being before all else clear about the proper phrasing for the subjects and 'motifs' of the piece, and then following this through in the minutest detail.

People cannot be reminded too often that on the organs of the seventeenth century it was not possible to play in as quick a tempo as one might wish to. The keys moved so stiffly and had to be depressed so far, that a good moderato itself was something of an achievement. Since, then, Bach must have conceived his Preludes and Fugues in the moderate tempo in which they could be played on his own organs, we, too, must hold fast to this fact as giving us the tempo which is authentic and appropriate.

It is well known that Hesse, in accordance with the Bach tradition which had come down to him, used to play the organ compositions in an extremely quiet tempo.

If the wonderful animation of the Bach line of melody is properly brought out by perfect phrasing, the listener does not feel the rate of playing slow even if it keeps within the limits of a moderato.

Since on the organ it is impossible to accent individual notes, the phrasing must be worked out without any support from such accentuation. Plastic rendering of Bach on the organ means, therefore, giving listeners the illusion of accents through perfect phrasing. It is because this is not yet recognized as the first requirement of all organ-playing in general, and of the playing of Bach in particular, that one so seldom hears Bach's compositions satisfactorily rendered. And how perfectly plastic must the playing be, when it has further to triumph over the acoustic perils of a large church.

To organists, then, who are familiar only with the

modern organ, Widor and I stand for an appropriate rendering of Bach's organ compositions which is in many respects new to them, in contrast to the modern showy style with which they are familiar. Along with this, we cannot but point out again and again how difficult it is to secure this style of rendering on the modern organ, which in respect of tone is so little suited to the purpose. We expected that the demands which Bach's works make on the organ would do more to popularize the ideal of the real, fine-toned organ than any number of essays on organ-building. And we have not been disappointed.

It was only the first five volumes of the new edition containing the Sonatas, the Concertos, the Preludes, and the Fugues that we could complete before my departure for Africa. The three volumes containing the Choral Preludes we intended to complete during my first period of leave in Europe, on the foundation of rough drafts to be made by me in Africa.

By the publisher's desire our work was published in three languages. The divergencies between the French text, on the one hand, and the German, together with the English which is based on it, on the other, arise from the fact that in respect of the details as to which our opinions differed, Widor and I had agreed that in the French edition his ideas, which fitted better the peculiarities of the French organs, should be dominant, while in the German and the English mine should, taking, as they did, more into account the character of the modern organ.

The outbreak of war so soon afterwards and the consequent disturbance of international dealings in the book trade, which still continues, have brought it about that our work, which was published in New York, was bought almost exclusively in English-speaking countries, for which, indeed, it was primarily designed. Its price was fixed on the dollar basis, and that alone made it after the war practically unsaleable in Germany and France.

Owing to various circumstances, and because other tasks always got in the way, I have again and again been obliged to postpone the publication of the three volumes of Choral Preludes.

CHAPTER XIII

FIRST ACTIVITIES IN AFRICA

1913-1917

In the afternoon of Good Friday, 1913, my wife and I left Günsbach; in the evening of March 26th we embarked at Bordeaux.

At Lambaréné the missionaries gave us a very hearty welcome. They had unfortunately not been able to erect the little buildings of corrugated iron in which I was to begin my medical activity, for they had not secured the necessary labourers. The trade in okoume wood, which was just beginning to flourish in the Ogowe district, offered any native who was fairly capable better paid work than he could find on the mission-station. So at first I had to use as my consulting-room an old fowl-house close to our living quarters, but in the late autumn I was able to move to a corrugated-iron building down by the river, 26 feet long and 13 feet wide, with a roof of palm-leaves. It contained a small consulting-room, an operation-room of similar proportions, and a still smaller dispensary. Round about this building there came gradually into existence a number of large bamboo huts for the accommodation of the native patients. The white patients found quarters in the mission-house and in the doctor's little bungalow.

From the very first days, before I had even found time to unpack the drugs and instruments, I was beseiged by sick people. The choice of Lambaréné as the site of the hospital had been made on the strength of the map and of the facts given us by Mr. Morel, the missionary, a native of Alsace, and it proved to be in every respect a happy one. From a distance of one to two hundred miles around, from upstream or downstream, the sick could be brought to me in canoes along the Ogowe and its affluents. The chief diseases I had to deal with were malaria, leprosy, sleeping sickness, dysentery, framboesia, and phagedenic ulcers, but I was surprised at the number of cases of pneumonia and heart disease which I discovered. There was much work too with urinary diseases. Surgical treatment was called for chiefly by hernia and elephantiasis tumours. Hernia is much commoner among the natives in Equatorial Africa than among us white people. If there is no medical man in the neighbourhood, every year sees a number of unfortunate mortals doomed to die a painful death from strangulated hernia from which a timely operation might have saved them. My first surgical intervention was in a case of that kind.

Thus I had during the very first weeks full opportunity for establishing the fact that physical misery among the natives is not less but even greater than I had supposed. How glad I was that in defiance of all objections I had carried out my plan of going out there as a doctor.

Great was the joy of Dr. Nassau, the aged founder of the mission-station at Lambaréné, when I sent to him in America the news that it was once more supplied with a doctor.

At first I was much hindered in my work by being unable to find natives who could serve as interpreters and orderlies. The first who showed himself worth anything was one who had been a cook, Joseph Azoawani by name, who stayed with me, though I could not pay him so much as he had earned in his former calling. He gave me some valuable hints about how to deal with the natives, though upon the one which he thought the most important I was unable to act. He advised me to refuse as patients those whose lives, so far as we could see, we were not likely to save, Again and again he held up to me the example of the fetich doctors who would have nothing to do with such cases, in order to endanger as little as possible their reputation as healers.

But on one point I had later to admit that he was right. One must never, when dealing with primitives, hold out hopes of recovery to the patient and his relatives, if the case is really hopeless. If death occurs without warning of it having been given, it is concluded that the doctor did not know the disease would have this outcome because he had not diagnosed it correctly. To native patients one must tell the truth without reservation. They wish to know it and they can endure it, for death is to them something natural. They are not afraid of it, but face it calmly. If after all the patient unexpectedly recovers, so much the better for the doctor's reputation. He ranks thereafter as one who can cure even fatal diseases.

Valiant help was given in the hospital by my wife, who had been trained as a nurse. She looked after the severe cases, superintended the linen and the bandages, was often busy in the dispensary, kept the instruments in proper condition, made all the preparations for the operations, herself then administering the anaesthetics, while Joseph acted as assistant. That she managed successfully the complicated work of an African household, and yet could find every day some hours to spare for the hospital was really a wonderful achievement.

To induce the natives to submit to operations needed no great skill in persuasion from me. A few years before a Government doctor, Jauré-Guibert by name, had stayed for a short time at Lambaréné on one of his journeys and performed some successful operations, on the strength of which my very modest surgical skill met with a trustful reception. Fortunately I did not lose a single one of those patients on whom I first operated.

At the end of a few months of work the hospital had to find every day accommodation for about forty patients. I had, however, to provide shelter not only for these but for the companions who had brought them long distances in canoes, and who stayed with them in order to paddle them back home again.

The actual work, heavy as it was, I found a lighter burden than the care and responsibility which came with it. I belong unfortunately to the number of those medical men who have not the robust temperament which is desirable in that calling, and so are consumed with unceasing anxiety about the condition of their severe cases and of those on whom they have operated. In vain have I tried to train myself to that equanimity which makes it possible for a doctor, in spite of all his sympathy with the sufferings of his patients, to husband, as is desirable, his spiritual and nervous energy.

those that were in the catechism. So she was ploughed, and had to offer herself for the examination again six months later.

I found preaching a great joy. It seemed to me a glorious thing to be allowed to preach the sayings of Jesus and Paul to people to whom they were quite new. As interpreters I had the native teachers of the Mission School, who translated each sentence at once into the language of the Galoas or of the Páhuins, or sometimes into both in succession.

The little spare time that was at my disposal in the first year at Lambaréné I devoted to work on the three last volumes of the American edition of Bach's organ music.

For keeping up my organ-playing I had the magnificent piano with pedal attachment, built specially for the Tropics, which the Paris Bach Society had presented to me in recognition of my many years of service as their organist. At first, however, I had not the heart to practise. I had accustomed myself to think that this activity in Africa meant the end of my life as an artist, and that the renunciation would be easier if I allowed fingers and feet to get rusty with disuse. One evening, however, as, in melancholy mood, I was playing one of Bach's organ fugues, the idea came suddenly upon me that I might after all use my free hours in Africa for the very purpose of perfecting and deepening my technique. I immediately formed a plan to take, one after another, compositions by Bach, Mendelssohn, Widor, César Franck, and Max Reger, study them carefully down to the smallest detail, and learn them by heart, even if I had to spend weeks or months on any particular piece. How I enjoyed being able to practise at leisure and in quiet, without any slavery to time through being due to play at concerts, even though occasionally I could not find more than a bare half-hour in the day for the purpose!

My wife and I had now completed our second dry season in Africa, and were beginning to sketch out plans for going home at the opening of the third, when on August 5th, 1914, the news came that war had broken out in Europe. On the evening of that very day were were informed that we must consider ourselves to be prisoners of war; we might, indeed, for the present remain in our own house, but we must stop all intercourse with either white people or natives, and obey unconditionally the regulations of the black soldiers who were assigned us as guards. One of the missionaries and his wife, who like ourselves were Alsatians, were also interned at the Lambaréné mission-station.

The only thing about the war which the natives understood at first was that it was all over with the timber trade, and that all commodities had become dearer. It was only later, when many of them were transported to Cameroon to serve as carriers for the active forces, that they began to understand what the war really meant.

As soon as it became known that of the white men who used to live on the Ogowe ten had already fallen, an old savage remarked: "What, so many men killed already in this war! Why don't their tribes meet to talk out the palaver? How can they ever pay for all these dead men?" For in native warfare those who fall, whether among the conquerors or the conquered, have to be paid for by the opposite side. This same savage expressed the criticism that Europeans kill each other merely out of cruelty, because of course they don't want to eat the dead.

That white people were making prisoners of other whites and putting them under the authority of black soldiers was something incomprehensible to the natives. What a torrent of abuse my black guards came in for from the people of the neighbouring villages because they thought they were "the Doctor's masters."

When I was forbidden to work in the Hospital, I thought at first that I would proceed to the completion of my book on St. Paul. But another subject at once forced itself upon me, one which I had had in my mind for years, and which the war was now making a real live issue: the problem of our civilization. So on the second day of my internment, still quite amazed at being able to sit down at my writing-table early in the morning as in the days before I took up medicine, I set to work on the Philosophy of Civilization.

My first incitement to take up this subject I had received in the summer of 1899 at the house of the Curtius family in Berlin. Hermann Grimm and others were conversing there one evening about a sitting of the Academy from which they had just come, when suddenly one of them— I forget which it was—came out with: "Why, we are all of us just nothing but 'Epigoni'!"[1] It struck home with me, like a flash of lightning, because it put into words what I myself felt.

As early as my first years at the University I had begun to feel misgivings about the opinion that mankind is constantly developing in the direction of progress. My impression was that the fire of its ideals was burning low without anyone noticing it or troubling about it. On a number of occasions I had to acknowledge that public opinion did not reject with indignation inhumane ideas which were publicly disseminated, but accepted them, and that it approved of, as opportune, inhumane courses of action taken by governments and nations. Even for what was just and expedient as well there seemed to me to be only a luke-warm zeal available. From a number of signs I had to infer the growth of a peculiar intellectual and spiritual fatigue in this generation which is so proud of what it has accomplished. It seemed as if I heard its members arguing to each other that their previous hopes for the future of mankind had been pitched too high, and that it was becoming necessary to limit oneself to striving for what was attainable. The slogan which was given out for all countries, *Realpolitik*, meant the approbation of a short-sighted nationalism, and compromises with forces and tendencies which had been resisted hitherto as hostile to progress. One of the clearest indications of decline for me was the fact that superstition, which had hitherto been banished from educated circles, was again thought fit for admission to society.

When about the end of the century men began to take a retrospective review of every field of human activity in order to determine and fix the value of their achievements,

[1] *Epigoni* (Gk. ἐπίγονοι: lit. After born). A Latin word used of the generation following those who lived in a great age; inheritors of a great past. The contemporaries of James I may be called Epigoni of the great Elizabethans.—TRANSLATOR'S NOTE.

this was done with an optimism which to me was incomprehensible. It seemed to be assumed everywhere not only that we had made progress in inventions and knowledge, but also that in the intellectual and ethical spheres we lived and moved at a height which we had never before reached, and from which we should never decline. My own impression was that in our mental and spiritual life we were not only below the level of past generations, but were in many respects only living on their achievements . . . and that not a little of this heritage was beginning to melt away in our hands.

And now—here was someone giving expression to the criticism which I myself had silently and half unconsciously passed upon our age! After that evening at Professor Curtius's house I was always, along with my other work, inwardly occupied with another book, which I entitled *Wir Epigonen* (" We Inheritors of a Past"). I often put before friends the thoughts contained in it, but they usually took them as just interesting paradoxes and manifestations of a *fin-de-siècle* pessimism. After that I kept my ideas strictly to myself, and only in sermons allowed my doubts about our civilization and our spirituality to find expression.

And now war was raging as a result of the downfall of civilization.

"We Inheritors of a Past," then, had in reality no longer any meaning. The book had been conceived as a criticism of civilization. It was meant to demonstrate its decline and to draw attention to the accompanying dangers. But if the catastrophe had already come about, what good was deliberation about the causes, which were now patent to everyone?

The book which had thus become out of date I thought of writing for my own sake. Could I be certain the pages would not be taken from a prisoner of war? And was there any prospect of my seeing Europe again?

In this attitude of entire detachment I began the work and went on with it when I was again allowed to go about and devote myself to the sick. For at the end of November we were released from our internment, thanks to Widor's exertions, as I afterwards learnt. Even before that the

order which kept me away from the sick had proved incapable of enforcement. White and black alike had pro-
tested against being deprived without any perceivable
reason of the services of the only doctor for hundreds of
miles around. The District Commandant had consequently
found himself compelled to give now to one, now to
another, a note for my guards, telling them to let the
bearer see me because he needed my help.

But when I resumed my medical activities in com-
parative freedom. I still found time to occupy myself with
the book on civilization. Many a night did I sit at it,
thinking and writing with deepest emotion as I thought
of those who were lying in the trenches.

At the beginning of the summer of 1915 I awoke from
a sort of stupor. Why only criticism of civilization? Why
content myself with analysing ourselves as *Epigoni*? Why
not go on to something constructive?

So now I began a search for the knowledge and convictions to which we must refer the will to civilization
and the power to realize it. "We Inheritors of a Past"
expanded into a work dealing with the restoration of
civilization.

As I worked I became clear about the connexion between
civilization and world-view (*Weltanschauung*), and I recognized that the catastrophe of civilization started from the
catastrophe of world-view.

The ideals of true civilization had become powerless,
because the idealistic world-view in which they are rooted
has been gradually lost to us. All the happenings which
come about within nations and within mankind as a whole
arise out of spiritual causes which are contained in the
prevailing world-view.

But what is civilization?

We may take as the essential element in civilization
the ethical perfecting of the individual and of society as
well. But at the same time, every spiritual and every
material step in advance has a significance for civilization.
The will to civilization is then the universal will to progress which is conscious of the ethical as the highest
value for all. In spite of the great importance we attach

to the triumphs of knowledge and achievement, it is nevertheless obvious that only a humanity which is striving after ethical ends can in full measure share in the blessings brought by material progress and become master of the dangers which accompany it. To the generation which had adopted a belief in an immanent power of progress realizing itself, in some measure, naturally and automatically, and which thought that it no longer needed any ethical ideals but could advance to its goal by means of knowledge and achievement alone, terrible proof was being given by its present position of the error into which it had sunk.

The only possible way out of the present chaos is for us to adopt a world-view which will bring us once more under the control of the ideals of true civilization which are contained in it.

But what is the nature of the world-view on which the universal will to progress and the ethical alike are founded and in which they are linked together with the other?

It consists in an ethical affirmation of the world and of life.

What is world- and life-affirmation?

To us Europeans and to people of European descent everywhere the will to progress is something so natural and so much a matter of course that it never occurs to us to recognize that it is rooted in a world-view, and springs from an act of the spirit. But if we look about us in the world, we see at once that what is to us such a matter of course is in reality anything but that. To Indian thought all effort directed to triumphs in knowledge and power and to the improvement of man's outer life and of society as a whole is mere folly. It teaches that the only sensible line of conduct for a man is to withdraw entirely into himself and to concern himself solely with the deepening of his inner life. He has nothing to do with what may become of human society and of mankind. The deepening of one's inner life, as Indian thought interprets it, means that a man surrenders himself to the thought of "no more will to live," and by abstention from action and by every sort of life denial reduces his earthly existence to a condition of being which has no content beyond a waiting for the cessation of being.

It is interesting to trace the origin of this idea, so contrary to nature, of world and life denial. It had at first nothing whatever to do with any world-view, but was a magical conception of the Indian priests of early times. These believed that by detachment from the world and from life they could become in some measure supernatural beings, and obtain power over the gods. In accordance with this idea arises the custom that the Brahmin, after living part of his life in the normal way and founding a family, terminates his life in complete renunciation of the world.

In the course of time this world- and life-negation which originally formed the Brahmin's privilege was developed into a world-view which claimed to be valid for men as such.

It depends on the world-view, then, whether there is any will-to-progress or not. The world-view of world- and life-negation excludes it; that of world- and life-affirmation demands it. Among primitive and half-primitive peoples too, whose unformed world-view has not yet reached the problem of world affirmation or negation, there is no will to progress. Their ideal is the simplest life with the least possible trouble.

Even we Europeans have only in the course of time and through a change in our world-view arrived at our will to progress. In antiquity and in the Middle Ages there was nothing more than attempts at it. Greek thinking does try to reach a world-view of world- and life-affirmation, but it fails in the attempt and ends in resignation. The world-view of the Middle Ages is determined by the ideas of primitive Christianity as brought into harmony with Greek metaphysics. It is fundamentally world and life negating because the interest of that stage of Christianity was concentrated on a super-sensible world. All that in the Middle Ages made itself felt as world- and life-affirmation is a fruit of the active ethic contained in the preaching of Jesus and of the creative forces of the fresh and unspoilt new peoples on whom Christianity had imposed a world-view which was in contradiction to their nature.

Then little by little the world- and life-affirmation that was already germinating among the peoples formed as a result of the *Völkerwanderung* (the Great Migration) begins to manifest itself. The Renaissance proclaims its rejection of the world and life negating world-view of the Middle Ages. And an ethical character is given to this new world- and life-affirmation by its taking over from Christianity the ethic of love taught by Jesus. This, as an ethic of activity, is strong enough to throw off the world-view of life- and world-negation in which it arose, to unite itself with the new world- and life-affirmation, and thereby to reach the ideal of realizing a spiritual and ethical world within the natural world.

The striving for material and spiritual progress, then, which characterizes the peoples of modern Europe, has its source in the world-view to which these peoples have come. As a result of the Renaissance and the spiritual and religious movements bound up with it, men have entered on a new relation to themselves and to the world, and this has aroused in them a need to create by their own activities spiritual and material values which shall help to a higher development of individuals and of mankind. It is not the case that the man of modern Europe is enthusiastic for progress because he may hope to get some personal advantage from it. He is less concerned about his own condition than about the happiness which he hopes will be the lot of coming generations. Enthusiasm for progress has taken possession of him. Impressed by his great experience of finding the world revealed to him as constituted and maintained by forces which carry out a definite design, he himself wills to become an active, purposeful force in the world. He looks with confidence towards new and better times which shall dawn for mankind, and learns by experience that the ideals which are held and acted upon by the mass of people do win power over circumstances and remould them.

It is on his will to material progress, acting in union with the will to ethical progress, that the foundations of modern civilization are being laid.

There is an essential relationship between the modern European world-view of ethical world- and life-affirmation

E*

and those of Zarathustra and of Chinese thought, as the latter meets us in the writings of Kungtse (Confucius), Mengtse (Mencius), Mitse (Nicius), and the other great ethical thinkers of China. In each of these we can see the striving to remould the circumstances of peoples and of mankind with the intention of progress, even if the efforts are not so powerful as those of modern Europe. Within the region influenced by the religion of Zarathustra and in China, there were actually established, as in Europe, civilizations which met the demands of an ethical world- and life-affirmation. But each met with a tragic end. The neo-Persian civilization of the Zarathustran world-view was blotted out by Islam. Chinese civilization is hampered in its natural development and threatened with decay by the pressure exerted upon it by European ideas and pro- blems, and by confusion wrought in the country's political and economic condition.

In modern European thought there is being enacted a tragedy, in that by a slow but irresistible process the bonds originally existing between world- and life-affirmation and the ethical are becoming slack and are finally being severed. The result that we are coming to is that European humanity is being guided by a will-to-progress that has become merely external and has lost its bearings.

World- and life-affirmation can produce of itself only a partial and imperfect civilization. Only if it becomes in- ward and ethical can the will-to-progress which results from it possess the requisite insight to distinguish the valuable from the less valuable, and strive after a civiliza- tion which does not consist only in achievements of know- ledge and power, but before all else will make men, both individually and collectively, more spiritual and more ethical.

But how could it come about that the modern world- view of world- and life-affirmation, ethical as it was originally, changed and became non-ethical?

The only possible explanation is that it was not really founded on thought. The thought out of which it arose was noble and enthusiastic but not deep. The intimate connexion of the ethical with world- and life-affirmation was for it a matter of feeling and experience rather than of proof. It took the side of world- and life-affirmation and of the ethical, without having penetrated their inner nature and their inward connexion.

This noble and valuable world-view, then, being rooted in belief rather than in thought which penetrated to the real nature of things, was bound to wither and lose its power over the minds of men. All subsequent thinking about the problems of ethics and of the relation of man to his world could not but expose the weak points in this world-view, and thereby help to hasten its decay. Its activity took effect in this direction even when its intention was to give support, for it never succeeded in replacing the inadequate foundation by one that was adequate. Again and again the new foundations and the underpinning masonry which it had taken in hand showed themselves too weak to support the building.

Thanks to my apparently abstract, yet absolutely practical thinking about the connexion of civilization with world-view, I had come to see the decay of civilization as a result of a growing impotence in the traditional modern world-view of ethical world- and life-affirmation, an impotence which there was no arresting. It had become clear to me that, like so many other people, I had clung to that world-view from inner necessity, without troubling at all about how far it could really be proved by thought.

I had got so far during the summer of 1915, But what was to come next?

Was the difficulty soluble which till now had seemed insoluble? Or had we to regard the world-view through which alone civilization is possible as an illusion within us which never ceases to stir our hearts yet never really gets dominion over us?

To continue holding it up to our generation as something to be believed seemed to me foolish and hopeless. Only if it offers itself to us as something desired from the depth of thought can it become spiritually our own.

At bottom I remained convinced that the mutual connexion between world- and life-affirmation and the ethical, declared to belong to that world-view which it had been found hitherto impossible to carry out fully, had come from a presentiment of the truth. So it was necessary to undertake to grasp as a necessity of thought by fresh, simple, and sincere thinking the truth which had hitherto been only suspected and believed in although so often proclaimed as proved.

In undertaking this I seemed to myself to be like a man who has to build a new and better boat to replace a rotten one in which he can no longer venture to trust himself to the sea, and yet does not know how to begin.

For months on end I lived in a continual state of mental excitement. Without the least success I let my thought be concentrated, even all through my daily work at the hospital, on the real nature of world- and life-affirmation and of ethics, and on the question of what they have in common. I was wandering about in a thicket in which no path was to be found. I was leaning with all my might against an iron door which would not yield.

All that I had learnt from philosophy about ethics left me in the lurch. The conceptions of the Good which it had offered were all so lifeless, so unelemental, so narrow, and so destitute of content that it was quite impossible to bring them into union with world- and life-affirmation. Moreover philosophy could be said never to have concerned itself with the problem of the connexion between civilization and world-view. The modern world- and life-affirmation had become to it such a matter of course that it had felt no need for coming to clear ideas about it.

To my surprise I had also to establish the fact, that the central province of philosophy, into which meditation about civilization and world-view had led me, was practically unexplored land. Now from this point, now from that, I tried to penetrate to its interior, but again and again I had to give up the attempt. I was already exhausted and disheartened. I saw, indeed, the conception needed before me, but I could not grasp it and give it expression.

While in this mental condition I had to undertake a longish journey on the river. I was staying with my wife on the coast at Cape Lopez for the sake of her health—it was in September 1915—when I was summoned to visit Madame Pelot, the ailing wife of a missionary, at N'Gômô, about 160 miles upstream. The only means of conveyance I could find was a small steamer, towing an overladen barge, which was on the point of starting. Except myself, there were only natives on board, but among them was Emil Ogouma, my friend from Lambaréné. Since I had been in too much of a hurry to provide myself with enough food for the journey, they let me share the contents of their cooking-pot. Slowly, we crept upstream, laboriously feeling—it was the dry season—for the channels between the sandbanks. Lost in thought I sat on the deck of the barge, struggling to find the elementary and universal conception of the ethical which I had not discovered in any philosophy. Sheet after sheet I covered with disconnected sentences, merely to keep myself concentrated on the problem. Late on the third day, at the very moment when, at sunset, we were making our way through a herd of hippopotamuses, there flashed upon my mind, unforeseen and unsought, the phrase, "Reverence for Life." The iron door had yielded: the path in the thicket had become visible. Now I had found my way to the idea in which world- and life-affirmation and ethics are contained side by side! Now I knew that the world-view of ethical world- and life-affirmation, together with its ideals of civilization, is founded in thought.

What is Reverence for Life, and how does it arise in us?

If man wishes to reach clear notions about himself and his relation to the world, he must ever again and again be looking away from the manifold, which is the product of his thought and knowledge, and reflect upon the first, the most immediate, and the continually given fact of his own consciousness. Only if he starts from this can he arrive at a thinking world-view.

Descartes makes thinking start from the sentence "I think; so I must exist" (*Cogito, ergo sum*), and with his beginning thus chosen he finds himself irretrievably on the road to the abstract. Out of this empty, artificial act of thinking there can result, of course, nothing which bears on the relation of man to himself, and to the universe. Yet in reality the most immediate act of consciousness has some content. To think means to think something. The

most immediate fact of man's consciousness is the assertion: "I am life which wills to live, in the midst of life
which wills to live," and it is as will-to-live in the midst
of will-to-live that man conceives himself during every
moment that he spends in meditating on himself and the
world around him.

As in my will-to-live there is ardent desire for further
life and for the mysterious exaltation of the will-to-live
which we call pleasure, while there is fear of destruction
and of that mysterious depreciation of the will-to-live
which we call pain: so too are these in the will-to-live
around me, whether it can express itself to me, or remains
dumb.

Man has now to decide what his relation to his will-to-
live shall be. He can deny it. But if he bids his will-to-live
change into will-not-to-live, as is done in Indian and indeed
in all pessimistic thought, he involves himself in self-
contradiction. He raises to the position of his world and
life view something unnatural, something which is in
itself untrue, and which cannot be carried to completion.
Indian thought, and Schopenhauer's also, is full of incon-
sistencies because it cannot help making concessions time
after time to the will-to-live which persists in spite of all
world and life denial, though it will not admit that the
concessions are really such. Negation of the will-to-live is
self-consistent only if it is really willing actually to put an
end to physical existence.

If man affirms his will-to-live, he acts naturally and
honestly. He confirms an act which has already been
accomplished in his instinctive thought by repeating it in
his conscious thought. The beginning of thought, a beginning which continually repeats itself, is that man does
not simply accept his existence as something given, but
experiences it as something unfathomably mysterious. Life-
affirmation is the spiritual act in which he ceases to live
unreflectively and begins to devote himself to his life with
reverence, in order to raise it to its true value. To affirm life
is to deepen, to make more inward, and to exalt the will-
to-live.

At the same time the man who has become a thinking
being feels a compulsion to give to every will-to-live the

same reverence for life that he gives to his own. He experiences that other life in his own. He accepts as being good : to preserve life, to promote life, to raise to its highest value life which is capable of development; and as being evil : to destroy life, to injure life, to repress life which is capable of development. This is the absolute, fundamental principle of the moral, and it is a necessity of thought.

The great fault of all ethics hitherto has been that they believed themselves to have to deal only with the relations of man to man. In reality, however, the question is what is his attitude to the world and all life that comes within his reach. A man is ethical only when life, as such, is sacred to him, that of plants and animals as that of his fellow-men, and when he devotes himself helpfully to all life that is in need of help. Only the universal ethic of the feeling of responsibility in an ever-widening sphere for all that lives—only that ethic can be founded in thought. The ethic of the relation of man to man is not something apart by itself : it is only a particular relation which results from the universal one.

The ethic of Reverence for Life, therefore, comprehends within itself everything that can be described as love, devotion, and sympathy whether in suffering, joy, or effort.

The world, however, offers us the horrible drama of Will-to-Live divided against itself. One existence holds its own at the cost of another : one destroys another. Only in the thinking man has the Will-to-Live become conscious of other will-to-live, and desirous of solidarity with it. This solidarity, however, he cannot completely bring about, because man is subject to the puzzling and horrible law of being obliged to live at the cost of other life, and to incur again and again the guilt of destroying and injuring life. But as an ethical being he strives to escape whenever possible from this necessity, and as one who has become enlightened and merciful to put a stop to this disunion (*Selbstentzweiung*) of the Will-to-Live so far as the influence of his own existence reaches. He thirsts to be permitted to preserve his humanity, and to be able to bring to other existences release from their sufferings.

The Reverence for Life, therefore, which has arisen in the thinking Will-to-Live, contains world- and life-affirmation and the ethical fused together. Its aim is to create values, and to realize progress of different kinds which shall serve the material, spiritual, and ethical development of men and mankind. While the unthinking modern world- and life-affirmation stumbles about with its ideals of power won by discovery and invention, the thinking world- and life-affirmation sets up the spiritual and ethical perfecting of mankind as the highest ideal, and an ideal from which alone all other ideals of progress get their real value.

Through ethical world- and life-affirmation we reach a power of reflection which enables us to distinguish between what is essential in civilization and what is not. The stupid arrogance of thinking ourselves civilized loses its power over us. We venture to face the truth that with so much progress in knowledge and power true civilization has become not easier but harder. The problem of the mutual relationship between the spiritual and the material dawns upon us. We know that we all have to struggle with circumstances to preserve our humanity, and that we must be anxiously concerned to turn once more towards hope of victory the almost hopeless struggle which many carry on to preserve their humanity amid unfavourable social circumstances.

A deepened, ethical will to progress which springs from thought will lead us back, then, out of uncivilization and its misery to true civilization. Sooner or later there must dawn the true and final Renaissance which will bring peace to the world.

Now there stood out clearly before my mind the plan of the whole Philosophy of Civilization. It divided itself as if automatically into four parts: (1) On the present lack of civilization and its causes; (2) a discussion of the idea of Reverence for Life in connexion with the attempts made in the past by European philosophy to provide foundations for the world-view of ethical world- and life-affirmation; (3) exposition of the world-view of Reverence for Life; (4) concerning the civilized state.

The writing of the second part, the description of European philosophy's tragic struggle for ethical world- and life-affirmation, was forced upon me by the inward necessity I felt for getting to know the problem I was dealing with in its historical development, and of compre- hending the solution I offered as the synthesis of all previous ones. That I once more succumbed to this temptation I have never regretted. Through my coming to an understanding of other thought, my own became clearer.

Some of the philosophical works needed for this historical task I had by me. What others I needed were sent to me by J. Strohl, Professor of Zoology at Zürich, and his wife. And the well-known Bach singer, Robert Kaufmann of Zürich, whom I had so often accompanied on the organ, made it his business, with the help of the Office des Internés Civils at Geneva, to keep me, as well as might be, in touch with the world.

Without haste I put on paper, one after another, rough drafts in which I collected and sifted the material without reference to the structure of the treatise already planned. Along with that I began to write out single sections in full. I felt it every day to be a great mercy that while others had had to be killing, I could not only save life but even work as well to bring nearer the coming of the Era of Peace.

Fortunately my supply of drugs and bandages did not give out, for by one of the last boats which arrived before the outbreak of war I had received a big supply of all necessary things.

The rainy season of 1916-17 we spent on the coast, because my wife's health had suffered from the sultry air of Lambaréné. A timber merchant placed at our disposal a house at Chienga near Cape Lopez at the mouth of one of the branches of the Ogowe. It was the home of the man who looked after his timber-rafts, but as a consequence of the war it now stood empty. In return for his kindness I joined those of his native labourers who were still on the spot in the work of rolling on to dry land the many okoume logs which had been already tied together in rafts, so that during the long interval which might elapse before cargoes could again be shipped to Europe they should not fall victims to the bore-worm (*Teredo navalis*). This heavy work—we often needed hours to roll up on to the shore one of these logs weighing from two to three tons—was only possible at high tide. When the tide was out, I sat at my Philosophy of Civilization, so far as my time was not claimed by patients.

CHAPTER XIV

GARAISON AND S. RÉMY

In September 1917, just after I had resumed my work in Lambaréné, the order was issued that we were to be taken at once, in a ship which was just due, to Europe, to be placed in a camp for prisoners of war. Fortunately the ship was a few days late, so that we had time, with the help of the missionaries and a few natives, to pack our belongings in cases, the drugs and instruments as well, and to stow them all in a small building of corrugated iron.

The taking with me of the sketches for the Philosophy of Civilization was not to be thought of. They might have been confiscated at any customs examination. I therefore entrusted them to the American missionary, Mr. Ford, who was just then working at Lambaréné. He—as he admitted to me—would have liked best to throw the heavy packet into the river, because he considered philosophy to be unnecessary and harmful. However, he was willing, of his Christian charity, to keep it, and send it to me at the end of the war. Still, in order that whatever might happen something of my work should be saved, I spent two nights making a summary of it in French, containing the leading ideas of the whole, and the order of the parts already finished. That it might appear to the censors who would have to deal with it to be remote from actual life and therefore inoffensive, I inserted suitable chapter-headings and made it look like an historical study of the Renaissance. I did in fact thus secure its escape from the confiscation which on several occasions threatened it.

Two days before our departure I had to operate with all haste, amid packed and half-packed cases, on a strangulated hernia.

Just as we had been taken on board the river steamer and the natives were shouting to us an affectionate farewell from the bank, the Father Superior of the Catholic Mission came on board, waved aside with an authoritative gesture the native soldiers who tried to prevent his approach, and shook hands with us: "You shall not leave this country," he said, "without my thanking you both for all the good that you have done it." We were never to see each other again. Shortly after the war he lost his life on board the *Afrique*, the ship which took us to Europe, when she was wrecked in the Bay of Biscay.

At Cape Lopez a white man, whose wife I had once had as a patient, crept up to me and offered me some money in case I had none. How thankful I was now for the gold which I had taken with me on the chance of war breaking out! An hour before we started I had visited an English timber merchant whom I knew well, and had exchanged it advantageously for French notes, which my wife and I now carried sewn into our clothing.

On the liner we were given in charge to a white N.C.O., who had to see that we had no intercourse with anyone except the steward definitely assigned to us, and who at certain appointed hours took us on deck. Since writing was impossible, I filled up my time with learning by heart some of Bach's fugues, and Widor's Sixth Organ Symphony.

Our steward—whose name, if I remember right, was Gaillard—was very good to us. Towards the end of the voyage he asked us whether we had noticed that he had treated us with a kindness rarely shown to prisoners. "Your meals," he told us somewhat pompously, "I always served with everything quite clean, and there was not more dirt in your cabin than in the others" (a quite correct expression in view of the very relative cleanliness that was the rule on the African ships during the war). "Can you guess," he continued, "why I did this? Certainly not because I expected a good tip. One never expects that from prisoners. Why then? I'll tell you. A few months ago a Mr. Gaucher, whom you had had for months as a patient in your hospital, travelled home in this ship in one of my cabins. Gaillard, he said to me, it may happen that before long you will be taking the Lambaréné doctor to Europe as a prisoner. If he ever does travel on your ship, and should you be able to help him in any way, do so for my sake. Now you know why I treated you well."

At Bordeaux we were put for three weeks in the Caserne de Passage (Temporary Barracks)[1] in the Rue de Belleville, in which during the war interned foreigners were lodged. There I at once developed dysentery. Fortunately I had in my baggage some emetin with which I fought it, but I was destined to suffer for a long time afterwards from its sequelæ.

We were taken next to the great Internment Camp at Garaison in the Pyrénees. The order to hold ourselves ready for departure during the night we mistakenly failed to interpret of the immediately succeeding night, so we had packed nothing when about midnight two gendarmes came with a carriage to take us away. As they were angry at what they supposed to be our disobedience, and packing by the light of one miserable candle was a very slow proceeding, they got impatient, and wanted to take us off, leaving our baggage behind. Finally, however, they had pity on us, and themselves helped to collect our possessions and to stuff them into our trunks. Often since then has the recollection of those two gendarmes made me behave patiently with others, when I felt that impatience was justifiable!

When we were delivered at Garaison, and the N.C.O. on guard inspected our baggage, he stumbled on a French translation of the *Politics* of Aristotle, which, with a view to the work on the Philosophy of Civilization I had brought with me : "Why, it's incredible!" he stormed : "they're actually bringing political books into a Prisoners of War Camp!" I shyly remarked to him, that the book was written long before the Birth of Christ. "Is that true, you scholar there?" he asked of a soldier who was standing near. The latter corroborated my statement. "What! People talked politics as long ago as that, did they?" he questioned back. On our answering in the affirmative, he gave his decision : "Anyhow, we talk them differently to-day from what they did then, and, so far as I am concerned, you can keep your book."

Garaison (Provençal for *guérison*, healing) was once a large monastery to which sick people made pilgrimages from long distances. After the separation of Church and

---

[1] Used normally for troops on their way to or from the Colonies.— TRANSLATOR'S NOTE.

State it stood empty, and was in a state of decay when, at the outbreak of war, hundreds of nationals of enemy states, men, women, and children were housed in it. In the course of a twelvemonth it was put into comparatively good condition by artisans who happened to be among those interned. The Governor, when we were there, was a retired colonial official named Vecchi, a Theosophist, who carried out his duties not only with fairness but with kindness, a fact which was the more gratefully recognized because his predecessor had been strict and harsh.

On the second day after our arrival as I stood shivering in the courtyard, a prisoner introduced himself to me as Mill-engineer Borkeloh, and asked what he could do to serve me. He was in my debt (he said) because I had cured his wife. That was the case, although I did not know the wife any more than she knew me. But at the beginning of the war I had given to the representative of a Hamburg timber firm, Richard Classen by name, who had been sent from Lamba-réné to a prisoner-of-war camp in Dahomey, a good supply of quinine, Blaud's pills, emetin, arrhenal, bromnatrium, sleeping draughts, and other drugs for himself and the other prisoners whom he would meet, putting on each bottle ample directions for use. From Dahomey he was taken to France and found himself in the same camp as Mr. Borkeloh and his wife. Hence, when Mrs. Borkeloh lost her appetite and let her nerves get below par, she was given some of the drugs which Mr. Classen had, as by a miracle, preserved through all the inspections of the baggage, and she made a good recovery. I now got my fee for this cure in the shape of a table, which Mr. Borkeloh made for me out of wood that he had torn loose somewhere in the loft. Now I could write and . . . play the organ. For before we left the boat I had begun some organ practice by using a table as manual and the floor as pedals, as I had done already when I was a boy.

A few days later I was asked by the eldest of the Gipsy Musicians, who were fellow-prisoners, whether I was the Albert Schweitzer whose name occurred in Romain Rolland's book *Musiciens d'aujourd'hui*. On my replying in the affirmative he let me know that he and his fellows would regard me from now onwards as one of themselves.

That meant that I might be present when they played in the loft, and that my wife and I had a right to a serenade on our birthdays. And in fact my wife did awake on her birthday to the sounds of the valse in *Hoffmann's Tales*, wonderfully played. These gipsy performers, who used to play in the fashionable cafés at Paris, had been allowed when taken prisoners to keep their instruments as the tools of their calling, and now they were allowed to practise in the camp.

Not long after our arrival some new-comers arrived from another camp which had been broken up. They at once began to grumble at the bad way in which the food was prepared and to reproach their fellow-prisoners who occupied the much envied posts in the kitchen with not being fit for their job. Great indignation thereat among these, who were cooks by profession and had found their way to Garaison from the kitchens of the first-class hotels and restaurants of Paris! The matter came before the Governor, and when he asked the rebels which of them were cooks, it turned out that there was not a single cook among them! Their leader was a shoemaker, and the others had such trades as tailoring, hat-making, basket-weaving, or brush-making. In their previous camp, however, they had applied themselves to do the cooking and declared that they had mastered the art of preparing food in large quantities so that it was just as tasty as when prepared in small quantities. With Solomon-like wisdom the Governor decided that they should take over the kitchen for a fortnight as an experiment. If they did better than the others, they should keep the posts. Otherwise they would be put under lock and key as disturbers of the peace. On the very first day they proved with potatoes and cabbage that they had not claimed too much, and every succeeding day was a new triumph. So the non-cooks were created 'Cooks', and the professional cooks were turned out of the kitchen! When I asked the shoemaker what was the secret of their success, he replied: "One must know all sorts of things, but the most important is to do the cooking with love and care." So now, if I learn that once more someone has been appointed Minister of some department about the work of which he knows nothing, I do not get as excited over it as I used to, but screw myself up to the hope that he will prove just as fit for his job as the Garaison shoemaker proved to be for his.

I was, strange to say, the only medical man among the interned. When we came the Governor had strictly forbidden me to have anything to do with the sick, since that was the business of the official Camp Doctor, an old country practitioner from the neighbourhood. Later on, however, he thought it only just that I should be allowed to let the camp benefit by my professional knowledge as it did by that of the dentists, of whom there were several among us. He even placed at my disposal a room which I could use for the purpose. As my baggage contained chiefly drugs and instruments, which the sergeant had let me retain after the inspection, I had available for use almost everything that I needed for treatment of the sick. I was able to give especially effective help to those who had been brought there from the colonies, as well as to the many sailors who were suffering from tropical diseases.

Thus I was once more a doctor. What leisure time I had left I gave to the Philosophy of Civilization (I was then drafting the chapters on the Civilized State), and practising the organ on table and floor.

As a medical man I got a glimpse of the manifold misery that prevailed in the camp. The worst off were those who suffered physically under the confinement. From the moment when we could go down into the courtyard till the trumpet signal which at dusk drove us out of it, they kept walking round and round looking out over the walls at the glorious white shimmering chain of the Pyrenees. They had no longer inner energy enough to occupy themselves with anything. If it rained, they stood apathetically about in the passages. Most of them, moreover, were suffering from malnutrition, because with the lapse of time they had contracted a distaste for the monotonous fare, although it was, for a prisoner-of-war camp, not in itself bad. Many suffered, too, from the cold, since most of the rooms could not be heated. For these people, weakened in body and soul, the slightest ailment meant a real illness which it was very hard to get at and treat correctly. In many cases the

depression was sustained by lamentation over their loss of
the position which they had secured in a foreign land. They
did not know where to go nor what to do when the gates
of Garaison should open and let them out. Many had married French wives and had children who could speak
nothing but French. Could they expect these to leave their
homes, or could they condemn themselves, after the war,
to a renewal, in the foreign land, of their previous struggle
for tolerance and employment?

In the courtyard and the corridors there were daily
battles among these pale, cold children of the Internment
Camp, most of whom were French-speaking. Some were
for the Entente, some were on the side of the Central
Powers.

To anyone who kept in some measure healthy and
vigorous the camp offered much that was interesting,
owing to the fact that people from many nations and of
almost every calling were to be found there. Housed in it
were : scholars and artists, especially painters, who had
been caught in Paris by the war; German and Austrian
shoemakers and ladies'-tailors, who had been employed by
the big Paris firms; bank directors, hotel managers, waiters,
engineers, architects, artisans, and business men who had
made their homes in France and her colonies; Catholic
missionaries and members of religious orders from the
Sahara, wearing white clothing with the red fez; traders
from Liberia and other districts of the West Coast of Africa;
merchants and commercial travellers from North America,
South America, China, and India who had been taken
prisoner on the high seas; the crews of German and
Austrian merchantmen who had suffered the same fate;
Turks, Arabians, Greeks, and nationals of the Balkan States,
who had for various reasons been deported in the course
of the operations in the East, and among them Turks with
wives who went about veiled. What a motley picture did
the courtyard offer twice a day when the roll was called!

To improve one's education one needed no books in the
camp. For everything he could want to learn there were
men with specialized knowledge at his disposal, and of this
unique opportunity for learning I made liberal use. About
banking, architecture, factory building and equipment,

cereal growing, furnace building, and many other things I picked up information which I should probably never have acquired elsewhere.

Perhaps the worst sufferers were the artisans, thus condemned to idleness. When my wife secured some material for a warm dress, quite a number of tailors offered to make it for nothing, merely in order to have some cloth in their hands once more, and needle and thread between their fingers.

Permission to go occasionally and help the farmers of the neighbourhood in their work was sought not only by those who knew something about agriculture but by many who were not accustomed to physical work of any sort. The least eagerness for activity was really shown by the numerous sailors. Their mode of life on board ship had taught them how to pass the time together in the most unassuming way.

At the beginning of 1918 we were informed that a certain number of the 'notables' in the camp, chosen from each initial letter, would be picked out and sent to a reprisals camp in North Africa, if I remember right, unless by a date named such and such measures taken by the Germans against the civil population of Belgium were rescinded. We were all advised to send this news home, so that our relatives might do what was necessary to save us from this fate. 'Notables,' i.e. bank directors, hotel managers, merchants, scholars, artists, and such folk, were chosen because it was assumed that such a fate would attract more attention in their home districts than it would if inflicted on members of the obscure majority. This proclamation brought to light the fact that among our notables were many persons who were not such at all. Head waiters, when delivered here, had given their profession as hotel directors so as to count for something in the camp; shop-assistants had elevated themselves to the rank of merchants. Now they bewailed to everyone they met the danger which threatened them on account of the rank they had assumed. However, all ended well. The measures taken against the Belgians were rescinded and Garaison's notables, whether genuine or fictitious, had for the present no reprisals camp to be afraid of.

When after a long and severe winter spring at last came, there came also an order that my wife and I were to be sent to a camp at S. Rémy de Provence, which was intended for Alsatians only. In vain had we begged for the rescinding of this order: the Governor that he might keep his camp doctor, and we that we might remain in the camp where we had made ourselves at home.

At the end of March we were transferred to S. Rémy. The camp there was not as cosmopolitan as that at Garaison, and was occupied chiefly by teachers, foresters, and railway employees. But I met there many people whom I knew, among them the young Günsbach schoolmaster, John Iltis, and a young pastor named Liebrich, who had been one of my pupils. He had permission to hold services on Sundays, and, as his curate, I got a good many opportunities of preaching.

The rule of the Governor, a retired Police Commissioner from Marseilles named Bagnaud, was fairly mild. Characteristic of his jovial temperament was the answer he used to give to the question whether such and such a thing were allowed. "Rien n'est permis! Mais il y a des choses qui sont tolérées, si vous vous montrez raisonnables!" ("Nothing is allowed! But there are certain things which are tolerated, if you show yourselves reasonable!") Since he could not pronounce my name, he used to call me 'Monsieur Albert.'

The first time I entered the big room on the ground floor which was our day-room, it struck me as being, in its unadorned and bare ugliness, strangely familiar. Where, then, had I seen that iron stove, and the flue-pipe crossing the room from end to end? The mystery was solved at last: I knew them from a drawing of Van Gogh's. The building in which we were housed, once a monastery in a walled-in garden, had till recently been occupied by sufferers from nervous or mental disease. Among them at one time was Van Gogh, who immortalized with his pencil the desolate room in which to-day we in our turn were sitting about. Like us, he had suffered from the cold stone floor when the mistral blew! Like us, he had walked round and round between the high garden walls!

As one of the interned was a doctor, I had at first nothing to do with the sick, and could sit the whole day over the sketches for the volume on the Civilized State. When, later on, my colleague was exchanged and allowed to go home, I became camp doctor, but the work was not as heavy here as at Garaison.

The bleak winds of Provence did not suit my wife, who in the mountain air of Garaison had improved considerably in health. And she could not get accustomed to the stone floors. I, too, felt far from well. Ever since my attack of dysentery at Bordeaux I had been conscious of a continually increasing languor, which I tried in vain to master. I easily got tired, and found myself unable, as did my wife also, to join in the walks which on fixed days the inmates of the camp were allowed to take in charge of soldiers. The walks were always at a rapid pace because the prisoners wanted to get as much exercise out of them as possible, and to go as far from camp as time permitted.

We were thankful indeed that on those days the Governor used to take us and other weaklings out himself.

CHAPTER XV

BACK IN ALSACE

FOR my wife's sake, who suffered much from the confinement and from home sickness, I was glad indeed when, about the middle of July, it was disclosed to me that we were all, or nearly all, going to be exchanged, and should be able in a few days to return home through Switzerland. My wife did not learn, fortunately, that my name was missing from the list of those to be released which the Governor had received. During the night of July 12th we were roused, a telegraphic order having been received that we should at once make our preparations for departure, and this time every name was on the list. As the sun rose we dragged our baggage into the courtyard for the examination. The sketches for the Philosophy of Civilization which I had put on paper here and at Garaison, and had already laid before the Camp Censor, I was allowed to take with me when he had put his stamp upon a certain number of pages. As the convoy passed through the gate I ran back to see the Governor once more, and found him, sitting, sorrowful, in his office. He felt the departure of his prisoners very much. We still write to each other, and he addresses me as *"mon cher pensionnaire"* ("My dear boarder").

At the station at Tarascon we had to wait for the arrival of our train in a distant goods-shed. My wife and I, heavily laden with our baggage, could hardly get along over the shingle between the lines. Thereupon a poor cripple whom I had treated in the camp came forward to help us. He had no baggage because he possessed nothing, and I was much moved by his offer, which I accepted. While we walked along side by side in the scorching sun, I vowed to myself that in memory of him I would in future always keep a look-out at stations for heavily laden people, and help them. And this vow I have kept. On one occasion, however, my offer made me suspected of thievish intentions!

Between Tarascon and Lyons we were charmingly

received at one station by a committee of ladies and gentlemen, and escorted to tables loaded with good things. While
we were enjoying them, however, our entertainers became
curiously embarrassed, and, after a few hurried words to
each other, they withdrew. They had realized that we were
not the guests for whom the welcome and the meal had
been intended. They expected people from the occupied
area in Northern France who, after a short period of internment, were being dispatched by the Germans to France
through Switzerland, and now had to be kept for a time in
Southern France. When the arrival of a *train d'internés*
was announced with the time allowed before its departure,
the committee which had been formed to look after these
deported people as they passed through took it for granted
that we were the travellers they were expecting, and they
only became aware of their mistake when they heard their
guests speaking not French but Alsatian. The situation was
so comical that it ended with the disillusioned committee
joining good-humouredly in the laughter. But the best of it
all was that the majority of our party, since it all happened
so quickly and they were so fully occupied with eating,
noticed nothing, and journeyed on in the honest belief that
they had done fitting honour to a good meal which had
been intended for them!

During the remainder of the journey our train got longer
and longer through the coaches from other camps which
were attached to it one after another at different stations.
Two of them were filled with basket and kettle menders,
scissor-grinders, tramps, and gipsies, who were also being
exchanged.

At the Swiss frontier our train was held up for a considerable time till a telegram brought the news that the train
conveying those for whom we were being exchanged had
also reached the Swiss frontier.

Early on July 15th we arrived at Zürich. To my astonishment I was called out of the train by Arnold Meyer, the
Professor of Theology, Robert Kaufmann, the singer, and
other friends who had gathered to welcome me. They had
known for weeks that I should be coming! During the
journey to Constance we stood the whole time at the
windows and could not see enough of the well-cultivated

fields and the clean houses of Switzerland. We could hardly grasp the fact that we had got into a land that had no experience of the war.

Dreadful was the impression we received in Constance. Here we had before our eyes for the first time the starvation of which till then we had only known by hearsay. None but pale, emaciated people in the streets! How wearily they went about! It was surprising that they could still stand!

My wife got permission to go to Strassburg at once with her parents, who had come to meet us. I had to spend another day in Constance with the others, and wait till all the necessary formalities were completed. I got to Strassburg during the night. Not a light was burning in the streets. Not a glimmer of light showing from any dwelling-house! On account of attacks from the air the city had to be completely dark. I could not hope to reach the distant garden suburb where my wife's parents lived, and I had much trouble in finding the way to Frau Fischer's house near S. Thomas's.

Since Günsbach was within the sphere of military operations, many visits and many entreaties were needed to get me permission to try to find my father. Trains still ran as far as Colmar, but the ten miles from there towards the Vosges had to be done on foot.

So this was the peaceful valley to which I had bidden farewell on Good Friday 1913! There were dull roars from guns on the mountains. On the roads one walked between lines of wire-netting packed with straw, as between high walls. These were intended to hide the traffic in the valley from the enemy batteries on the crest of the Vosges. Everywhere there were brick emplacements for machine guns! Houses ruined by gun-fire! Hills which I remembered covered with woods now stood bare. The shell-fire had left only a few stumps here and there. In the villages one saw posted up the order that everyone must always carry a gas-mask about with him.

Günsbach, the nearest spot to the trenches that was still inhabited, owed it to the hills among which it was concealed that it had not long before been destroyed by artillery fire. Among crowds of soldiers and between lines of battered houses the inhabitants went about their business as if there were no war going on. That they could not bring home the second hay-crop from the meadows by day was now as much a matter of course to them as the duty of rushing to the cellars whenever the alarm was given, or the fact that they might at any moment receive an order to quit the village, leaving all their goods behind because an attack was threatened. My father had become so indifferent to danger that when bombardments were going on he used to remain in his study instead of making for the cellars like everyone else. That there had once been a time when he did not share the vicarage with officers and soldiers he could no longer imagine.

But anxiety about the harvest weighed heavily on people who had become indifferent to the war. A terrible drought prevailed. The corn was drying up; the potatoes were being ruined; on many meadows the grass-crop was so thin that it was not worth while to mow it; from the byres resounded the bellowing of hungry cattle. Even if a storm-cloud rose above the horizon it brought not rain but wind which robbed the soil of its remaining moisture, and clouds of dust which there flew the spectre of starvation.

Meanwhile my wife also had obtained permission to come to Günsbach.

I kept hoping in vain that among my native hills I should get rid of my languor, together with the now slight, now severe attacks of the fever from which I began to suffer in the last weeks at S. Rémy. But I got worse and worse, till at the end of August the high fever and the torturing pains made me conclude that they were an after effect of the dysentery I had successfully got over at Bordeaux, and that an immediate surgical operation was needed. Accompanied by my wife I dragged myself six kilometres in the direction of Colmar before we could find a vehicle of any sort. On September 1st I was operated on by Professor Stolz in Strassburg.

As soon as I was to some extent capable of work the Mayor of Strassburg, Mr. Schwander, offered me a position as a doctor at the Municipal Hospital, an offer which I joyfully accepted, for I really did not know how I was going to

CHAPTER XVI

PHYSICIAN AT THE HOSPITAL AND PREACHER AT S. NICHOLAS'

ʹRING the little free time which my two posts left me, I
:upied myself with Bach's Choral Preludes that I might
mediately get ready for the press the manuscript I had
ɪfted in Lambaréné for the three last volumes of the
nerican edition, should it ever again come into my
ɪssession. But as the parcel seemed never to be coming
d the American publisher, too, showed no desire to begin
blication at once, I put this work on one side and took
again the Philosophy of Civilization. Nor have I ever
t, in spite of the pressure brought to bear on me by the
ɪce more enterprising publisher, managed to bring out
e three volumes of Choral Preludes.

While waiting for the Philosophy of Civilization manu-
ript from Africa I occupied myself with studying the
eat world-religions and the world-views which they
ɪplied. Just as I had already examined philosophy up to
-day to see how far it represents ethical life- and world-
ɪrmation as providing the impulse to civilization, so I
ɪw sought to make clear to what extent world- and life-
ɪrmation, world- and life-negation, and ethics are con-
ined in Judaism and Christianity, in Islam, in the religion
Zarathustra, in Brahminism, Buddhism, and Hinduism,
ɪd in the religious side of Chinese thought. In this inves-
ɪation I found full confirmation of my view that
vilization is based upon ethical world- and life-affirma-
ɪn.

The religions which decisively deny the world and life
ɪahminism and Buddhism) show no interest in civilization.
ɪe Judaism of the prophetic period, the almost contemporary
ɪigion of Zarathustra, and the religious thought of the Chinese
:clude in their ethical world- and life-affirmation strong
ɪpulses to civilization. They want to improve social conditions,

live. I was allotted two women's wards in the dep
for diseases of the skin. At the same time I was ap
once more curate at S. Nicholas'. I also am deeply
to the Chapter of S. Thomas's for placing at my disp
unoccupied parsonage belonging to the church
Nicholas Embankment, although, being only cura
no claim on it.

After the Armistice, under the terms of which
passed from German rule to French, I had for a
carry on the services at S. Nicholas' by myself. Mr
who on account of his anti-German utterances
removed from his post by the German administra
not yet been reappointed by the French, and Mr.
successor to Mr. Knittel, had been compelled
because he was not sufficiently well disposed to th

During the Armistice period and the two follow
I was to the Customs officials at the Rhine Bridg
known personality, because I frequently went ov
with a rücksack full of provisions in order to s
from there to starving friends in Germany. I made
point of helping in this way Frau Cosima Wagne
aged painter Hans Thoma, together with his siste
Hans Thoma I had known for years through Frau
Schumm, whose late husband and he had been y
together.

and they call men to purposeful action in the service of common aims which ought to be realized, whereas the pessimistic religions let men continue to pass their time in solitary meditation.

The Jewish prophets Amos and Isaiah (760-700 B.C.), Zarathustra (7th century B.C.), and Kungtse (560-480 B.C.) mark the great turning-point in the spiritual history of mankind. Between the eighth and sixth centuries B.C. thinking men belonging to three nations, living in widely separated countries and having no relations whatever with one another rise one and all to the perception that the ethical consists not in submission to traditional national customs, but in the active devotion of individuals to their fellow-men or to aims which should produce an improvement of social conditions. In this great revolution begins the spiritual humanizing of mankind and, with that, the civilization which is capable of the highest development.

Christianity and Hinduism are neither world and life affirming nor world and life denying without qualification; each contains the two principles side by side and in a state of tension with each other. Consequently they can range themselves on the side of both affirmation of civilization and its negation.

Christianity denies civilization because owing its birth to expectation of the end of the world it shows no interest in the improvement of conditions in the natural world. But at the same time, it vigorously affirms civilization so far as it contains an active ethic. It was as a destructive force to civilization that it revealed itself in the ancient world, and it is partly responsible for the fact that the attempts of later Stoicism to reform the world and produce an ethical mankind remained ineffective. At the same time the ethical views of the later Stoicism, as we know them from the writings of Epictetus and others, came very near to those of Jesus. The determining factor in the situation, however, was the connexion of the Christian ethic with a world- and life-denying world-view.

In modern times, under the influence of the Renaissance, the Reformation, and the thinkers of the Age of Enlightenment (*Aufklärung*), Christianity laid aside the world and life denial which clung to it as a survival from the primitive Christian expectation of the end to the world, and allowed room within itself for world- and life-affirmation. It thus changed into a religion which could work for a realization of civilization.

As such a religion it took part in the struggle against ignorance, want of purpose, cruelty, and injustice out of which in modern times a new world emerged. It was only because the powerful ethical energies of Christianity allied themselves with the will-to-progress which characterized the world- and life-affirmation of the modern world, and worked in the service of the modern age that the seventeenth and eighteenth centuries were capable of doing the work for civilization for which we have to thank them.

In proportion, however, to the extent to which the world- and life-negation which had been repressed in the eighteenth century begins to acquire importance in it again through medieval and later tendencies, Christianity ceases to be a force making for civilization and begins to attract attention as a hindrance to it, as is shown by the history of our own time.

In Hinduism world- and life-affirmation has never succeeded in getting the mastery over world- and life-negation. In India there never came a break with the traditional pessimism, such as was brought about by powerful thinkers in the Christianity of the sixteenth, seventeenth, and eighteenth centuries. Hinduism, therefore, in spite of its ethical tendency, was never in a position to accomplish in the regions where it prevailed a work for civilization which was comparable to that of Christianity.

Islam can be called a world-religion only in virtue of its wide extension. Spiritually it could not develop to be such because it never produced any thinking about the world and mankind which penetrated to the depths. If ever any such thought stirred within it, it was suppressed in order to maintain the authority of traditional views. Nevertheless the Islam of to-day carries within it stronger tendencies to mysticism and to greater ethical depth, than appearances would lead one to suppose.

While I was busy with tasks like these I received, a few days before Christmas 1919, through Archbishop Söderblom, an invitation to deliver some lectures, after Easter 1920, for the Olaus-Petri Foundation at the University of Upsala. This request came to me entirely unexpected. Ever since the war I had felt, in my seclusion at Strassburg, rather like a coin that has rolled under a piece of furniture and has remained there lost. Once only had I got into touch again with the outer world; that was in October 1919, when, having with much trouble secured permission to travel, I scraped together every shilling I could and went to Barcelona to let my friends of the Orféo Catalá once more hear me play the organ. This first emergence into the world let me see that as an artist I was still of some value.

On the return journey I had as fellow-passengers, from Tarascon to Lyons, some sailors belonging to the cruiser *Ernest Renan*. When I asked them what sort of a man it was, whose name they had on their caps, they answered: "We've never been told anything about him. Probably it is the name of some dead general."

In learned circles I could have believed myself entirely forgotten but for the affection and kindness shown by me by the theological faculties at Zürich and Berne.

For the subject of my lectures in Upsala I chose the problem of world- and life-affirmation and ethics in philosophy and the world-religions. When I set to work on them I was still without the chapters of the Philosophy of Civilization which had been left behind in Africa; so I had to write them over again. At first that made me very unhappy, but I noticed later on that his repetition of the work was not unprofitable, and I got reconciled to my fate. It was only in the summer of 1920, after my return from Upsala, that the manuscript from Africa at last reached me.

In Upsala I found for the first time an echo to the thoughts which I had been carrying about with me for five years. In the last lecture, in which I developed the fundamental ideas of the ethic of Reverence for Life, I was so moved that I found it difficult to speak.

I came to Sweden a tired, depressed, and still ailing man —for in the summer of 1919 I had had to undergo a second operation. In the magnificent air of Upsala, and the kindly atmosphere of the Archbishop's house, in which my wife and I were guests, I recovered my health and once more found enjoyment in my work.

But there still weighed upon me the burden of the debts which I had contracted with the Paris Missionary Society and Parisian acquaintances during the war to make possible the carrying on of the hospital. During a walk with me the Archbishop learnt about this anxiety, and advised me to make the experiment of giving organ recitals and lectures in Sweden, to which country the war had brought considerable financial gains. He also gave me introductions to several cities. A theological student, Elias Söderström (who died in the mission field a few years later), offered to be my travelling companion. Standing near me on the platform or in the pulpit he translated my lectures on the Forest Hospital sentence by sentence in such a lively way that in a few moments the audience had forgotten that they were listening to a translated discourse. What an advantage it was to me now that in the services at Lambaréné I had mastered the art of speaking through the mouth of an interpreter! What is most important in that is to speak in short, simple, and clearly constructed sentences, to go through the address with the interpreter with the greatest possible care beforehand, and to deliver it in the shape which he expects. With this preparation the interpreter has to make no effort to understand the meaning of the sentence to be translated; he catches it like a ball which he throws on at once to the listeners. By following this plan one makes it possible to deliver through an interpreter even scientific addresses, and it is a much better way than for the speaker to inflict torture on himself and his hearers by speaking in a language of which he is not fully master.

Though they are not large, the wonderfully resonant old Swedish organs pleased me greatly. They were admirably adapted to my method of rendering Bach's music.

In the course of a few weeks I had collected by concerts and lectures so much money that I could at once pay off the most pressing of my debts.

When in the middle of July I quitted Swedish soil on which my experience had been so happy, I had firmly made up my mind to take up again my work at Lambaréné. Till then I had not ventured to think of it, but had familiarized myself with the idea of returning to academic circles as a teacher. Some hints received before my departure for Sweden pointed to Switzerland as the country on which in that case I might set my hopes. In 1920 I was made an Hon. D.D. by the Theological Faculty at Zürich.

CHAPTER XVII

THE BOOK OF AFRICAN REMINISCENCES

AGAIN at home I set to work at once writing down my recollections of Africa under the title of *Zwischen Wasser und Urwald* ("On the Edge of the Primeval Forest"). The Lindblad publishing house at Upsala had commissioned me to write such a book, but it was not an easy task for I was limited to so many thousand words. When I had finished I had to throw several thousand overboard, and the choice of these gave me more trouble than writing the whole book. Finally the whole chapter about the timber trade in the jungle ought to have been dropped out, but at my urgent request the publisher accepted the manuscript with the superfluous section still forming part of it.

The fact that I was compelled to count my words was, after all, advantageous for the book, and since then I have held myself down—even in the exposition of my Philosophy of Civilization—to the greatest possible conciseness in the expression of my ideas.

Zwischen Wasser und Urwald appeared in Swedish, translated by Baroness Greta Lagerfelt, in 1921. In the same year it came out in German (first in Switzerland), and then in English with the title of *On the Edge of the Primeval Forest*, translated by my friend C. T. Campion. Later on it was published in Dutch, French, Danish, and Finnish.

The fine illustrations which adorn the book are in most cases from photographs taken in the summer of 1914, while he was in the neighbourhood of Lambaréné for the purpose of buying supplies of timber, by Mr. Richard Classen of Hamburg, whom, when later on he became a prisoner of war I supplied with drugs. Having to give an account of my activity in the West African primeval forest gave me an opportunity of expressing myself also on the difficult problems of colonization among primitive peoples.

Have we white people the right to impose our rule on primitive and semi-primitive peoples—my experience has been gathered among such only? No, if we only want to rule over them and draw material advantage from their country. Yes, if we seriously desire to educate them and help them to attain to a condition of well-being. If there were any sort of possibility that these peoples could live really by and for themselves, we could leave them to themselves. But as things are, the world trade which has reached them is a fact against which both we and they are powerless. They have already through it lost their freedom. Their economic and social relations are shaken by it. An inevitable development brought it about that the chiefs, with the weapons and money which commerce placed at their disposal, reduced the mass of the natives to servitude and turned them into slaves who had to work for the export trade to make a few select people rich. It sometimes happened too that, as in the days of the slave trade, the people themselves became merchandise, and were exchanged for money, lead, gunpowder, tobacco and brandy. In view of the state of things produced by world trade there can be no question with these peoples of real independence, but only whether it is better for them to be delivered over to the mercies, tender or otherwise, of rapacious native tyrants or to be governed by officials of European states.

That of those who were commissioned to carry out in our name the seizure of our colonial territories many were guilty of injustice, violence, and cruelty as bad as those of the native chiefs, and so brought on our heads a load of guilt, is only too true. Nor of the sins committed against the natives to-day must anything be suppressed or whitewashed. But willingness to give these primitive and semi-primitive people of our colonies an independence which would inevitably end in enslavement to their fellows, is no way of making up for our failure to treat them properly. Our only possible course is to exercise for the benefit of the natives the power we actually possess, and thus provide a moral justification for it. Even the hitherto prevailing 'imperialism' can plead that it has some qualities of ethical value. It has put an end to the slave trade; it has stopped the perpetual wars which the primitive peoples used to wage with one another, and has thus given a lasting peace to large portions of the world; it endeavours in many ways to produce in the colonies conditions which shall render more difficult the exploitation of the population by world trade. I dare not picture what the lot of the native lumbermen in the forests of the Ogowe district would be if the Government authorities which at the present time preserve their rights for them in opposition to the merchants, both white and black, should be withdrawn.

What so-called self-government means for primitive and semi-primitive peoples can be gathered from the fact that in the Black Republic of Liberia, domestic slavery and what is far worse, the compulsory shipment of labourers to other countries, have continued down to our own day. They were both abolished on October 1st, 1930—on paper.

The tragic fact is that the interests of colonization and those of civilization do not always run parallel, but are often in direct opposition to each other. The best thing for primitive peoples would be that, in such seclusion from world trade as is possible, and under an intelligent administration, they should rise by slow development from being nomads and semi-nomads to be agriculturists and artisans, permanently settled on the soil. That, however, is rendered impossible by the fact that these peoples themselves will not let themselves be withheld from the chance of earning money by selling goods to world trade, just as on the other hand world trade will not abstain from purchasing native products from them and depositing manufactured goods in exchange. Thus it becomes very hard to carry to completion a colonization which means at the same time true civilization. The real wealth of these peoples would consist in their coming to produce for themselves by agriculture and handicrafts as far as possible all the necessities of their life. Instead of that they are exclusively bent on providing the materials which world trade requires, and for which it pays them good prices. With the money thus obtained they procure from it manufactured goods and prepared foodstuffs, thereby making home industry impossible, and often even endangering the stability of their own agriculture. This is the condition in which all primitive and semi-primitive peoples find themselves who can offer to world trade rice, cotton, coffee, cocoa, minerals, timber, and similar things.

Whenever the timber trade is good, permanent famine reigns in the Ogowe region, because the natives neglect the making of new plantations in order to fell as many trees as possible. In the swamps and the forest in which they find this work they live on imported rice and imported preserved foods, which they purchase with the proceeds of their labour.

Colonization, then, in the sense of civilization, means trying to ensure that among the primitive and semi-primitive peoples who are in danger in this way, only so much labour-power is allowed to be engaged for the export trade as is not needed for home industry and for that proportion of their agriculture

F*

which produces the foodstuffs needed at home. The more thinly any colony is populated, the more difficult it is to reconcile the interests of a sound development of the country with those of world trade. A rising export trade does not always prove that a colony is making progress; it may also mean that it is on the way to ruin.

Again, road and railway construction shows itself as a difficult problem amid a primitive population. Roads and railways are necessary in order that the horror of transport by carriers may be ended; that in times of famine foodsuffs may be conveyed into the threatened regions; and that trade may prosper. At the same time there is a danger that they may imperil the beneficial development of the country. They do that when they call for more labour-power than the country can normally spare for them. Account must be taken, too, of the fact that colonial road and railway construction involves great loss of human life, even when—and this is unfortunately not always the case—the best possible provision is made for the lodging and provisioning of the labourers. It may happen, too, that the district which the road or the railway was meant to serve is ruined by it. The opening up of any region must therefore be undertaken only after full consideration. The public works which are taken in hand because they are held to be necessary and also possible, must be carried on slowly, in some cases even with occasional cessations of work, for in that way, as experience has shown, many lives can be saved.

In the interest of the development of the country it may become necessary to transplant remote villages to the neighbourhood of the railway or the road. But only when no other course it possible should there be encroachment in this and other ways on the human rights of the natives. How much disaffection is provoked again and again in the colonies by the compulsory application of measures which are expedient only in the imagination of some official who wants to draw attention to himself!

With regard to the question, much discussed to-day, of the justifiableness or not of forced labour, my standpoint is that the native may under no circumstances be compelled by the authorities to work for any period, either short or long, for any private undertaking, not even if the labour is accepted as a substitute for a tax, or for statutory labour due to the state. The only labour which may be imposed on the natives is what has to be done in the interests of the public well-being, and is done under the supervision of state officials.

Nor must it be thought that the native can be trained to

labour by requiring him to pay ever-increasing taxes. He is indeed obliged to work to obtain the money needed for such taxes, but this concealed forced labour will not, any more than the unconcealed, change him from an indolent to an industrious man. Injustice cannot produce a moral result.

In every colony in the world the taxes are to-day already so high that they can only with difficulty be paid by the population. Colonies everywhere have, for want of thought, been burdened with loans the interest on which can hardly be raised.

The problems of native education are mixed up with economic and social problems, and are not less complicated than the latter.

Agriculture and handicraft are the foundations of civilization. Only where that foundation exists are the conditions given for the formation and persistence of a stratum of population which can occupy itself with commercial and intellectual pursuits. But with the natives in the colonies—and they themselves demand it—we proceed as if not agriculture and handicraft, but reading and writing, were the beginnings of civilization. From schools which are mere copies of those of Europe they are turned out as 'educated,' persons, that is, who think themselves superior to manual work, and want to follow only commercial or intellectual callings. All those who are unable to secure acceptable employment in the offices of the business houses or of the Government sit about as idlers or grumblers. It is the misfortune of all colonies—and not only of those with primitive or semi-primitive populations!—that those who go through the schools are mostly lost to agriculture and handicraft instead of contributing to their development. This change of class, from lower to higher, produces thoroughly unhealthy economic and social conditions. Proper colonization means educating the natives in such a way that they are not alienated from agriculture and handicraft but attracted to them. Intellectual learning should in every colonial school be accompanied by the acquisition of every kind of manual skill. For their civilization it is more important that the natives should learn to burn bricks, to build, to saw logs into planks, to be ready with hammer, plane, and chisel, than that they should be brilliant at reading and writing, and even be able to calculate with $a + b$, and $x + y$.

But the most important thing of all is that we cry 'Halt!' to the dying out of the primitive and semi-primitive peoples. Their existence is threatened by alcohol, with which commerce supplies them, by diseases which we have taken to them, and

by diseases which already existed among them, but which, like
sleeping sickness, were first enabled to spread by the intercourse which colonization brought with it. To-day that disease
is a peril to millions.

The harm which the importation of alcohol means for these
people cannot be counteracted by forbidding brandy and rum
while allowing wine and beer as before. In the colonies wine
and beer are much more dangerous beverages than in Europe,
because, to enable them to keep good in tropical and sub-
tropical regions, pure alcohol is always added to them. The
absence of brandy and rum is amply made up for by an
enormously increased consumption of wine and beer of this
description. The share that alcohol has in the ruin of these
peoples can, therefore, only be prevented by absolute prohibi-
tion of the importation of all alcoholic drinks, of whatever sort.

In nearly all colonies the struggle against disease has been
undertaken with too little energy and was begun too late. That
it can be carried on to-day with some prospect of success we
owe to the weapons which the latest medical science has put
into our hands.

The necessity for taking medical help to the natives in our
colonies is frequently argued on the ground that it is worth
while to preserve the human material without which the
colonies would become valueless. But the matter is in reality
something much more important than a question of economics.
It is unthinkable that we civilized peoples should keep for ourselves alone the wealth of means for fighting sickness, pain, and
death, which science has given us. If there is any ethical thinking at all among us, how can we refuse to let these new dis-
coveries benefit those who, in distant lands, are subject to even
greater physical distress than we are? In addition to the
medical men who are sent out by the governments, and who
are never more than enough to accomplish a fraction of what
needs doing, others must go out too, commissioned by human
society as such. Whoever among us has through personal
experience learnt what pain and anxiety really are must help
to ensure that those who out there are in bodily need obtain
the help that came to him. He belongs no more to himself
alone; he has become the brother of all who suffer. On the
"Brotherhood of those who bear the mark of pain" lies the
duty of medical work, work for humanity's sake, in the
colonies. Commissioned by their representatives, medical men
must accomplish among the suffering in far-off lands what is
crying out for accomplishment in the name of true civilization.

In reliance upon the elementary truth which is embodied in

the idea of the "Brotherhood of those who bear the mark of pain," I ventured to found the Forest Hospital at Lambaréné. That truth was recognized, and is now spreading.

Finally, let me urge that whatever benefit we confer upon the peoples of our colonies is not beneficence but atonement for the terrible sufferings which we white people have been bringing upon them ever since the day on which the first of our ships found its way to their shores. Colonial problems, as they exist to-day, cannot be solved by political measures alone. A new element must be introduced; white and coloured must meet in an atmosphere of the ethical spirit. Then only will mutual understanding be possible.

To work for the creation of that spirit means helping to make the course of world politics rich in blessings for the future.

CHAPTER XVIII

GÜNSBACH AND JOURNEYS ABROAD

On the Sunday before Palm Sunday 1921 I had the joy of playing the organ at the first performance of Bach's S. Matthew Passion at the Orféo Catalá in Barcelona—the very first time that this work was performed in Spain.

In April 1921 I resigned my two posts at Strassburg, reckoning to depend in future for my living on my pen and my organ-playing. In order to work in quiet at the Philosophy of Civilization I moved, with my wife and child—a daughter born to us on January 14th, my own birthday, in 1919—to my father's homely vicarage at Günsbach. For occasional quarters ·in Strassburg, where I often had to spend considerable periods to consult the Library, I had an attic in the house of the widow of Pastor Dietz-Härter, who lived in an old house in the Knoblochgasse.

My work was, indeed, often interrupted by journeys. From various universities I received invitations to give lectures on the Philosophy of Civilization or on the problems of Primitive Christianity. It was necessary, too, to raise by lectures on the Hospital at Lambaréné funds for continuing the work, and I had to give organ recitals to provide support for myself and my family during the years when I should again be in Africa.

In the autumn of 1921 I was in Switzerland, and from there I went in November to Sweden. At the end of January I left Sweden for Oxford in order to deliver at Mansfield College the Dale Memorial Lectures. After that I lectured at the Selly Oak College at Birmingham (on "Christianity and the Religions of the World"), at Cambridge (on "The Significance of Eschatology"), and in London to the Society for the Study of the Science of Religion (on "The Pauline Problem"). I also gave a number of organ recitals in England.

In the middle of March 1922 I returned to Sweden from England to give more concerts and lectures. Scarcely was I home when I went again for weeks to give lectures and concerts in Switzerland.

In the summer of 1922 I was able to work at the Philosophy of Civilization undisturbed.

In the autumn I went again to Switzerland, and after that I gave some lectures on Ethics at Copenhagen, by invitation of the Theological Faculty of the University. With these were combined organ recitals and lectures in various towns of Denmark.

In January 1923 I lectured on the "Philosophy of Civilization" at Prague, by invitation of Professor Oscar Kraus. I thus began a warm friendship with this loyal pupil of Brentano.

How wonderful were the experiences vouchsafed me during these years! When I first went to Africa I prepared to make three sacrifices: to abandon the organ, to renounce the academic teaching activities, to which I had given my heart, and to lose my financial independence, relying for the rest of my life on the help of friends.

These three sacrifices I had begun to make, and only my intimate friends knew what they cost me.

But now there happened to me, what happened to Abraham when he prepared to sacrifice his son. I, like him, was spared the sacrifice. The piano with pedal attachment, built for the Tropics, which the Paris Bach Society had presented to me, and the triumph of my own health over the tropical climate had allowed me to keep up my skill on the organ. During the many quiet hours which I was able to spend with Bach during my four and a half years of loneliness in the jungle I had penetrated deeper into the spirit of his works. I returned to Europe, therefore, not as an artist who had become an amateur, but in full possession of my technique and privileged to find that, as an artist, I was more esteemed than before.

For the renunciation of my teaching activities in Strassburg University I found compensation in opportunities of lecturing in very many others.

And if I did for a time lose my financial independence, I was able now to win it again by means of organ and pen.

That I was let off the threefold sacrifice I had already offered was for me the encouraging experience which in all the difficulties brought upon me, and upon so many others, by the fateful post-war period has buoyed me up, and made me ready for every effort and every renunciation.

In the spring of 1923 the two first volumes of the Philosophy of Civilization were finished, and they were published that same year. The first bears the title of *Verfall und Wiederaufbau der Kultur* ("The Decay and Restoration of Civilization")[1] and the second that of *Kultur und Ethik* ("Civilization and Ethics").

In the first I describe the relations which subsist between Civilization and World-view.

Responsibility for the decay of civilization lies at the door of nineteenth-century philosophy. It did not understand how to keep alive the mental disposition to civilization which existed in the period of the *Aufklärung*. It should have recognized its task as being the continuation of the work in elemental thinking about ethics and world-view, which was left incomplete by the eighteenth century. Instead of that, it lost itself during the nineteenth century more and more deeply in the unelemental. It renounced its connexion with man's natural search for a word-view, and became merely a science of the history of philosophy. It provided itself with a world-view out of a combination of history and natural science. This, however, turned out to be quite lifeless, and failed to preserve any disposition to civilization.

Then, just at the time when the civilization-world-view became powerless, civilization was threatened on its material side. The machine age brought upon mankind conditions of existence which made the possession of civilization difficult. And because men had no civilization-world-view to hold on to, tendencies obstructive to civilization produced their effects without encountering any opposition from men. As an over-occupied being, no longer capable of any real collectedness, man fell a victim to spiritual dependence, to superficiality of every kind, to wrong valuations of the facts of history and actual life, to a nationalism which sprang from those valuations, and finally to a terrifying lack of humane feeling.

We must use, then, new methods of thinking to get back again to a world-view containing the ideals of true civilisation. If we only begin again to reflect at all on ethics and our

[1] *Verfall und Wiederaufbau der Kultur.* 65 pages. 1923. (C. H. Beck, Munich; Paul Haupt, Bern.) Also in English, Swedish, Danish, and Dutch translations.

spiritual relation to the world, we are already on the road which leads back from uncivilization to civilization.

Civilization I define in quite general terms as spiritual and material progress in all spheres of activity, accompanied by an ethical development of individuals and of mankind.

In *Civilization and Ethics* I unroll the history of the tragic struggle of European thought to reach the world-view of ethical world and life affirmation.[1] I would gladly have depicted at the same time the struggle for a civilization-world-view as it develops in the world-religions, but that design I had to abandon because it would have made the book too long. I therefore limit myself to a few short allusions to the subject.

I intentionally avoid technical philosophical phraseology. My appeal is to thinking men and women whom I wish to provoke to elemental thought about the questions of existence which occur to the mind of every human being.

What is it that takes place in the vain struggle for ethics and for a deep world and life affirmation?

Ancient thought made mighty efforts to represent the ethical as the reasonable, and to understand world and life affirmation as having a meaning. But by an inexorable logic it is led to the necessity of surrendering itself to resignation. This surrender expresses itself in its adoption as its ideal of the wise man who refuses all activity in the world.

It is only in the later Stoicism of Marcus Aurelius, Epictetus, and others that a confident ethical world-view breaks through, which imposes it as a duty on the individual man to work in the world with the object of creating better material and spiritual conditions. This late-Stoic world-view is to a certain extent the forerunner of that which later, in the age of the *Aufklärung*, wins authority over men's minds as the reasonable. At this first appearance on the stage of history it is unable to establish its position or to unfold its reforming powers. The great Stoic emperors, it is true, are devoted to it, and they attempt under its influence to arrest the decadence of the ancient world, which was already in full swing. Over the

[1] *Kultur und Ethik.* 280 pages. 1923. (C. H. Beck, Munich; Paul Haupt, Bern.) English edition, A. & C. Black, 1923 and 1929. Dutch edition, 1931.

masses, however, this world-view never obtains any influence.

How do the late-Stoicism and the Rationalism of the eighteenth century attain to ethical world- and life-affirmation? By not accepting the world as it is, but by conceiving the course of world events as the expression of a rational, ethical world-will. The world- and life-affirming ethical will of man interprets in terms of itself the force which is working itself out in the course of world-events. A life-view clothes itself with a world-view, but is not clear what it is doing; it believes, on the contrary, that it is itself a result of knowledge of the nature of the world.

What takes place here is repeated wherever philosophy reaches an ethical world- and life-affirmation. It deduces this principle from an interpretation of the course of world-history which seeks to make this course intelligible, as having a meaning and being in some way or other directed to ethical ends. Further, this interpretation makes man enter through his own ethical activity into the service of this world-purpose.

With Confucius, also, and Zarathustra their ethical world- and life-affirmation goes back to an explanation of the world which is similarly presupposed.

Such an interpretation of the world is no longer undertaken by Kant, Fichte, Hegel, and the other great thinkers of the speculative philosophy in the simple, naïve fashion of the ethical rationalism of the eighteenth century. They reach their explanation by complicated operations of thought. These end in the theory that the world-view of ethical world- and life-affirmation is to be secured from the correct solution of the problem of the theory of knowledge, or from the logical comprehension of how pure Being develops into the world of happenings in space and time.

In the artificial method of thinking employed by these great systems, the educated people of the early nineteenth century believe that they possess this world-view of ethical world- and life-affirmation as a proved necessity of thought. Their joy, however, is of short duration. About the middle of that century under the pressure of a realistic and scientific method of thinking these logical castles in the air crumble and collapse. A period of severe disenchantment sets in, and thought gives up all attempt to make this world comprehensible by either force or artifice. It is ready to resign itself to coming to terms with reality as it is, and to take from it motives for activtiy which are inconsonance with ethical world- and life-affirmation. But it soon learns by experience that reality refuses to provide what is expected from it. The world it not patient of any interpretation which gives a definite place to ethical activity on the part of mankind.

Thought, it is true, does not accept this negative result with all its implications. But the result announces itself in the fact that the world-view of ethical world- and life-affirmation and the ideals of civilization involved in it have no longer any influence in the world.

There is no hope of success for any attempt that thought might still make, to attain through some other interpretation of the world to ethical world- and life-affirmation.

The world-view of Reverence for Life follows from taking the world as it is. And the world means the horrible in the glorious, the meaningless in the full of meaning, the sorrowful in the joyful. However it is looked at it remains to many a riddle.

But that does not mean that we need stand before the problem of life at our wits' end because we have to renounce all hope of comprehending the course of world-events as having a meaning. Reverence for Life brings us into a spiritual relation with the world which is independent of all knowledge of the universe. Through the dark valley of resignation it leads us by an inward necessity up to the shining heights of ethical world- and life-affirmation.

We are no longer obliged to derive our live-view from knowledge of the world. In the disposition to Reverence for Life we possess a life-view founded on itself, in which there stands, firm and ready for us, the ethical world-view we are in search of. It renews itself in us every time we look thoughtfully at ourselves and the life around us.

It is not through knowledge, but through experience of the world that we are brought into relation with it. All thinking which penetrates to the depths ends in ethical mysticism. What is rational is continued into what is non-rational. The ethical mysticism of Reverence for Life is rationalism thought to a conclusion.

While I was correcting the proofs of *Civilization and Ethics*, I was already packing cases for my second voyage to Africa.

In the Autumn of 1923 the printing was interrupted for a time because the printing-works belonging to the publisher of the German edition, which was situated in Nördlingen (Bavaria), was requisitioned by the State to help in the production of the mass of paper money which was needed on account of the inflation.

That I was able to take up again my work in the jungle I owed to the evangelical parishes in Alsace, Switzerland, Sweden, Denmark, England, and Czecho-Slovakia which had been moved by my lectures to provide money for it, and to kind personal friends such as I now had in most of the countries of Europe.

Before leaving for Africa I also got ready for the press the lectures which I delivered at Selly Oak College in Birmingham, on "Christianity and the Religions of the World."[1] They seek to define the nature of these religions from the philosophic standpoint according to the greater or smaller degree of importance allowed in the convictions underlying them to world- and life-affirmation, to world- and life-negation, and to ethics. Unfortunately I was obliged to confine within too small a compass this epitome of my examination of these religions, since I had to publish it in the form of those lectures.

My writing down, in the intervals of packing, of the recollections of my childhood and youth is connected with a visit to my friend Dr. O. Pfister, the well-known Zürich psycho-analyst. In the early summer of 1923, while travelling across Switzerland from West to East, I had to wait two hours in Zürich, and went to visit him. He relieved my thirst and gave me an opportunity to stretch out and rest my weary body. But he at the same time made me narrate to him, just as they came into my mind, some incidents of my childhood, that he might make use of them in a young people's magazine. Soon afterwards he sent me a copy of what he had taken down in shorthand during those two hours. I asked him not to publish it, but to leave it to me to complete. Then, shortly before my departure to Africa, one Sunday afternoon when it was pelting with rain and snow alternately, I wrote down as an epilogue to what I had narrated, thoughts that used to stir me when I looked back upon my youth.[2]

---

[1] *Das Christentum und die Weltreligionen.* 59 pages. 1924. (C. H. Beck, Munich; Paul Haupt, Bern.) *Christianity and the Religions of the World.* (Allen & Unwin, London, 1923.) Later Danish, Swedish, Dutch, and Japanese editions.

[2] *Aus meiner Kindheit und Jugendzeit.* 64 pages. 1924. (Paul Haupt, Bern; C. H. Beck, Munich.) *Memoirs of Childhood and Youth.* (Allen & Unwin, London, 1924.) Later Swedish, Dutch, Danish, and French editions.

CHAPTER XIX

THE SECOND PERIOD IN AFRICA

1924-1927

ON February 14th, 1924, I left Strassburg. My wife could not accompany me this time because of a breakdown in her health. For the fact that she so far sacrificed herself as to acquiesce under these circumstances in my resumption of work at Lambaréné, I have never ceased to be grateful to her. I was accompanied by a young Oxford student of Chemistry, Noël Gillespie, whom his mother entrusted to me for a few months as a helper.

When we embarked at Bordeaux I came under suspicion with the Customs officer who examined the baggage of travellers outwards. I was taking with me four potato-sacks full of unanswered letters, which I meant to answer during the voyage. He had never yet encountered a traveller with so many letters, and as at that time the transfer of French money to other countries was strictly forbidden— a traveller was only allowed to take 5,000 francs with him —he could not help supposing that there was money hidden in those letters. He therefore spent an hour and a half examining them, one by one, till, on getting to the bottom of the second sack, he shook his head and gave it up as useless.

After a long voyage on the Dutch cargo-boat *Orestes*, which gave me an opportunity of getting to know better the places along the West Coast, I found myself at sunrise on April 19th, Easter Eve, once more in Lambaréné.

All that still remained of the Hospital was the small building of corrugated iron, and the hardwood skeleton of one of the big bamboo huts. During the seven years of my absence all the other buildings had decayed and collapsed. The path leading from the Hospital to the doctor's bungalow on the hill was so completely over-grown with grass and creepers that I could scarcely trace its windings. The first job, then, was to give the minimum of necessary repairs to the rotten and leaky roofs of the bungalow and the two Hospital buildings which were still standing. Next I re-erected the fallen buildings, a work which took me several months, and was so fatiguing that I was quite unable to give my evenings, as I had planned, to working over the manuscript of the *Mysticism of S. Paul* which was begun in 1911 and which I had brought now for the second time to Africa.

My life during those months was lived as a doctor in the mornings, and as a master-builder in the afternoons. Just as during my previous stay, there were unfortunately no labourers to be had, since the timber trade, which was flourishing again after the war, absorbed all the labour power that was to be found.

I had, therefore, to accept as my helpers a few 'volunteers' who were in the Hospital as companions of the patients or as convalescents, and worked without enthusiasm unless, indeed, they thought it preferable to disappear and hide themselves on the days when they were wanted.

One day during these early weeks there came to have his midday meal with us an elderly timber merchant, who had more or less 'gone African.' When we got up from table he thought he ought to say something nice to me, so he said: "Doctor, I know you play the harmonium beautifully. I am fond of music too, and if I had not to rush away so as to get home before the storm bursts, I would ask you to play me one of Goethe's Fugues."

The number of patients kept steadily increasing, so during 1924 and 1925 I sent for two doctors and two nurses from Europe.

At last, in the autumn of 1925, the Hospital could be said to have been rebuilt, and I was enjoying the prospect of being able to give my evenings to the work on S. Paul. Then—since all over the country the timber-felling had caused the cultivation of foodstuffs to be neglected—a severe famine began. At the same time there set in a terrible epidemic of dysentery. These two occurrences occupied fully myself and my helpers for many months. We had to make numerous journeys in our two motor-boats, the *Tak sa mycket* and the *Raarup* (one of them a present from Swedish, the other from Jutland friends) to collect rice wherever we could, if there was nothing else to be had with which to feed our Hospital inmates.

The dysentery epidemic made clear to me the necessity of removing the Hospital to a larger site. It could not spread out over land belonging to the Mission because all that was at my disposal was shut in by water, swamp, or steep hill. The buildings which could be erected on it sufficed well enough for the fifty patients and their attendants of the earlier period, but not for the 150 whom we had now to provide for every night.

I had, indeed, already become conscious of this during the rebuilding, but I had hoped that the huge number of patients was something only temporary. Now, however, the dysentery epidemic showed me in addition the danger which threatened the Hospital because I had no isolation ward for infectious cases. Owing to the impossibility of keeping the dysentery patients separate from the rest, as is always desirable, the whole Hospital was getting infected. It was a dreadful time!

Another great defect was the absence of sufficient accommodation for mental patients. I often found myself in the position of being unable to take in dangerous lunatics, because our only two cells were occupied.

So with a heavy heart I forced myself to the decision to remove the Hospital to a spot three kilometres (nearly two miles) up the river where it could be extended as much as was necessary. My confidence in the supporters of my work allowed me to venture to use the removal as an opportunity for replacing with huts of corrugated iron the old ones of bamboo with the raffia-leaf roofs which were everlastingly needing repair. To protect the Hospital against river floods and from the torrents which washed down from the hills after heavy storms I became a modern prehistoric man, and erected it as a village on piles, but a village of corrugated iron.

The professional work in the Hospital I now left almost entirely to my colleagues, Dr. Nessmann (an Alsatian), Dr. Lauterburg (a Swiss), and Dr. Trensz (an Alsatian who came to relieve Dr. Nessmann). I myself now for a year and a half became overseer of the labourers who cut down the

vegetation on the chosen site and worked on the buildings.
This job I was obliged to undertake myself because the
ever-changing squad of 'volunteers' recruited from the
attendants of the patients and from convalescents well
enough to work, would acknowledge no authority save
that of the 'old' Doctor. It was while I was foreman of a
troop of workmen hewing down trees that the news
reached me of the Philosophical Faculty of the German
University of Prague having conferred on me the honorary
degree of Doctor.

As soon as the building site had been cleared, I started
making the land near it ready for cultivation. What a joy
it was to win fields from the jungle!

Year after year since then work has been carried on
with the object of producing a Garden of Eden round the
Hospital. Hundreds of young fruit trees, which we have
grown from pips, have already been planted. Some day
there must be so much fruit growing here that all can
take what they please, and there will no longer be such
a crime as stealing. We have already got to that stage
with the fruits of the papaya, the mango-trees, and the
oil-palms. The papaya we planted in such numbers
are already producing more fruit than the Hospital needs,
while of mango-trees and oil-palms there were so many
already growing in the forest around that when the trees
about them had been cut down they formed regular groves.
As soon as ever they were delivered from the creepers
which were strangling them, and from the giant trees
which overshadowed them, they at once began to bear.

These fruit trees were, of course, not aboriginal elements
in the forest. The mangoes had made their way into the
forest from the villages which once stood along the river
bank; the oil-palms had sprung up from kernels which the
parrots had carried off from the trees near the villages
and then had dropped. The jungle of Equatorial Africa
contains no indigenous trees with edible fruits. The
traveller whose supplies give out during his journey is
doomed to starvation. It is well known that the banana
clumps, the manioc clumps, the oil-palms, the mango-trees
and many other vegetable growths which supply human
food are not natives of Equatorial Africa, but were intro-

duced by Europeans from the West Indian Islands and other tropical countries.

Unfortunately fruit cannot be stored here, on account of the damp and the heat. As soon as it is picked it begins to decay.

For the large amount of plantains required for feeding the patients I shall still, in spite of the Garden of Eden, have to resort to importation from the neighbouring villages. The plantains which I grow with paid labour cost me, in fact, much more than those which the natives bring me from their own plantations, which are always favourably situated near water. But the natives possess hardly any fruit-trees because they do not live permanently at one spot, but are constantly moving their villages to some new site.

Since even plantains cannot be stored, I have also to keep a considerable stock of rice in case there are not enough plantations in bearing in the neighbourhood.

The fact that I did not at once begin building a new Hospital but rebuilt the old one was by no means a misfortune. It enabled us to accumulate experiences which now came in very useful. We had only one native worker who stayed with us all through the rebuilding, a carpenter named Monenzali, but without him I could not have carried out the undertaking. During the last few months I had also the help of a young carpenter from Switzerland.

So again this second time that I was working in Africa my plan of returning to Europe at the end of two years came to nothing. I had to stay there for three and a half. In the evenings I found myself so tired out and so dulled by the continual going about in the sun that I, so to say, never got as far as writing. My remaining energy sufficed for nothing beyond regular practice on my piano with its pedal attachment. *The Mysticism of S. Paul* remained, therefore, unfinished, but during these years I made progress in music.

This second period of activity in Africa is described in the *Mitteilungen aus Lambaréné*.[1] They contain sketches

[1] *Mitteilungen aus Lambaréné*. 1st and 2nd Parts (spring 1924–autumn 1925). 164 pages. 3rd Part (autumn 1925–summer 1927). 74 pages. (C. H. Beck, Munich.) Swedish, English, American, and Dutch trans-

written at intervals during the work, for the information of friends and supporters.

During my absence the work which had to be done for the support of the Hospital was in the hands of Mrs. Emmy Martin at Strassburg, the Rev. Hans Bauer, D.D., at Basel, and my brother-in-law, the Rev. Albert Woytt at Oberhausbergen, near Strassburg. Without the self-denying help of these and other volunteers the undertaking, now so much expanded, could not be carried on.

Some of the new buildings were finished, when, on January 21st, 1927, the transfer of the patients from the old Hospital to the new was effected. That evening on the last journey we made, I took with me the mental patients. Their guardians never tired of representing to them that in the new Hospital they would live in cells with floors of wood. In the old cells the floor had been just the damp earth.

When I made my tour of the Hospital that evening, there resounded from every fire and every mosquito-net the greeting : "It's a good hut, Doctor, a very good hut!" So now for the first time since I began to work in Africa my patients were housed as human beings should be!

In April 1927 I was able to hand over the superintendence of the labourers engaged in deforestation around the Hospital to Mrs. C. E. B. Russell, who had just arrived, for she possessed the talent of getting them to obey her. Under her leadership a beginning was also made with the laying out of a plantation. Since then it has been my experience on the whole that the authority of a white woman is more readily recognized by our primitives than that of us men.

By about the middle of the summer of the same year I completed several more wards. Then I was in possession of a Hospital in which, if need should be, we were in a position to accommodate 200 patients and those who accompanied them. During recent months the number had been between 140 and 160. Provision was made also for

lations. The English edition (1931) bears the title *More from the Primeval Forest* (A. & C. Black), and the American *The Forest Hospital at Lambaréné* (Henry Holt, New York).

the isolation of dysentery patients. The building for the mental patients was erected from a fund established by the Guildhouse congregation in London in memory of a deceased member, Mr. Ambrose Pomeroy-Cragg.

And now, after making the most necessary arrangements for the internal affairs of the Hospital, I could leave it to my colleagues and think of going home. On July 21st I left Lambaréné. With me there travelled also Miss Mathilde Kottmann, who had worked in the Hospital since the summer of 1924, and the sister of Dr. Lauterburg. Miss Emma Haussknecht was left at Lambaréné, but some nurses came before long to help in the work.

CHAPTER XX

TWO YEARS IN EUROPE. A THIRD PERIOD IN AFRICA

OF the two years which I spent in Europe a good part was occupied with travelling to give lectures and organ recitals.

The autumn and winter of 1927 I spent in Sweden and Denmark. In the spring and early summer of 1928 I was in Holland and England; in the autumn and winter in Switzerland, Germany, and Czecho-Slovakia.

In 1929 I undertook several recital-tours in Germany. When not travelling, I lived with my wife and child at the mountain health-resort of Königsfeld in the Black Forest, or at Strassburg.

I was caused much work and worry by having to find and send out to Lambaréné as soon as possible doctors and nurses to replace those who had to return to Europe sooner than they expected, either because they could not stand the climate there, or on account of family circumstances, I secured as fresh medical men Dr. Mündler, Dr. Hediger, Dr. Stalder, and Mlle. Dr. Schnabel, all from Switzerland. We were all much saddened by the death of a Swiss doctor, Dr. Eric Dölken, who in October 1929, on the voyage to Lambaréné, died suddenly in the harbour of Grand Bassam, probably from a heart attack.

All my spare time in Europe I spent in getting ready for the press my book on *The Mysticism of Paul the Apostle*.[1] I did not wish to take the manuscript with me to Africa a third time, and I soon found myself once more at home in the subject-matter. Chapter after chapter came slowly into existence.

S. Paul's mysticism of Being in Christ finds its explanation in

[1] *Die Mystik des Apostels Paulus.* 405 pages. 1930. (J. C. B. Mohr (Siebeck), Tübingen.) A few days after finishing the English translation (A. & C. Black, the translator, Mr. W. Montgomery, died suddenly. The translation was finally revised, and the book seen through the press by Professor F. C. Burkitt of Cambridge.

the conception which the apostle has of the coming of the Messianic Kingdom and of the End of the World. On the strength of the views which, like his fellow-believers of those earliest days, he had taken over from Judaism, he supposes that those who believe in Jesus as the coming Messiah will live with Him in the Messianic Kingdom in a supernatural mode of existence, while their unbelieving contemporaries and the people of previous generations ever since the Creation must first rest in the grave. It is only at the close of the Messianic Kingdom, which, though supernatural, is nevertheless conceived as transitory, that, in accordance with the late-Jewish view, the General Resurrection takes place and is followed by the Last Judgment. Not till then does Eternity begin, in which God "is all in all," that is, all things return to God.

The fact that those who believe in Christ as the Messiah enter upon the post-Resurrection mode of being sooner than all other men through their participation in membership of the Messianic Kingdom, is explained by S. Paul as due to their having a special sort of corporeal existence in common with Christ. Their belief in Him is only a manifestation of the fact that God chose them out from all eternity to be companions of the Messiah. In virtue of this union with Him, which is both mystical and natural (at once), the forces which, working in Him, effected His death and resurrection, begin from that very time to work for the same results in them. These believers cease to be natural men like others. They become beings who are in process of changing from their natural condition to a supernatural one, and now wear the appearance of natural men only as a kind of veil which, when the Messianic Kingdom is revealed, they will at once throw off. In a mysterious fashion they are already dead and risen with Christ and in Him, and similarly will shortly live with Him in the mode of existence on which He entered at His resurrection.

In the mysticism of "being-in-Christ" and of having "died and risen with Christ," we have, therefore, an extension of the eschatological expectation. The belief in the imminent manifestation of the Kingdom is extended in S. Paul's thought into a conviction that with the death and resurrection of Jesus the change of the natural into the supernatural has already begun. We have, therefore, to do with a mysticism which is based on the assumption of a great cosmic happening.

From this knowledge of the meaning of union with Christ there follows, for S. Paul, the ethic which is to be practised. With the Jewish Law believers have nothing more to do, since that is valid for natural men only. For the same reason it must not be imposed on heathen who have come to believe in Christ. He who has entered into union with Christ knows what is ethical directly from the spirit of Christ in which he is a sharer.

While for other believers ecstatic discourses and convulsive raptures mean the surest proof of the possession of the Spirit, S. Paul turns the doctrine of the Spirit into ethical channels. According to him the Spirit which believers possess is the Spirit of Jesus, in which they have become participators because of the mysterious fellowship with Him which they enjoy. This Spirit of Jesus is the heavenly life-force which is preparing them for existence in the post-resurrection condition, just as it effected the resurrection itself in Him. At the same time it is the power which compels them, through their being different from the world, to approve themselves as men who have ceased to belong to this world. The highest proof of the Spirit is love. Love is the eternal thing which men can already on earth possess as it really is.

Thus in the eschatological mysticism of fellowship with Christ everything metaphysical has an ethical significance. The supremacy of the ethical in religion S. Paul establishes for all time in the saying, "And now abideth faith, hope and love, these three, but the greatest of these is love." This ethical interpretation of what it is to be a Christian he shows in himself by an activity full of service.

The saying of Jesus about bread and wine as His body and blood S. Paul interprets in accordance with his doctrine of the mystical fellowship with Christ, and therefore makes the meaning of the Supper consist in the fact that those who partake of it do by that eating and drinking enter upon fellowship with Jesus. Baptism, as the beginning of redemption through Christ, is for him the beginning of dying and rising again with Christ.

The doctrine of justification by faith only, which has for centuries been accepted as the central element of S. Paul's religion, is in reality a conception of the primitive doctrine of the atoning death of Jesus which has been made to harmonize with the mysticism of fellowship with Christ. In order to meet his Jewish-Christian opponents more successfully S. Paul undertakes to formulate the belief in the atoning significance of the sacrificial death of Jesus in such a way that it carries with it that certainty of the Law having no longer any validity at all which follows from the mysticism of fellowship with Christ. He thus succeeds, as against the Jewish Christians, in refusing to allow to works—he means works of the Jewish Law—any value at all as an addition to faith, whereas he can and does in his mysticism demand ethical deeds as a proof of fellowship with Christ.

The doctrine of justification by faith only which was produced for the struggle against Jewish Christianity has acquired a great importance since then because at all periods those who rebelled against the externalising of Christianity with a righteousness produced by works have appealed to it and, with the help of S. Paul's authority, have won their case. On the other hand the artificial logic with which S. Paul seeks to represent this doctrine as already contained in the Old Testament has given rise to a mistaken opinion about him. He was denounced as the man who had substituted a complicated dogma for the simple Gospel of Jesus. In reality, however, S. Paul, in spite of the Rabbinic element which clings here and there to his method of arguing, is a powerful elemental thinker. He puts forward the simple Gospel of Jesus not in the letter but in the spirit. While he works out the eschatological belief in Jesus and the Kingdom of God into his mysticism of fellowship with Christ, he gives it a shape in which it proves capable of outlasting the decay of the eschatological expectation and winning recognition, under every subsequent world-view, as an ethical Christ-mysticism. By thus thinking out to its furthest consequences the eschatological belief in Christ he advances thoughts about our relation to Jesus, which ethically and spiritually are final and good for all time, even if we do find their source in the metaphysic of eschatology.

There is, then, in S. Paul no Greek element at all. He does, however, in fact give the Christian belief a form in which it can be assimilated by the Greek spirit. Ignatius and Justin, in whose thought this process is completed, do nothing more than translate the mysticism of fellowship with Christ into Greek terms.

The last chapter of *The Mysticism of Paul the Apostle* I wrote in December 1929 on board ship between Bordeaux and Cape Lopez, and the Preface the day after Christmas on board the river-steamer which was taking to Lambaréné myself, my wife, Dr. Anna Schmitz, and Miss Marie Secretan, who came to work in the laboratory.

On this my third arrival I unfortunately again found building to be done. During a serious epidemic of dysentery, which was coming to an end just as I arrived, the wards had been found too small. So the neighbouring building for mental patients had to be devoted to those suffering from dysentery, and a new one had to be erected for the insane. By reason of experiences accumulated in the meantime, the new cells were made stronger and at the same time lighter and more airy than the old. After that I had, further to build a large ward with separate beds for severe cases, an airy and at the same time thief-proof storeroom for food supplies, and rooms for the native Hospital orderlies. All this work I carried out in the course of a twelvemonth with the help of our loyal native carpenter, Monenzali, in addition to my work in the Hospital. At the same time the Hospital was provided with large cement reservoirs for rain water, and enriched with an airy building of the same material, which serves us as dining-room and common-room.

Towards Easter 1930 my wife had unfortunately to return to Europe, since she felt the climate telling on her.

In the course of the summer a new Alsatian medical man, Dr. Meyländer, arrived.

The Hospital is now known over an area hundreds of kilometres wide. People who have spent weeks on the journey come to us for operations. The kindness of friends in Europe enables us to be in possession of an operating-room which is fitted out with everything necessary; to have in the Dispensary a store of all the drugs that we require, even of the often rather expensive ones needed for the treatment of colonial diseases. Further, it makes it possible for us to give sufficient nourishment to the many sick people who are too poor to buy their own food. So now it is fine to be working at Lambaréné, and the more so because we now have sufficient doctors and nurses to do all that is needed without our having to work ourselves to exhaustion. How can we thank sufficiently the friends of the Hospital who have made such a work possible!

Because at the Hospital there is still hard work, but no longer as formerly, work beyond our powers, I find myself fresh enough in the evening to turn to intellectual work. Very often, indeed, this leisure-time work has to be intermitted for days and weeks, when I am so full of anxiety about the surgical cases and the serious medical ones that I can think about nothing else for the time. Similarly this simple narrative of my life and activities, which I had planned to be my first literary work during this present stay in Africa, is getting spread out over months and months.

CHAPTER XXI

EPILOGUE

Two perceptions cast their shadows over my existence. One consists in my realization that the world is inexplicably mysterious and full of suffering; the other in the fact that I have been born into a period of spiritual decadence in mankind. I have become familiar with and ready to deal with each through the thinking which has led me to the ethical world- and life-affirmation of Reverence for Life. In that principle my life has found a firm footing and a clear path to follow.

I therefore stand and work in the world as one who aims at making men less shallow and morally better by making them think.

With the spirit of the age I am in complete disagreement, because it is filled with disdain for thinking. That such is its attitude is to some extent explicable by the fact that thought has never yet reached the goal which it must set before itself. Time after time it was convinced that it had clearly established a world-view which was in accordance with knowledge and ethically satisfactory. But time after time the truth came out that it had not succeeded.

Doubts, therefore, could well arise as to whether thinking would ever be capable of answering current questions about the world and our relation to it in such a way that we could give a meaning and a content to our lives.

But to-day in addition to that neglect of thought there is also prevalent a mistrust of it. The organized political, social, and religious associations of our time are at work to induce the individual man not to arrive at his convictions by his own thinking but to make his own such convictions as they keep ready made for him. Any man who thinks for himself and at the same time is spiritually free, is to them something inconvenient and even uncanny. He does not offer sufficient guarantee that he will merge himself in their organization in the way they wish. All corporate bodies look to-day for their strength not so much to the spiritual worth of the ideas which they represent and to that of the people who belong to them, as to the attainment of the highest possible degree of unity and exclusiveness. It is in this that they expect to find their strongest power for offence and defence.

Hence the spirit of the age rejoices, instead of lamenting, that thinking seems to be unequal to its task, and gives it no credit for what, in spite of imperfections, it has already accomplished. It refuses to admit, what is nevertheless the fact, that all spiritual progress up to to-day has come about through the achievements of thought, or to reflect that thinking may still be able in the future to accomplish what it has not succeeded in accomplishing as yet. Of such considerations the spirit of the age takes no account. Its only concern is to discredit individual thinking in every possible way, and it deals with that on the lines of the saying: "Whosoever hath not, from him shall be taken away even that which he hath."

Thus, his whole life long, the man of to-day is exposed to influences which are bent on robbing him of all confidence in his own thinking. The spirit of spiritual dependence to which he is called on to surrender is in everything that he hears or reads; it is in the people whom he meets every day; it is in the parties and associations which have claimed him as their own; it pervades all the circumstances of his life.

From every side and in the most varied ways it is dinned into him that the truths and convictions which he needs for life must be taken by him from the associations which have rights over him. The spirit of the age never lets him come to himself. Over and over again convictions are forced upon him in the same way as, by means of the electric advertisements which flare in the streets of every large town, any company which has sufficient capital to get itself securely established, exercises pressure on him at every step he takes to induce him to buy their boot polish or their soup tablets.

By the spirit of the age, then, the man of to-day is forced into scepticism about his own thinking, in order to make him receptive to truth which comes to him from authority.

To all this constant influence he cannot make the resistance that is desirable because he is an overworked and distracted being without power to concentrate. Moreover, the mani-fold material trammels which are his lot work upon his mentality in such a way that he comes at last to believe himself unqualified even to make any claim to thoughts of his own.

His self-confidence is also diminished through the pres-sure exercised upon him by the huge and daily increasing mass of Knowledge. He is no longer in a position to take in as something which he has grasped all the new dis-coveries that are constantly announced; he has to accept them as fact although he does not understand them. This being his relation to scientific truth he is tempted to acquiesce in the idea that in matters of thought also his judgment cannot be trusted.

Thus do the circumstances of the age do their best to deliver us up to the spirit of the age.

The seed of scepticism has germinated. In fact, the modern man has no longer any spiritual self-confidence at all. Behind a self-confident exterior he conceals a great inward lack of confidence. In spite of his great capacity in material matters he is an altogether stunted being, because he makes no use of his capacity for thinking. It will ever remain incomprehensible that our generation, which has shown itself so great by its achievements in discovery and invention, could fall so low spiritually as to give up thinking.

In a period which regards as absurd and little worth, as antiquated and long ago left far behind, whatever it feels to be in any way akin to rationalism or free thought, and which even mocks at the vindication of inalienable human rights which was secured in the eighteenth century, I acknowledge myself to be one who places all his confidence in rational thinking. I venture to say to our generation that it must not think it has done with rationalism because the rationalism of the past had to give place first to Roman-ticism, and then to a *Realpolitik* which is coming to dominate the spiritual sphere as well as the material. When it has run the gauntlet of the follies of this universal

Realpolitik and has thereby got itself into deeper and deeper misery, both spiritual and material, it will discover at last that there is nothing for it to do but trust itself to a new Rationalism, deeper and more efficient than the old, and in that seek its salvation.

Renunciation of thinking is a declaration of spiritual bankruptcy. Where there is no longer a conviction that men can get to know the truth by their own thinking, scepticism begins. Those who work to make our age sceptical in this way, do so in the expectation that, as a result of renouncing all hope of self-discovered truth, men will end by accepting as truth what is forced upon them with authority and by propaganda.

But their calculations are wrong. No one who opens the sluices to let a flood of scepticism pour itself over the land must expect to be able to bring it back within its proper bounds. Of those who let themselves get too disheartened to try any longer to discover truth by their own thinking, only a few find a substitute for it in truth taken from others. The mass of people remain sceptical. They lose all feeling for truth, and all sense of need for it as well, finding themselves quite comfortable in a life without thought, driven now here, now there, from one opinion to another.

But the acceptance of authoritative truth, even if that truth has both spiritual and ethical content, does not bring scepticism to an end; it merely covers it up. Man's unnatural condition of not believing that any truth is discoverable by himself continues, and produces its natural results. The city of truth cannot be built on the swampy ground of scepticism. Our spiritual life is rotten throughout because it is permeated through and through with scepticism, and we live in consequence in a world which in every respect is full of falsehood. We are not far from shipwreck on the rock of wanting to have even truth organized.

Truth taken over by a scepticism which has become believing has not the spiritual qualities of that which originated in thinking. It has been externalized and rendered torpid. It does obtain influence over a man, but it is not capable of uniting itself with him to the very marrow of his being. Living truth is that alone which has its origin in thinking.

Just as a tree bears year after year the same fruit and yet fruit which is each year new, so must all permanently valuable ideas be continually born again in thought. But our age is bent on trying to make the barren tree of scepticism fruitful by tying fruits of truth on its branches.

It is only by confidence in our ability to reach truth by our own individual thinking, that we are capable of accepting truth from outside. Unfettered thought, provided it be deep, never degenerates into subjectivity. With its own ideas it stirs those within itself which enjoy any traditional credit for being true, and exerts itself to be able to possess them as knowledge.

Not less strong than the will to truth must be the will to sincerity. Only an age which can show the courage of sincerity can possess truth which works as a spiritual force within it.

Sincerity is the foundation of the spiritual life.

With its depreciation of thinking our generation has lost its feeling for sincerity and with it that for truth as well. It can therefore be helped only by its being brought once more on to the road of thinking.

Because I have this certainty I oppose the spirit of the age, and take upon myself with confidence the responsibility of taking my part in the rekindling of the fire of thought.

Thought on the lines of Reverence for Life is by its very nature peculiarly qualified to take up the struggle against scepticism. It is elemental.

Elemental thinking is that which starts from the fundamental questions about the relations of man to the universe, about the meaning of life, and about the nature of goodness. It stands in the most immediate connexion with the thinking which impulse stirs in everyone. It enters into that thinking, widening and deepening it.

Such elemental thinking we find in Stoicism. When as a student I began going through the history of philosophy I found it difficult to tear myself away from Stoicism, and to pursue my way through the utterly different thinking which succeeded it. It is true that the results produced by Stoic thought were far from satisfying me, but I had the feeling that this simple kind of philosophizing was the right one, and I could not understand how people had come to abandon it.

Stoicism seemed to me great in that it goes straight for its goal; that it is universally intelligible, and is at the same time profound; that it makes the best of the truth which it recognizes as such, even if it is unsatisfying; that it puts life into such truth by the earnestness with which it devotes itself to it; that it possesses the spirit of sincerity; that it urges men to collect their thoughts, and to become more inward; and that it arouses in them the sense of responsibility. I felt, too, that the fundamental thought of Stoicism is true, namely that man must bring himself into a spiritual relation with the world, and become one with it. In its essence Stoicism is a nature-philosophy which ends in mysticism.

Just as I felt Stoic thinking to be elemental, so I felt that of Lao-tse to be the same, when I became acquainted with his Tao-te-King. For him, too, the important thing is that man shall come, by simple thinking, into a spiritual relation to the world, and prove his unity with it by his life.

There is, therefore, an essential relationship between Greek Stoicism and Chinese. The only distinction between them is that the former had its origin in well-developed, logical thinking, the latter in intuitive thinking which was undeveloped and yet marvellously profound.

This elemental thinking, however, which emerges in European as in extra-European philosophy, is unable to retain the leadership it has won; it must resign that position to the unelemental. It proves a failure because its results are not satisfying. It cannot see any meaning in the impulse to activity and to ethical deeds which is contained in the will-to-live of the spiritually developed man. Hence Greek Stoicism gets no further than the ideal of resignation, Lao-tse no further than the kindly inactivity which to us Europeans seems so curious.

The ultimate explanation of the history of philosophy is that the thoughts of ethical world- and life-affirmation which are natural to man can never acquiesce contentedly in the results of simple logical thinking about man and his relation to the universe, because they cannot fit themselves into it properly. They therefore compel thinking to take to roundabout roads, along which they hope to reach their goal. Thus there arises side by side with elemental thinking an unelemental, in various forms, which grows up round the other and often entirely conceals it.

These roundabout roads which thinking takes lead especially in the direction of an attempted explanation of the world which shall represent the will to ethical activity in the world as purposive. In the late-Stoicism of an Epictetus and a Marcus Aurelius, in the Rationalism of the eighteenth century, and in that of Kung-tse (Confucius), Meng-tse (Mencius), Mi-tse (Micius), and other Chinese thinkers, the philosophy which starts from the elemental problem of the relation of man to the world reaches an ethical world- and life-affirmation by tracing the course of world-events back to a world-will with ethical aims, and claiming man for service to it. In the thinking of Brahmanism, and of the Buddha, as in the Indian systems generally, and in the philosophy of Schopenhauer, the opposite explanation of the world is put forward, namely that the Life which runs its course in space and time is purposeless, and must be brought to an end. The sensible attitude of man to the world is therefore to die to the world and to life.

Side by side with this form of thinking which, so far, at any rate, as its starting-point and its interests are concerned, has remained elemental, there enters the field, especially in European philosophy, another form which is completely unelemental in that it no longer has as its central point the question of man's relation to the world. It busies itself with the problem of the nature of knowledge, with logical speculations, with natural science, with psychology, with sociology, and with other things, as if philosophy were really concerned with the solution of all these questions for their own sake, or as if itself consisted merely in the sifting and systematizing of the results of the various sciences. Instead of urging man to constant meditation on himself and his relation to the world, this philosophy presents him with results of epistemology, of logical speculation, of natural science, of psychology, or of sociology, as matters according to which alone he is to shape his view of his life and his relation to the world. On all these things it discourses to him as if he were not a being who is in the world and lives his life in it, but one who is stationed near it, and contemplates it from the outside.

Because it approaches the problem of the relation of man to the universe from some arbitrarily chosen standpoint, or perhaps passes it by altogether, this unelemental European philosophy lacks unity and consistency, and shows itself more or less restless, artificial, eccentric, and fragmentary. At the same time, it is the richest and the most universal. In its systems, half-systems, and no-systems, which succeed and interpenetrate each other, it is able to contemplate the problem of world-view from every side, and in every possible perspective. It is also the most practical in that it deals with the natural sciences, history, and ethical questions more profoundly than the others do.

The world-philosophy of the future will owe its origin less to efforts to reconcile European and non-European thought, than to those made to reconcile elemental and unelemental thinking.

From the intellectual life of our time mysticism stands aside. It is in essence a form of elemental thinking, because it is directly occupied in enabling the individual man to put himself into a spiritual relation with the world. It despairs, however, of this being possible by means of logical thinking, and falls back on intuition, within which imagination can be active. In a certain sense, then, the mysticism also of the past goes back to a mode of thinking which tries roundabout routes. Since with us only that knowledge which is a result of logical thinking is accepted as truth, the convictions which make up the mysticism above described, cannot become our spiritual possession in the form in which they are expressed and declared to be proved. Moreover, they are not in themselves satisfying. Of all the mysticism of the past it must be said that its ethical content is too slight. It puts men on the road of inwardness, but not on that of a living ethic. The truth of a world-view must be proved by the fact that the spiritual relation to life and the universe into which that world-view brings us makes us into inward men with an active ethic.

Against the lack of thought, then, which characterizes our age nothing effective can be done either by the unelemental thinking which takes the round-about route in the explanation of the world, or by mystical intuition. Power over scepticism is given only to that elemental thinking which takes up and develops the simple thinking which is natural in all men. The unelemental thinking on the other hand, which sets before men certain results of thinking at which it has in one way or another arrived, is not in a position to sustain their own thinking, but takes it from them in order to put another kind in its place. This acceptance of another kind of thinking means a disturbance and weakening of one's own. It is a step towards the acceptance of truth from outside, and thus a step towards scepticism. It was in this way that the great systems of German philosophy which when they appeared were taken up with such enthusiasm, prepared at the beginning of the nineteenth century the ground upon which later on scepticism developed.

To make men thinking beings once more, then, means to make them resort to their own way of thinking that they may try to secure that knowledge which they need for living. In the thinking which starts from Reverence for Life there is to be found a renewal of elemental thinking. The stream which has been flowing for a long distance underground comes again to the surface.

The belief that elemental thinking is now arriving at world- and life-affirmation, which it has hitherto vainly striven to reach, is no self-deception, but is connected with the fact that thinking has become thoroughly realistic.

It used to deal with the world as being only a totality of happenings. With this totality of happenings the only spiritual relation which man can reach is one in which, acknowledging his own natural subordination to it, he secures a spiritual position under it by resignation. To attribute any meaning and purpose to his own activities is impossible with such a conception of the world. He cannot possibly place himself at the service of this totality of happenings which crushes him. His way to world- and life-affirmation and to the ethical is barred.

It thereupon attempts, but in vain, to grasp by means of some sort of explanation of the world what elemental thinking, hindered by this lifeless and incomplete representation of the world, cannot reach in the natural way. This thinking is like a river which on its way to the sea is held up by a range of mountains. Its waters try to find a passage to the sea by roundabout ways. In vain. They only pour themselves into other valleys and fill them. Then, centuries later, the damned up waters manage to break through.

The world does not consist of happenings only; it contains life as well, and to the life in the world, so far as it comes within my reach, I have to be in a relation which is not only passive but active. By placing myself in the service of that which lives I reach an activity, exerted upon the world, which has meaning and purpose.

However simple and obvious a proceeding it may seem to be when once accomplished, to replace that lifeless idea of the world by a real world which is full of life, a long period of evolution was needed, nevertheless, before it became possible. Just as the solid rock of a mountain range which has risen from the sea first becomes visible when the layers of chalk which covered it have been eroded and washed away by the rain, so, in questions of world-view, is realist thinking overlaid by unrealistic.

The idea of Reverence for Life offers itself as the realistic answer to the realistic question of how man and the world are related to each other. Of the world man knows only that everything which exists is, like himself, a manifestation of the Will-to-Live. With this world he stands in a relation of passivity and of activity. On the one hand he is subordinate to the course of events which is given in this totality of life; on the other hand he is capable of affecting the life which comes within his reach by hampering or promoting it, by destroying or maintaining it.

The one possible way of giving meaning to his existence is that of raising his natural relation to the world to a spiritual one. As a being in a passive relation to the world he comes into a spiritual relation to it by resignation. True resignation consists in this: that man, feeling his subordination to the course of world-happenings, wins his way to inward freedom from the fortunes which shape the outward side of his existence. Inward freedom means that he finds strength to deal with everything that is hard in his lot, in such a way that it all helps to make him a deeper and more inward person, to purify him, and to keep him calm and peaceful. Resignation, therefore, is the spiritual and ethical affirmation of one's own existence. Only he who has gone through the stage of resignation is capable of world-affirmation.

As a being in an active relation to the world he comes into a spiritual relation with it by not living for himself alone, but feeling himself one with all life that comes within his reach. He will feel all that life's experiences as his own, he will give it all the help that he possibly can, and will feel all the saving and promotion of life that he has been able to effect as the deepest happiness that can ever fall to his lot.

Let a man once begin to think about the mystery of his life and the links which connect him with the life that fills the world, and he cannot but bring to bear upon his own life and all other life that comes within his reach the principle of Reverence for Life, and manifest this principle by ethical world- and life-affirmation expressed in action. Existence will thereby become harder for him in every respect than it would be if he lived for himself, but at the same time it will be richer, more beautiful, and happier. It will become, instead of mere living, a real experience of life.

Beginning to think about life and the world leads a man directly and almost irresistibly to Reverence for Life. Such thinking leads to no conclusions which could point in any other direction.

If the man who has once begun to think wishes to persist in his mere living he can do so only by surrendering himself, whenever this idea takes possession of him, to thoughtlessness, and stupefying himself therein. If he perseveres with thinking he can come to no other result than Reverence for Life.

Any thinking by which men assert that they are reaching scepticism or life without ethical ideals, is not thinking but thoughtlessness which poses as thinking, and it proves itself to be such by the fact that it is unconcerned about the mystery of life and the world.

Reverence for Life contains in itself Resignation, World- and Life-Affirmation, and the Ethical, the three essential elements in a world-view, as mutually interconnected results of thinking.

Up to now there have been world-views of Resignation, world-views of World- and Life-Affirmation, and world-views which sought to satisfy the claims of the Ethical. Not one has there been, however, which has been able to combine the three elements. That is possible only on condition that all three are conceived as essentially products of the universal conviction of Reverence for Life, and are recognized as being all contained in it. Resignation and World- and Life-Affirmation have no separate existence of their own by the side of the Ethical; they are its lower octaves.

Having its origin in realistic thinking, the ethic of Reverence for Life, is realistic, and brings man to a realistic and steading facing of reality.

It may seem, at first glance, as if Reverence for Life were something too general and too lifeless to provide the content of a living ethic. But thinking has no need to trouble as to whether its expressions sound living enough, so long as they hit the mark and have life in them. Anyone who comes under the influence of the ethic of Reverence for Life will very soon be able to detect, thanks to what that ethic demands from him, what fire glows in the lifeless expression. The ethic of Reverence for Life is the ethic of Love widened into universality. It is the ethic of Jesus, now recognized as a necessity of thought.

Objection is made to this ethic that it sets too high a value on natural life. To this it can retort that the mistake made by all previous systems of ethics has been the failure to recognize that life as such is the mysterious value with which they have to deal. All spiritual life meets us within natural life. Reverence for Life, therefore, is applied to natural life and spiritual life alike. In the parable of Jesus, the shepherd saves not merely the soul of the lost sheep but the whole animal. The stronger the reverence for natural life, the stronger grows also that for spiritual life.

The ethic of Reverence for Life is found particularly strange because it establishes no dividing-line between higher and lower, between more valuable and less valuable life. For this omission it has its reasons.

To undertake to lay down universally valid distinctions of value between different kinds of life will end in judging them by the greater or lesser distance at which they seem to stand from us human beings—as we ourselves judge. But that is a purely subjective criterion. Who among us knows what significance any other kind of life has in itself, and as a part of the universe?

Following on such a distinction there comes next the view that there can be life which is worthless, injury to which or destruction of which does not matter. Then in the category of worthless life we come to include, according to circumstances, different kinds of insects, or primitive peoples.

To the man who is truly ethical all life is sacred, including that which from the human point of view seems lower in the scale. He makes distinctions only as each case comes before him, and under the pressure of necessity, as, for example, when it falls to him to decide which of two lives he must sacrifice in order to preserve the other. But all through this series of decisions he is conscious of acting on subjective grounds and arbitrarily, and knows that he bears the responsibility for the life which is sacrificed.

I rejoice over the new remedies for sleeping-sickness, which enable me to preserve life, whereas I had previously to watch a painful disease. But every time I have under the microscope the germs which cause the disease, I cannot but reflect that I have to sacrifice this life in order to save other life.

I buy from natives a young fish-eagle, which they have caught on a sand-bank, in order to rescue it from their cruel hands. But now I have to decide whether I shall let it starve, or kill every day a number of small fishes, in order to keep it alive. I decide on the latter course, but every day I feel it hard that this life must be sacrificed for the other on my responsibility.

Standing, as he does, with the whole body of living creatures under the law of this dilemma (*Selbstentzweiung*) in the will-to-live, man comes again and again into the position of being able to preserve his own life and life generally only at the cost of other life. If he has been touched by the ethic of Reverence for Life, he injures and destroys life only under a necessity which he cannot avoid, and never from thoughtlessness. So far as he is a free man he uses every opportunity of tasting the blessedness of being able to assist life and avert from it suffering and destruction.

Devoted as I was from boyhood to the cause of the protection of animal life, it is a special joy to me that the universal ethic of Reverence for Life shows the sympathy with animals which is so often represented as sentimentality, to be a duty which no thinking man can escape. Hitherto ethics have faced the problem of man and beast either uncomprehending or helpless. Even when sympathy with the animal creation was felt to be right, it could not be brought within the scope of ethics, because ethics were really focussed only on the behaviour of man to man.

When will the time come when public opinion will tolerate no longer any popular amusements which depend on the ill-treatment of animals!

The ethic, then, which originates in thinking is not "according to reason," but non-rational and enthusiastic. It marks off no skilfully defined circle of duties, but lays upon each individual the responsibility for all life within his reach, and compels him to devote himself to helping it.

Any profound world-view is mysticism, in that it brings men into a spiritual relation with the Infinite. The world-view of Reverence for Life is ethical mysticism. It allows union with the infinite to be realized by ethical action. This ethical mysticism originates in logical thinking. If our will-to-live begins to think about itself and the world, we come to experience the life of the world, so far as it comes within our reach, in our own life, and to devote our will-to-live to the infinite will-to-live through the deeds we do. Rational thinking, if it goes deep, ends of necessity in the non-rational of mysticism. It has, of course, to deal with life and the world, both of which are non-rational entities.

In the world the infinite will-to-live reveals itself to us as will-to-create, and this is full of dark and painful riddles for us; in ourselves it is revealed as will-to-love, which will through us remove the dilemma (*Selbstentzweiung*) of the will-to-live.

The world-view of Reverence for Life has, therefore, a religious character. The man who avows his belief in it, and acts upon the belief, shows a piety which is elemental. Through the active ethic of love with its religious character, and through its inwardness, the world-view of Reverence for Life is essentially related to that of Christianity. Hence there is a possibility that Christianity and thought may now meet in a new relation to each other which will do more than the present one to promote spiritual life.

Christianity has once already entered into a connexion with thought, namely during the period of Rationalism in the eighteenth century. It did so because thought met it with an enthusiastic ethic which was religious in character. As a matter of fact, however, thought had not produced this ethic itself, but had, without knowing it, taken it over from Christianity. When, later on, it had to depend solely upon its own ethic, this latter proved to have in it so little life and so little religion that it had not much in common with Christian ethics. Then the bonds between Christianity and active thought were loosened, and the situation to-day is that Christianity has completely withdrawn into itself, and is concerned only with the propagation of its own ideas, as such. It no longer sees any use in proving them to be in agreement with thought, but prefers that they be regarded as something altogether outside it, and occupying a superior position. It loses, however, thereby its connexion with the spiritual life of the time and the possibility of exercising any real influence upon it.

The emergence of the world-view of Reverence for Life now summons it to face once more the question whether it will or will not join hands with Thought which is ethical and religious in character.

Christianity has need of thought that it may come to the consciousness of its real self. For centuries it treasured the great commandment of love and mercy as traditional truth without recognizing it as a reason for opposing slavery, witch-burning, torture, and all the other ancient and mediæval forms of inhumanity. It was only when it experienced the influence of the thinking of the Age of Enlightenment (*Aufklärung*[1]) that it was stirred into entering the struggle for humanity. The remembrance of this ought to preserve it for ever from assuming any air of superiority in comparison with Thought.

Many people find pleasure to-day in talking continually of how 'shallow' Christianity became in the age of Rationalism. Justice surely demands that we should find out and admit how much compensation was made for that 'shallowness' by the services rendered by that Christianity. To-day torture has been re-established. In many states the system of Justice acquiesces without protest in the most infamous tortures being applied, before and simultaneously with the regular proceedings of police and prison officials, in order to extract confessions from those accused. The sum-total of misery thus caused every hour passes imagination. But to this renewal of torture the Christianity of to-day offers no opposition even in words, much less in deeds, and similarly it makes hardly any effort to counter the superstitions of to-day. And even if it did resolve to venture on resisting these things and on undertaking other things such as the Christianity of the eighteenth century accomplished, it would be unable to carry out its intention because it has no power over the spirit of the age.

To make up to itself for the fact that it does so little to prove the reality of its spiritual and ethical nature, the Christianity of to-day cheats itself with the delusion that it is making its position as a Church stronger year by year. It is accommodating itself to the spirit of the age by adopting a kind of modern worldliness. Like other organized bodies it is at work to make good, by ever stronger and more uniform organization, its claim to be a body justified by history and practical success. But just in proportion as it gains in external power, it loses in spiritual.

Christianity cannot take the place of thinking, but it must be founded on it.

In and by itself it is not capable of mastering lack of

[1] *Aufklärung*=Illumination. The name given to the period of the eighteenth century made notable by the influence of the progressive thinkers: Montesquieu (1689-1755). Voltaire (1694-1778), Rousseau (1712-1778), Diderot (1713-1784), and others.—Translator's Note.

thought and scepticism. The only age which can be receptive for the imperishable elements in its own thoughts is
one animated by an elemental piety which springs from
thinking.

Just as a stream is preserved from gradually leaking
away, because it flows along above subsoil water, so does
Christianity need the subsoil water of elemental piety
which is the fruit of thinking. It can only attain to real
spiritual power when men find the road from thought to
religion no longer barred.

I know that I myself owe it to thinking that I was able to
retain my faith in religion and Christianity.

The man who thinks stands up freer in the face of traditional religious truth than the man who does not, but the
profound and imperishable elements contained in it he
assimilates with much more effect than the latter.

The essential element in Christianty as it was preached
by Jesus and as it is comprehended by thought, is this, that
it is only through love that we can attain to communion
with God. All living knowledge of God rests upon this
foundation: that we experience Him in our lives as Will-
to-Love.

Anyone who has recognized that the idea of Love is the
spiritual beam of light which reaches us from the Infinite,
ceases to demand from religion that it shall offer him complete knowledge of the supra-sensible. He ponders, indeed,
on the great questions: What the meaning is of the evil in
the world; how in God, the great First Cause, the will-to-
create and the will-to-love are one; in what relation the
spiritual and the material life stand to one another, and in
what way our existence is transitory and yet eternal. But
he is able to leave these questions on one side, however
painful it may be to give up all hope of answers to them.
In the knowledge of spiritual existence in God through love
he possesses the one thing needful.

"Love never faileth: but . . . whether there be knowledge
it shall be done away," says S. Paul.

The deeper piety is, the humbler are its claims with
regard to knowledge of the supra-sensible. It is like a path
which winds between the hills instead of going over them.

The fear that the Christianity which is favourably

inclined to the piety originating in thought will step into pantheism is unreal. Every form of living Christianity is pantheistic in that it is bound to envisage everything that exists as having its being in the great First Cause of all being. But at the same time all ethical piety is higher than any pantheistic mysticism, in that it does not find the God of Love in Nature, but knows about Him only from the fact that He announces Himself in us as Will-to-Love. The First Cause of Being, as He manifests Himself in Nature, is to us always something impersonal. But to the First Cause of Being, who becomes revealed to us as Will-to-Love, we relate ourselves as to an ethical personality. Theism does not stand in opposition to pantheism, but emerges from it as the ethically determined out of what is natural and undetermined.

Unfounded, too, is the doubt whether the Christianity which has passed through a stage of thinking can still bring home his sinfulness to the consciousness of man with sufficient seriousness. It is not where sinfulness is most talked about that its seriousness is most forcibly taught. There is not much about it in the Sermon on the Mount. But thanks to the longing for freedom from sin and for purity of heart which Jesus has enshrined in the Beatitudes, these form the great call to repentance which is unceasingly working on man.

If Christianity, for the sake of any tradition or for any considerations whatever, refuses to have itself interpreted in terms of ethico-religious thinking, it will be a misfortune for itself and for mankind.

What Christianity needs is that it shall be filled to over-flowing with the spirit of Jesus, and in the strength of that shall spiritualize itself into a living religion of inwardness and love, such as its destined purpose should make it. Only as such can it become the leaven in the spiritual life of mankind. What has been passing for Christianity during these nineteen centuries is merely a beginning, full of weaknesses and mistakes, not a full-grown Christianity springing from the spirit of Jesus.

Because I am devoted to Christianity in deep affection, I am trying to serve it with loyalty and sincerity. In no wise do I undertake to enter the lists on its behalf with the crooked and fragile thinking of Christian apologetic, but I call on it to set itself right in the spirit of sincerity with its past and with thought in order that it may thereby become conscious of its true nature.

My hope is that the emergence of an elemental mode of thought which must lead us to the ethico-religious idea of Reverence for Life, may contribute to the bringing of Christianity and thought closer to each other.

To the question whether I am a pessimist or an optimist, I answer that my knowledge is pessimistic, but my willing and hoping are optimistic.

I am pessimistic in that I experience in its full weight what we conceive to be the absence of purpose in the course of world-happenings. Only at quite rare moments have I felt really glad to be alive. I could not but feel with a sympathy full of regret all the pain that I saw around me, not only that of men but that of the whole creation. From this community of suffering I have never tried to withdraw myself. It seemed to me a matter of course that we should all take our share of the burden of pain which lies upon the world. Even while I was a boy at school it was clear to me that no explanation of the evil in the world could ever satisfy me; all explanations, I felt ended in sophistries, and at bottom had no other object than to make it possible for men to share in the misery around them, with less keen feelings. That a thinker like Leibnitz could reach the miserable conclusion that though this world is, indeed, not good, it is the best that was possible, I have never been able to understand.

But however much concerned I was at the problem of the misery in the world, I never let myself get lost in broodings over it; I always held firmly to the thought that each one of us can do a little to bring some portion of it to an end. Thus I came gradually to rest content in the knowledge that there is only one thing we can understand about the problem, and that is that each of us has to go his own way, but as one who means to help to bring about deliverance.

In my judgment, too, of the situation in which mankind finds itself at the present time I am pessimistic. I cannot make myself believe that that situation is not so bad as it seems to be, but I am inwardly conscious that we are on a road which, if we continue to tread it, will bring us into "Middle Ages" of a new character. The spiritual and material misery to which mankind of to-day is delivering itself through its renunciation of thinking and of the ideals which spring therefrom, I picture to myself in its utmost compass. And yet I remain optimistic. One belief of my childhood I have preserved with the certainty that I can never lose it : belief in truth. I am confident that the spirit generated by truth is stronger than the force of circumstances. In my view no other destiny awaits mankind than that which, through its mental and spiritual disposition, it prepares for itself. Therefore I do not believe that it will have to tread the road to ruin right to the end.

If men can be found who revolt against the spirit of thoughtlessness, and who are personalities sound enough and profound enough to let the ideals of ethical progress radiate from them as a force, there will start an activity of the spirit which will be strong enough to evoke a new mental and spiritual disposition in mankind.

Because I have confidence in the power of truth and of the spirit, I believe in the future of mankind. Ethical world- and life-affirmation contains within itself an optimistic willing and hoping which can never be lost. It is, therefore, never afraid to face the dismal reality, and to see it as it really is.

In my own life anxiety, trouble and sorrow have been allotted to me at times in such abundant measure that had my nerves not been so strong, I must have broken down under the weight. Heavy is the burden of fatigue and responsibility which has lain upon me without a break for years. I have not much of my life for myself, not even the hours I should like to devote to my wife and child.

But I have had blessings too : that I am allowed to work in the service of mercy; that my work has been successful; that I receive from other people affection and kindness in abundance; that I have loyal helpers, who identify themselves with my activity; that I enjoy a health which allows me to undertake most exhausting work; that I have a well-balanced temperament which varies little, and an energy which exerts itself with calmness and deliberation; and, finally, that I can recognize as such whatever happiness falls to my lot, accepting it also as a thing for which some thank-offering is due from me.

I feel it deeply that I can work as a free man at a time when an oppressive lack of freedom is the lot of so many, as also that though my immediate work is material, yet I have at the same time opportunities of occupying myself in the sphere of the spiritual and intellectual.

That the circumstances of my life provide in such varied ways favourable conditions for my work, I accept as something of which I would fain prove myself worthy.

How much of the work which I have planned and have in mind shall I be able to complete?

My hair is beginning to turn. My body is beginning to show traces of the exertions I have demanded of it, and of the passage of the years.

I look back with thankfulness to the time when, without needing to husband my strength, I could get through an uninterrupted course of bodily and mental work. With calmness and humility I look forward to the future, so that I may not be unprepared for renunciation if it be required of me. Whether we be workers or sufferers, it is assuredly our duty to conserve our powers, as being men who have won their way through to the peace which passeth all understanding.

LAMBARÉNÉ
    March 7th, 1931.

POSTSCRIPT

1932—1949

by Everett Skillings

BEFORE WORLD WAR II

IN the fall of 1931 near the end of his third period in Africa, Albert Schweitzer received an invitation from the city of Frankfort to give the address at the celebration of the hundredth anniversary of Goethe's death. He had just finished writing his autobiography and having a complete set of Goethe's works with him at Lambaréné, he turned his thoughts at once to the memorial oration, the outline for which he completed before setting sail for Europe in January. One of the four nurses returning with him, Miss Margaret Deneke of Oxford, who had supervised the gangs of native labourers during her stay in Africa, recalls that the members of the party were all in high spirits and that the voyage was a very happy one. Much work had just been accomplished at the Hospital : some new buildings, a new road and paths, and a new wharf at the riverbank had all been completed exactly according to schedule. Even on the boat the Doctor's days were planned. The best hours he spent in writing, but the evenings were given over to recreation. There was music of course and there were English lessons for the Doctor, "conducted like a humorous game," says his teacher. The Goethe memorial oration was completed just as the *Brazza* steamed into Bordeaux at the end of the eighteen-day journey.

The celebration at Frankfort took place on March 22, 1932. Beginning at the exact hour of Goethe's death, Schweitzer spoke to men and women many of whom were conscious that they were facing a great national tragedy. With prophetic insight he gave them a clear analysis of the causes of the catastrophe which was indeed hanging over

the whole world. Mrs. C. E. B. Russell, Schweitzer's friend
and co-worker, writes: "How inspiring was the occasion!
. . . The great opera house in the poet's birthplace was
packed to its utmost capacity with listeners, so spellbound
by the gravity of the only speaker, that for sixty-five
minutes one could, as the phrase goes, have heard a pin
drop but for the sound of his voice. Again and again he
referred to the present time as *grausig* (gruesome, frightful),
and he proclaimed that a gigantic repetition of the Faust
drama was being played on the world stage."

To quote from Schweitzer's oration:[1]

The cottage of Philemon and Baucis burns with a thousand
tongues of flame! In deeds of violence and murders a thousandfold, a brutalized humanity plays its cruel game! Mephis-
topheles leers at us with a thousand grimaces! In a thousand
different ways mankind has been persuaded to give up its
natural relations with reality, and to seek its welfare in the
magic formulas of some kind of economic and social witchcraft, by which the possibility of freeing itself from economic
and social misery is only still further removed!

And the tragic meaning of these magic formulas, to whatever
kind of economic and social witchcraft they may belong, is
always just this, that the individual must give up his own
material and spiritual personality and must live only as one
of the spiritually restless and materialistic multitude which
claims control over him.

Schweitzer, quite characteristically ends his address on a
somewhat more hopeful note. He says:

Not everything in history is ordained to be overthrown in
the process of constant change, as it seems to superficial
observers; on the contrary, ideals that carry within themselves
enduring worth will adjust themselves to changing circumstances and grow stronger and deeper in the midst of them.
Such an ideal is that of human personality. If it is given up,
then the human spirit will be destroyed, which will mean the
end of civilization, and even of humanity. . . .

Before two decades have come to an end, Frankfurt will
celebrate the two hundredth anniversary of the birthday of its

[1] The following excerpts are quoted from Albert Schweitzer, *Goethe:
Two Addresses*, trans. by C. R. Joy and C. T. Campion (Boston, Beacon
Press, 1948), pp. 55, 57, 58. Quoted by permission.

greatest son. May it be that he who gives the memorial address at that new festival may be able to state that the deep darkness which surrounds this one has already begun to lighten, that a race with a true feeling for reality is seeking to comprehend it, and is beginning to achieve a mastery over material and social needs, united in its resolve to remain loyal to the one true ideal of human personality.

During his stay in Europe from February, 1932, to March, 1933, in addition to the Goethe Oration, Schweitzer gave many lectures and concerts in Holland, England, Sweden, Germany, and Switzerland. "I recall," says Pierre van Paassen, "how Dr. Schweitzer once came to Zutphen [Holland] to preach the Christmas sermon when I was a guest at the manse. He arrived on a Monday, and Christmas fell on a Saturday. We did not see the great man all week, until finally, passing by the cathedral and hearing the organ, we found Dr. Schweitzer covered with dust and sweat, up in the loft busy cleaning the pipes. On Christmas he not only preached the sermon, but also played the organ to the astonishment of the churchgoers, who upon entering the cathedral, looked up in amazement when they heard the prelude and said: 'Is that our old organ!' Archbishop Söderblom told me that Schweitzer did the same thing once in Upsula. But there he worked for two months before he had the organ back to what it should have been."[1]

Schweitzer's most extended tours were usually in England. Beginning in early June, 1932, for several weeks, he lectured, gave organ recitals and visited friends in many parts of England. He broadcast from St. Margaret's, Westminster, and made recordings. He preached at Maude Royden's Guildhouse. He visited Scotland, for the first time, and with special interest because his mother, on account of Sir Walter Scott, had cherished for many years an unfulfilled desire to see that country.

During this visit to Britain, Schweitzer was the recipient of four honorary degrees: at Oxford (Divinity), at Edinburgh (Divinity and Music, granted in absentia the year before) and at St. Andrews (Laws). At St. Andrews he was asked to "stand" for the rectorship of the university to

[1] From *That Day Alone* by Pierre van Paassen by permission of Dial Press, Inc. Copyright 1941 by Pierre van Paassen.

succeed General Smuts, but he refused on the grounds of the insufficiency of his English. In Glasgow, where Living-stone received his medical training, a civic banquet was given in his honour.

In his prime, Schweitzer worked on a sixteen-hour schedule when he was on tour. His pace was fast and furious, but his immense reserves of energy were such that he could keep going on a minimum of food and sleep. After he had been working until four o'clock one morning a friend said to him, "You cannot burn a candle at both ends." But Schweitzer replied, "Oh, yes you can, if the candle is long enough."

While he is travelling he carries with him two linen bags, much like laundry bags, to hold his correspondence, which he cannot neglect lest it gets hopelessly ahead of him. As soon as he has answered a letter, it is transferred from one bag to another.

Before an organ recital he has been known to practice as long as eight hours. He and his assistant go up and down the stairs to the organ loft many times to get the effect of the various stops. This is necessary because no two organs are the same and, in order to render a perfect performance, he must before each recital, pencil in on the music the stops to be used.

In a letter to an American friend, Dr. Schweitzer tells about his manner of preparing and delivering a lecture : "I have it in written form and speak it word for word as I have written it. The translator studies the written text and goes over the lecture with me, sentence by sentence, so that when we stand before the public, there is no need of his searching what I say in order to interpret it. He knows it all by heart just as I do myself, and the lecture runs off so smoothly in two languages that the auditor shortly forgets that he is listening to a translated lecture. Naturally this practice represents a great deal of effort on my part and on the part of the interpreter; but it enables me to speak in foreign countries in a manner that is not annoying to the listeners."

After his return from England Schweitzer received many visitors at the Guest House in Günsbach, but most of his time until the day of his departure for Africa in March,

1933, was spent studying and writing about the Chinese and Indian philosophies. The Guest House is the headquarters in Europe for Dr. Schweitzer's work. Here Mme. Emmy Martin, his devoted and efficient secretary, carries on a vast correspondence with business firms over the purchase of drugs and other supplies; with friends in many countries who help support the Hospital; and with men and women from all over the world who beg for the privilege of working with him, believing that whether or not the Africans would benefit, at least *they* would. Here doctors and nurses on furlough from Lambaréné stop for a few days or for a much longer period. Miss Gloria Coolidge, the first American nurse to go to Lambaréné, spent several months at the Guest House with Mme. Martin, learning, from her many details of the work at the Hospital before embarking for Africa in January, 1948.

It is at Günsbach that Dr. Schweitzer does most of his writing while he is in Europe; but busy as he is, he always has time for visitors. Often he meets an expected guest at the station and carries or wheels the luggage the half-mile or so to the Guest House. He takes his visitors to walk through the beautiful old village and usually ends up at the church where he plays some Bach or Mendelssohn on the organ with the guest sitting beside him on the organ bench.

In the late twenties, President J. S. Bixler of Colby College, then at Harvard, was requested by President Lowell to call upon Schweitzer when he was in Europe and ask him if he would come to Boston to deliver the Lowell Lectures. This was the year before the Guest House was completed so Dr. Bixler was invited to come to Königsfeld in the mountains of the Black Forest, where Schweitzer's modest home still stands. Dr. Bixler writes:

The two visits I had with Dr. Schweitzer at that time mark one of the high points of my life. Three impressions stand out. First I remember being upset when he asked me if it was not time for what sounded like *Yotz*. I could not remember ever hearing the word, but when he sat down at the piano and started to drum away in syncopated time I realized it was *Jazz* he was talking about.

The second has to do with the large bundle of mail wrapped up with a strap which he threw into a far corner of the room,

showing his impatience with the vast volume of correspondence he had to keep up with, yet he had plenty of time and
patience for this completely unknown American who had
come in to see him.

The third and strongest impression of all is based on a
remark he made. He said, "I think the most important quality
in a person concerned with religion is absolute devotion to the
truth." I have often thought back on that remark and connected it with his scholarly passion for fact in *The Quest of the
Historical Jesus*. A few days later when he gave a Bach recital
at Freiburg he showed the same responsiveness to the claim of
the abstract idea. And when later he said that he had gone to
Africa in the name of common justice it seemed as if the
picture were complete.

For Dr. Schweitzer, devotion to *truth*, *beauty*, and *justice* is
a means of following through the religious desire "Not my will
but Thine be done."

Just before the Nazi collapse Schweitzer wrote to a
friend in America: "I received a cablegram from Alsace
that my house at Günsbach has not suffered from the
bombing that much of the Münster valley has had. All the
village of Günsbach is in good condition. Münster (2½ kilo-
meters from Günsbach) is in part destroyed. . . ."

In 1933, Mrs. Schweitzer left Königsfeld with their
daughter to settle in Lausanne where, as much as his travels
and work permitted, the Doctor spent his time when he
was in Europe. They had chosen Lausanne for the climate
and for the resources offered by the city for their daughter's
education. "This city, so sympathetic in itself," writes
Schweitzer, "had a particular attraction for us because of
dear friends who lived there."

At the end of his fourth period in Africa, Schweitzer
wrote an account of the work at the Hospital for his
English friends which appeared in the *Spectator*, September,
6, 1935. Here is a summary of this report:

A grateful white patient has presented the Hospital with a
large kerosene lamp so that now urgent operations can be performed at night. This of course precludes the use of ether as an
anesthetic because of the danger of fire, but a local or spinal
anesthetic is generally used in any case. During these years the
hospital has usually been filled to capacity largely on account

of the influenza epidemic. In this period also, as many as thirty patients might be waiting at one time for their turns at the operating table. [The natives believe that sickness and pain are caused by worms located in various parts of the body. Therefore they are very eager to be operated upon because they think as soon as the worm is removed, they will be well]. Recently when Dr. Goldschmid began a friendly conversation with a woman who lay on the operating table, in order to divert her attention and cheer her, while she received the injections for local anesthesia, he received the comment: "This is no time for gossip; get on with the cutting."

In the year 1934, 622 major operations were performed. On one day between one and one-thirty P.M. three patients from three different directions arrived at the Hospital with strangulated hernias. [Many men are afflicted with this ailment because their muscles have grown flabby from letting the women do most of the hard work.] The most common ailments requiring surgery are hernia, elephantiasis, and abdominal tumours. [Cancer and appendicitis have never been seen among the natives].

In February, 1934, Schweitzer is again in Europe spending the spring and summer, for the most part at Günsbach working upon the third volume of his Philosophy and upon the preparation of the Gifford Lectures. In that year Dr. Ernest Bueding, now at Western Reserve University, came in contact with Schweitzer under very interesting circumstances at the Pasteur Institute in Paris. He relates an incident which is characteristic of the Doctor's noble spirit and attitude towards medicine: "A group of research workers were engaged in preparing and studying a vaccine against yellow fever. They succeeded in obtaining a preparation which offered some degree of immunity. One day someone called from Colmar, Alsace, requesting information about this vaccine. He indicated that he would like to take it to Africa in order to vaccinate some patients in a hospital, as well as some other natives. When informed that serious side reactions may occur as a result of the administration of this vaccine, he said that he would only consider large scale vaccinations if he himself were first given this preparation in order to experience and evaluate the untoward effects. He was asked about his age and when

he said he was about sixty, the person in charge advised
strongly not to try this preparation on himself. This was to
no avail and the 'doctor from Colmar' replied that he would
come to Paris the next day in order to discuss the matter
further. He insisted that if the vaccine is considered safe
enough for the natives of Africa, it should be safe enough
for him. When this telephone conversation was discussed I
happened to be in the laboratory and I immediately won-
dered whether the 'doctor from Colmar' was not Dr. Albert
Schweitzer whose books had inspired my greatest admiration. My guess proved to be correct and I explained as well
as possible the great personality, the ideas, and the achievements of Dr. Schweitzer before his arrival the next
morning. When he reached the laboratory, the chief of the
latter tried again to convince him that it would be unwise
to try this experiment on himself. However, this was again
unsuccessful; he was determined to have the vaccination
performed. As a measure of precaution he was hospitalized
for two days at the Hospital Pasteur. Fortunately Dr.
Schweitzer had no serious reactions from this injection.
However he was a very "bad" patient because he could not
see why these precautions of keeping him inactive in the
hospital for two days should be taken."

In the autumn of 1934, Schweitzer visited England again
to deliver the Hibbert Lectures at Manchester College,
Oxford, on the subject, *Religion in Modern Civilization*. A
series of four, these were given between October, 16-25,
and, on alternate days of the same period, they were
repeated at London University. These lectures have not yet
been published, but a fairly adequate summary from
Schweitzer's own pen was contributed to *The Christian
Century*, November 21 and 28, 1934. The first and last para-
graphs of this summary follow:

I am going to discuss religion in the spiritual life and civilization of our time. The first question to be faced, therefore, is:
Is religion a force in the spiritual life of our age? I answer in
your name, and mine, "No!" .... There is [however] a longing
for religion among many who no longer belong to the churches.
I rejoice to concede this. And yet we must hold fast to the fact
that religion is not a force. The proof? The war. . . .

We wander in darkness now, but one with another we all have the conviction that we are advancing to the light; in that again a time will come when religion and ethical thinking will unite. This we believe, and hope and work for, maintaining the belief that if we make ethical ideals active in our lives, then the time will come when peoples will do the same. Let us look out toward the light and comfort ourselves in reflecting on what thinking is preparing for us.

In November Schweitzer went to Edinburgh for the Gifford Lectures which he delivered three times a week in a series of ten on *The Problem of Natural Philosophy and Natural Ethics*. In these, he traces the progress of human thought, beginning with the great thinkers of India, China, Greece, and Persia. The chapter on the Evolution of Indian Thought grew to such proportions that he decided to publish it as a separate book. The German edition, *Die Weltanschauung der Indischen Denker*, was published in 1934 by Beck in Munich; the French edition, *Les Grands Penseurs de l'Inde*, was translated by Schweitzer himself in 1936 and published in Paris the same year by Payot. It was translated into English with the title, *Indian Thought and Its Development*, by Mrs. C. E. B. Russell and published in London by Hodder and Stoughton in 1936, and in the United States by Henry Holt and Company the same year. Charles F. Andrews, the friend of Gandhi, assisted in the preparation of this book, particularly in connexion with the chapters dealing with modern Indian thought; also Professor Winternitz, the celebrated authority on India at Prague, looked over important pages which Schweitzer sent to him for criticism. There will be a volume on The Chinese Thinkers after he has been able to submit his work to an authoritative Sinologist, Schweitzer has said.

"The two courses of lectures (The Hibbert and the Gifford) overlap each other to some extent, and together represent a summary in homiletic form of the theme he has already developed in his *Philosophy of Civilization*."[1]

When Schweitzer was in Edinburgh for the Gifford

---

[1] This and the two following quotations are from Seaver, *Albert Schweitzer: The Man and His Mind* (New York, Harper & Bros., 1947), Quoted by permission.

Lectures, it happened that Sir Wilfred Grenfell was home from Labrador. A meeting was arranged between them by a mutual friend. "We began at once," says Schweitzer, "to question each other about the management of our hospitals. His chief trouble was the disappearance of reindeer for their periodic migrations; mine the loss of goats from theft and snake bites. Then we burst out laughing: we were talking not as doctors concerned with patients, but as farmers concerned with livestock."

When they left the home of their host, they were asked to sign the guest book. Grenfell wrote his name and then Schweitzer, struck by the humorous contrast between his own swarthy bulk and the much smaller frame of his trim, white-haired companion, wrote beneath his signature: *"L'Hippopotame est heureaux de recontrer l'Ours Blanc."*

On January 14th, 1935, the city of Strasbourg commemorated Schweitzer's sixtieth birthday by giving his name to one of its beautiful parks. At the end of February Schweitzer was again at Lambaréné but this time for a period of only seven months because he had promised to deliver a second series of Gifford Lectures in Edinburgh early in November. These were delivered in a series of twelve.

During this visit to Great Britain, his last one up to 1949, he gave concerts and lectures almost continually for over two months. Schweitzer has written: "For a part of this trip, my dear friend and translator, C. T. Campion was with me. It was our last time together, for some years later in Africa, I received news of his death."

That Schweitzer is greatly beloved throughout Britain is evidenced on all sides. His host at Leeds writes:[1] "I think we were a little apprehensive of his arrival at our modest manse. But as soon as he came into the room he put us all at our ease at once. He brought with him an atmosphere of good will and happiness. . . . I can see him now with my little daughter of seven on his knee playing tunes for her on the piano and guiding her little fingers over the keys."

[1] The three following quotations are from Seaver, *Albert Schweitzer: The Man and His Mind* (New York, Harper & Bros., 1947), pp. 149 ff. Quoted by permission.

At Peterborough the Dean "retains as the most vivid memory of his short visit, 'the tireless energy of a guest who in the space of a few hours could keep an appointment with a dentist, practice on the cathedral organ and work off a considerable correspondence; and of a lecturer who aided by the remarkable skill of his interpreter, could hold his audience spellbound, creating the illusion that we heard him speak in our own tongue. . . .'"

At Canterbury the Dean, Dr. Hewlett Johnson, writes:

Of course, the visit of Dr. Schweitzer was an outstanding event. He addressed some 150 or 200 people in my large drawing room . . . and his robust personality illuminated all he had to say. . . . It had been proposed that he and Dr. Grenfell and I, together with the Japanese Christian, Kagawa, should go on a mission of help to China at the time of the great flood in the previous year. Arrangements for that quarter, however, fell through and I alone went, and Dr. Schweitzer wrote to me to say how gladly he would have come, but that he was tied to his work in Africa, at which he would continue, for his strength allowed him to go on running in the same old pair of shafts, but like an old cart horse he might not run equally well in fresh shafts. . . .

It was the mingling of these many lighter touches with the general optimism, vitality, and buoyancy of the man that helped to build up in one's mind a figure of massive proportions, such as I have seldom met elsewhere. In a sense he and Grenfell were counterparts, but Schweitzer had the additional quality of deep scholarship and extensive learning which, however, he carried lightly and easily. The humanity of the man predominated over all other elements. . . .

In the spring of 1936, Schweitzer was lecturing and giving recitals in his beloved Switzerland, which has furnished so many doctors and nurses for the work at Lambaréné. The rest of the year he spent for the most part at his desk in the Guest House at Günsbach. He translated into French his book on the Indian philosophers and spent much time on the third volume of his *Philosophy of Civilization—Reverence for Life*. In October he made recordings on the organ of St. Aurelia's at Strasbourg for Columbia Records in London.

At the end of January he set sail for his sixth period in

Africa, carrying with him the manuscript for the "Third Volume," believing that now it would be possible for him to finish it. However, the increasing responsibilities of the hospital left him little time for this work. He was able, however, during 1938 to write a little volume of anecdotes upon the lives and ideas of the African natives. This book, entitled *Afrikanische Geschichten*, was published by Meiner in Leipzig in 1938; Payot in Paris issued the French edition in 1941; Allen and Unwin in London, the English edition *From My African Notebook*, in 1938; and Henry Holt, in New York in 1939.

In the year 1937, Schweitzer discovered a perennial spring near his Hospital which he dedicated to the memory of Miss Dorothy Mannering, one time honorary secretary of Dr. Maude Royden's Guildhouse Fellowship in London which had become one of Lambaréné's staunchest supporters. Schweitzer wrote to Miss Royden:

"I had the great good luck to come upon a spring of water which never runs dry. To prevent the walls from falling in, I had to line them with 750 big concrete blocks which Mlle. Haussknecht and I made."

In 1938, to commemorate the twenty-fifth anniversary of the founding of the Hospital at Lambaréné, the Europeans living in the Ogowé region presented Dr. Schweitzer with 90,000 francs with which to purchase an X-ray apparatus. With great foresight, however, he obtained their approval to buy instead a large supply of the most necessary drugs, a decision which proved, during the war years, to be a very wise provision.

THE WAR YEARS AND AFTER

AGAIN a world war confronted the Schweitzers. Even before 1937, it was clear to them that war was inevitable and might break out at any time, perhaps cutting off all European sources of support for their Hospital. So in 1937 and again in 1938, Mme. Schweitzer came to the United States on a lecture tour, raising funds, contacting old friends and making new ones. Their daughter, Rhena, came with her.

On the first of February, 1939, Dr. Schweitzer arrived

in Bordeaux for one of his periodic breaks in routine. He needed rest and went straight to Günsbach. But the dread of war hung heavy over Europe and he did not even unpack his baggage. Desiring to shelter the people to whom he had given nearly thirty years of his life, he returned to Bordeaux and sailed back to Africa on the same ship which had brought him to Europe. This time Mme. Schweitzer did not accompany him.

Soon after the war began, Dr. Schweitzer wrote the following to a friend in America :

We are all of us conscious that many of the natives are puzzling over the questions raised by the war. How can it be possible that the whites, who brought them the Gospel of Love, are now murdering each other, and throwing to the winds the commands of the Lord Jesus? When they put the question to us, we are helpless. If I am questioned on the subject by those who think, I make no attempt to explain or to extenuate, but say that we are in "front" of something terrible and incomprehensible. How far the ethical and religious authority of the white man among these children of nature is impaired by this war, we shall only be able to measure later on. I fear that the damage done will be very considerable.

Dr. Schweitzer wrote an account of the war years at Lambaréné which appeared in pamphlet form in the United States in January, 1947. Here are excerpts from this report :[1]

On March 3, 1939, aboard a little steamer, I entered once more the river Ogowé. With quaking heart I asked myself what events would have taken place before I next sailed out of this stream into the sea. During the months that followed I used all the funds of the Hospital to buy a store of drugs and other necessities, purchasing them in Africa or ordering them from Europe. Luckily nearly all of these consignments arrived before the outbreak of war.

In September we sent back to their homes a large proportion of the patients who had come from the interior for operations. From now on it was necessary to be economical with all materials and therefore we would operate only in the most urgent cases. We also dismissed all who were not seriously ill.

[1] *The Hospital at Lambaréné During the War Years*, 1939-1945. Pub. by The Albert Schweitzer Fellowship.

What sad days we spent sending these people home! Again and again we had to refuse the urgent entreaties of those who, in spite of all, wished to stay with us. Many of the homeward bound were able to travel by steamer or motorboat, but others had to make their way to distant villages by long and difficult jungle trails. At last they had all gone and the heart-rending scenes were at an end.

In March the liner *Brazza*, which for years had been running between Bordeaux and Equatorial Africa, was torpedoed near Cape Finisterre. She sank so quickly that few passengers were saved. Among those who perished were many from our district. And with her also was lost our last consignment of drugs and materials from Europe.

In the fall of 1940, the troops of General de Gaulle and those of Vichy were engaged in fighting for the possession of Lambaréné. Our Hospital is situated about two and one half miles up the Ogowé from the village and is separated from it by an arm of the river some six hundred yards wide. The crews of the aircraft on both sides were ordered by their leaders not to bomb the Hospital, so it escaped serious damage and became a haven of refuge for both white people and black. We protected ourselves against the numerous stray shots by reinforcing the wooden walls, which faced Lambaréné, with thick sheets of corrugated iron, of which we had a good store.

From the autumn of 1940 on, our colony possessed a government co-operating with the Allies, with the result that, for the most part, we were cut off from France and the continent of Europe, but could have intercourse with England and the United States and, from time to time, through England, with Sweden. But considerable time elapsed before postal arrangements with these countries began to function. For a while it was possible to buy everything at the trading posts in Africa and more than once merchants offered me considerable quantities of rice at a favourable price. It appeared that they were anxious to get rid of it because it was not the best quality and already harbored weevils. So a large quantity was practically forced upon me. Fortunately I had space to store it, and for three years it rendered great service in feeding our native patients. In this country a good stock of rice is always necessary because, between harvests periods recur when bananas and tapioca, which constitute the main diet of the natives, are scarce. It also happens, when a great deal of rain falls during the dry season, that famine conditions last for months. Luckily during the war we were spared famine caused in this way, but what I so greatly feared during the war years has now happened to us afterwards. In the summer of 1944 the rainfall in the dry season prevented the natives from burning over the forest they had cleared in order to plant. Fortunately a district officer further up country has insisted since 1942 on the population cultivating rice even though such plantations must be watched all of the time because of the constant depredations of innumerable birds. If I had not had the means to acquire a considerable stock of rice, I should have had to close the Hospital just as the schools were closed at the mission stations because there was no food for the children.

At the end of the year 1940 I had a splendid surprise. Word came from America that drugs and other things would be sent to me if I would say what I needed. It was over a year before the consignment finally arrived in May, 1942. The new drugs came just in the nick of time, for our supply was nearly used up. And there were not only drugs in the boxes, but also many other useful articles. Again and again while unpacking, shouts of joy resounded when we came across something which we especially needed. Of particular value were rubber gloves which fitted my hands. For months I had been obliged, when operating, to wear gloves too small for me. Those who had charge of the kitchens were in ecstasies over new cooking utensils. Later shipments supplemented this first one and replenished our stock. Shoes and spectacles received in 1943 were a great boon to many of us.

The donations received in 1941 were just sufficient to keep things going after a fashion, but what we received in 1942 and 1943 allowed us gradually to admit more patients. How grateful I am to faithful friends in the countries that have helped me, for now I can take in all the sick who are in great need. We are greatly encouraged in our work!

As we became more and more weary from the long stay in the oppressive climate, the work constantly increased. To a great extent this was due to the large number of white patients. For weeks at a time every available bed was occupied. The principal cause of this bad health, along with the tropical climate, is the absence of calcium in the diet. Fortunately we have had plenty of Swiss and American preparations of calcium as well as the French preparation of phosphorus which assists in the assimilation of calcium. We have also received preparations of liver and iron from England, America, and Switzerland.

The Government has taken over the fight against sleeping sickness so that our only concern now is to pass on to the "Colonial Sanitary Service" any patient in whom we suspect the disease. A large camp for these patients has been established a short distance down the river. Doctors or white assistants now visit every village in a given district and examine all the inhabitants to discover by microscopic tests whether germs of the disease are to be found in their blood or spinal fluid. Unfortunately at the present time this disease is increasing rather than diminishing in our region.

As usual we are much concerned with natives suffering from leprosy. The diphtheria toxoid received from England has been found to be effective. But these poor blacks lack the necessary patience to stay with us for the many months that the proper treatment requires. Scarcely do they feel better, scarcely do their ulcers show a tendency to heal, than they believe they can for the time being do without treatment. They leave the Hospital, only to return months later when their condition has become much worse. Recently there has been hope of important progress in the treatment of leprosy. French doctors in Madagascar have, since 1937, been making promising experiments with a drug obtained from a plant found on the island (*hydrocotylus asiatica*). With this treatment they are achieving rapid cures of leprous ulcers. In America a drug called promine is also being tried with success.

We are often reminded that ours is a jungle Hospital by the natives who arrive after being wounded by wild animals. The white ants too are a constant reminder. We are continually being stirred up by them, and their presence is only discovered when they have already done considerable damage. Then everything has to be cleared out in order to find out just where they made their entrance. How much labour and waste of time these wicked insects do cause! Nothing so far has been effective in keeping them out, but a ray of hope, in the use of DDT, is now held out to us.

We also suffer much from elephants, as they are constantly breaking, with devastating results, into the plantation belonging to the natives who supply the Hospital with bananas. As a result we are often hard up for food. How near the wild creatures of the forest come to us, I had an opportunity of realizing afresh a few weeks ago. As some natives had started making plantations on land belonging to the Hospital, I had to re-mark its boundaries. When I was supervising the setting of new posts, I heard behind me what I thought were human voices. I shouted to the labourers, "What's that? What are the women and children doing here?" Laughing, they replied, " 'These women and children' are chimpanzees who are excited at hearing your voice here in the forest."

With the onset of the war, the timber trade collapsed and consequently labour could be had cheap; so I resolved to undertake several pieces of work which had long been put off. More land needed to be cleared for cultivation. Our big garden on the slope near the river had begun to slide away during the rainy season. Several hundred yards of strong walls with deep foundations were needed to put an end to this devastating movement. The mere assembling of the stones involved a long and heavy piece of work, for they could not be found in the neighbourhood. It was necessary also to repair our streets which in the course of years had suffered from terrible thunderstorms. We built retaining walls to protect them from the water that rushes down from the hills behind. During the first two years of the war I spent nearly all of my afternoons with the labourers who were employed on these urgent undertakings, for they only work if they are supervised by a European.

Since 1941 a great change has been wrought in our country by the construction of roads which were a strategic necessity in war time. The highway now running from Capetown to Algiers passes through Lambaréné. Of course these new roads are very imperfect and to travel on them is anything but a pleasure. But they signify a great step in advance over the old method of travel.

During the spring and summer of 1939 two doctors and two nurses returned to their homes in Switzerland, one of the doctors just in time to exchange his pith helmet for a soldier's. That left the medical and surgical work to Dr. Ladislas Goldschmid, Dr. Anna Wildikann, and myself. Dr. Goldschmid, who began work here in 1933, had returned from a furlough in Europe in 1938. Dr. Wildikann, who worked at Lambaréné from 1935 to 1937, arrived for a second term of service in January, 1940, after accomplishing the incredible feat of reaching Bordeaux from her home in Riga in war time. Soon after Dr. Wildikann arrived, Mlle. Gertrud Koch returned to Switzerland by air after her third period of work here.

In 1943 Doctor Goldschmid spent several months' leave in the Belgian Congo and Dr. Wildikann, who had worked splendidly to keep everything going during his absence, went on leave for several months in 1944. From April, 1944 on, Dr. Goldschmid undertook to replace the government doctor at the sleeping sickness camp near us. After this he was at our disposal only on mornings when we operated and for two or three hours in the afternoons.

In the summer of 1941 my wife arrived at Lambaréné; as if by miracle she succeeded in getting from France to Lisbon and thence on a Portuguese steamer to a port of the Portuguese colony of Angola at the mouth of the Congo. After a detour through the Belgian Congo she arrived on August 2nd.

When the work of the Hospital was cut down at the beginning of the war, some of the nurses found employment elsewhere. We were finally left with only four nurses, Mlle. Nötzli and Mlle. Müller from Switzerland, Mlle. Maria Lagendijk, a Dutch woman, and Mlle. Emma Haussknecht from Alsace. My wife substituted for each one in turn and so made it possible for nurses who had worked without a break since the beginning of the war, to have a little relaxation. She also devoted herself to keeping in order all that was wanted for operations, gave assistance wherever it was needed and helped me with correspondence and writing. She has stood the strain of the exacting climate better than I had expected. She keeps going all day long and her help is very precious.

Early in June, 1943 Mlle. Nötzli, who had been with us since 1938, started home to Switzerland. After more than six months she finally reached the end of her journey. To replace her, Mlle. Koch returned to us in July after spending months collecting all the necessary documents for the enterprise. She brought with her from Switzerland a number of cases of drugs. As soon as she arrived she took over the kitchen and assisted Mlle. Maria, the Dutch nurse, who had to be careful because of ill health.

In the course of the year 1944 things became very difficult for us owing to the fact that Mlle. Maria was obliged to give up her work. In August she was sent to hospitals in the Cameroon mountains where she recovered sufficiently to fly to Paris in 1945, arriving there during the days of the liberation of Holland.

Now Mlle. Koch took over all of the work in the Hospital and Mlle. Emma undertook the kitchen as well as the housekeeping and the garden. For a long time we had only three nurses instead of four. It was then that we began to realize how tired we had become. The fatigue was due not only to the long sojourn in the hot, close climate, but to excessive work and overstrain. We confided to each other that, in order to carry on our daily work, we must continually strive to pull ourselves out of a deep depression.

We received the news of the end of the war in Europe at midday on May 7th. While I was sitting at my table, writing some urgent letters which must reach the river steamer by two o'clock, there appeared at my window a white patient who had brought his radio with him to the Hospital. He shouted to me that an armistice had been concluded in Europe. I had to keep on with my letters and then I had to go down to the Hospital for some appointments. But in the course of the afternoon the big Hospital bell was rung and our community gathered to hear the joyful news. After that, in spite of great fatigue, I had to drag myself to the plantation to see how the work was progressing. Not until evening could I begin to think and to imagine the meaning of the end of hostilities. While the palms were gently rustling outside in the darkness, I took from its shelf my little book with the sayings of Lao-tse, the Great Chinese thinker of the sixth century B.C., and read his impressive words on war and victory: "Weapons are disastrous implements, no tools for a noble being. Only when he cannot do otherwise, does he make use of them. Quiet and peace are for him the highest. He conquers, but he knows no joy in it. He who would rejoice in victory, would be rejoicing in murder. At the victory celebration, the general should take his place as is the custom at funeral ceremonies. The slaughter of human beings in great numbers should be lamented with tears of compassion. Therefore should he, who has conquered in battle, bear himself as if he were at a festival of mourning."

Now that the war was over in Europe, we expected that, within a reasonable time, fresh nurses and doctors would be able to come to our aid. But we were forced to abandon these cherished hopes. The formalities they had to go through before the journey could be undertaken, occupied months. Mlle. Kottman finally was able to fly to Libreville and reached Lambaréné early in August, where she started work at once to relieve Mlle. Haussknecht and myself as much as possible.

At the approach of the rainy season in September, 1945, my wife who had been at Lambaréné since August, 1941, returned to Europe. Since then she has been at Lambaréné only when better weather prevails, that is from May to September [of the years 1946 and 1947].

In October the long expected ship, the *Providence*, arrived to take home the Europeans of our colony. It embarked hundreds of them including a number from our district who had to get away as quickly as possible on account of their health. Many of these had been resident patients at our Hospital for a long time.

Since the war ended, prices have been steadily rising, so that before long I must be prepared for the cost of running the Hospital to be four times as great as formerly, however economical we are. Not only do we have to pay much more for all that we import, but also bananas and tapioca cost more

and that means also an increase in wages for the natives.
And we are hit hardest of all by the enormously increased fares
for travel to and from Europe, for in this matter no economy is
possible.

Emma Haussknecht, who was at Lambaréné without
vacation for eight years during the war period, wrote to
The Fellowship in 1946:

I am a nurse in Dr. Schweitzer's hospital. I started working
at Lambaréné twenty years ago and I have had the privilege
of spending the war years at the Hospital working with dear
Dr. Schweitzer. We are all awfully tired, but the Doctor is the
most courageous of all.

After the day's duties he plays on the piano with organ
pedals and from our rooms, in the silence of the night and
in the midst of the big forest, we enjoy the most perfect
recitals. The music hours are comfort and inner help. They
have meant so much to me during the years of separation from
home!

We cannot forget the helpfulness of the Lambaréné friends
in the USA during the war. We cannot imagine the region
here without the Hospital and its staff. The misery around us
makes us keen to continue as long as our strength holds out.

In the meantime, the middle of May, 1939, Mme.
Schweitzer and her daughter had set sail for Lambaréné.
This was Rhena's first visit to Africa and the occasion
gave them all great joy. The Doctor wrote to an American
friend: "I am so happy that my daughter is able to see
my Hospital. She is delighted with the six chimpanzees
and the five young antelopes that play around in the yard."
They returned to Europe before the war broke out and
Rhena joined her husband in Paris. She had married an
organ builder, M. Eckert, an Alsatian friend of long standing.

At the time of the collapse of the French government in
1940, Mme. Schweitzer, who had been spending some
time in Lausanne, was visiting the Eckerts in Paris. A letter
from Mme. Eckert to a friend in America describes their
tragic flight to the south of France. "Like so many other
people, we left Paris in June in our little car where we
had packed the most necessary things. My mother, my

husband, our little daughter, and I travelled across France. For about a month we lived on the roads, sleeping most of the time in our car and eating when we found something to eat."

Before they were finally settled in Lyon, where M. Eckert found employment and a tiny apartment, a second child was born to the Eckerts. In the summer of 1941 Mme. Schweitzer joined her husband in Africa and the Eckerts, later on, were able to get to Switzerland. M. Eckert took a position with an old-established firm of organ builders, the House of Kuhn in Zurich, of which he later became a director. The Eckerts now have four children. When the publishers of the new *Schweitzer Anthology* offered to send a number of copies to friends and supporters of the Hospital and asked for a list of names, Dr. Schweitzer responded: "I want the first four copies to go to the grandchildren I have never seen."

[Through the courtesy of Dr. A. A. Roback, editor of the *Albert Schweitzer Jubilee Book*, I use in what follows parts of my article, *Albert Schweitzer, Humanitarian*, in that book.]

Soon after the outbreak of the war, Schweitzer wrote to American friends that he did not know whether he should stay at Lambaréné with his co-workers to continue their humanitarian work, or whether they should close the Hospital and return to Europe when that could be done. Later, upon learning of his decision to keep the Hospital open, friends got together and formulated plans to enlist American support for his work.

Thus it came about that, late in 1939, The Albert Schweitzer Fellowship of America came into being. The title "Fellowship" was suggested by Schweitzer's use of the word in the last chapter of *On the Edge of the Primeval Forest*. He writes about "the fellowship of those who bear the mark of pain." He says: "Who are the members of this fellowship? Those who have learned by experience what physical pain and bodily anguish mean belong together the world over; they are united by a secret bond. One and all, they know the horrors of suffering to which man can be exposed; one and all they know the longing to be free from pain."

When Schweitzer was told of the plans being formulated, he wrote: "My mind is greatly relieved to hear that now I can receive help from America. It seems to me in the nature of a miracle. I shall never be able to thank you all sufficiently." He went on in this letter to explain the nature of his work which is not connected with any church or missionary society or any other organization. His one request was that the form of our association should be as simple as possible. He desires no rigid, impersonal setup, but rather direct personal touch from one individual to another, creating complete spontaneity of interest and spiritual concern for his undertaking.

By 1943 the interest in Schweitzer's work had increased to such an extent in America that a Pacific Coast Branch of the Fellowship was formed in California. This group has raised thousands of dollars for the African work and is stimulating ever-widening interest in that section of the country.

The harpsicordist, Mme. Alice Ehlers, who knew the Schweitzers in Europe has given a number of recitals in the West for the benefit of Lambaréné.

The organists of the United States, through their organization The American Guild of Organists, have done much to further the work. Mr. Edouard Nies-Berger, who as a boy in Strasbourg knew Schweitzer, has taken the lead in this matter and has given many benefit recitals.

From far-off Australia and New Zealand have come inquiries about The Albert Schweitzer Fellowship. They witness the international importance of the Schweitzers in their work of racial reconciliation. The director of the Presbyterian Church of Australia wrote: "It seems an amazing piece of internationalism that your acquaintance with a New Zealand chaplain, now in Italy, led you to write to me in Melbourne from Vermont about affairs in Africa."

On January 14th, 1945, Albert Schweitzer was seventy years old. On that day throughout the United States, musical circles, weekly journals, churches, and other organizations took note of the event. Dr. Schweitzer wrote to the Fellowship:

Your cable of January 14th informing me that you are sending funds has made me very happy. How very grateful I am to all the donors who have made this remittance possible. I also received a cable from Dr. Joy of the Unitarian Service Committee bringing me the best wishes of his committee and also those of the General Council of Congregational Churches and of friends of the Episcopal Church, and informing me that these three groups were cabling gifts for my Hospital. I always draw new energy from the evidences that come to me of the great sympathy for my work.

I had imagined that at the age of sixty-five and onward, I could entrust most of the work at the Hospital to the doctors who would come to Lambaréné to help me, so that I should be able to spend a number of months from time to time in Europe, occupied with completing some books and giving concerts for the Hospital. I even dreamed of some time taking several weeks' vacation. And here comes the war to supervene and change everything. I have known great crises of fatigue during these years, but I have been able to resist the debilitating climate and to keep going all day long.

The Christian Century, February 14th, 1945, commenting upon Schweitzer's seventieth birthday, says: "We hope he is given strength to complete his book, a volume of philosophy. What man is in a better position than he to appraise our fratricidal civilization and to urge it to return to that reverence for life which has been his own guiding principle. . . . We have no way of knowing what he did on that day but probably it was nothing markedly different from what he did on the eleven thousand other days which have passed since he built his Hospital there thirty years ago."

Dr. Schweitzer answered the surmise as to his doings on his birthday in a letter to the editor: "Alas, for the work I have to do, I should be thirty years old not seventy. . . . You wonder how I spent that day. It was a Sunday and I had even more to do than ordinarily. In the afternoon my colleague and I operated a case of strangulated hernia which had arrived that morning. I had several heart cases that worried me greatly. Moreover, the heat was excessive even for people accustomed to the torrid zone."

The seventieth birthday was also celebrated in London. The British correspondent to *The Christian Century*, the late Edward Shillito, wrote in the issue for February, 21st,

1945: "No Friendlier or more unaffected visitor has ever come to this country. Everywhere he is reverenced. . . . In a broadcast, it was pleasantly remembered how, when the chairman at one of his lectures asked him how he should be introduced, Schweitzer replied; 'Just say, this fellow who looks like a Scottish collie is Albert Schweitzer.' It was also recalled that, when he first played the organ in Westminster Abbey, a long queue of Londoners awaited patiently the hour when the doors were opened. . . . Dr. Micklem of Oxford dwelt in a radio talk on Schweitzer's eschatological interpretation of Jesus in terms of his own age, and not as if he were a child of our age, as previous interpreters of Jesus had done."

Since the war, several Americans have visited Dr. Schweitzer at his Hospital in Africa. Dr. Emory Ross, of the Foreign Missions Conference, who is the secretary-treasurer of The Albert Schweitzer Fellowship in America, and his wife were at Lambaréné in August, 1946. Here are excerpts from their diary:

This is one of the moments in life when I long for the pen of the most gifted muse to describe the experience that has been ours in visiting the famous mission hospital of the more famous Dr. Albert Schweitzer.

We arrived after dark, about 7.30. In the blackness of the night our faithful African crew got us out of the launch. Across the sand we ploughed for what seemed a long way; up some rough stone steps, up and up, by our flashlights. Then into the black forest. But some lights began to flicker here and there, and suddenly we were outside windows. Inside we saw a long room, with a long table spread, and folks around it. There were three or four kerosene lamps along the length of the table.

Just as we glimpsed this scene, they heard us and began getting up from the table. By the time we got around to the door Dr. Schweitzer was on the steps to greet us, and behind him Mrs. Schweitzer. Thus it was that we met this man whom we have always considered great, but whose true greatness was to grow and impress itself upon us in the few days we were privileged to spend in his presence, and in the presence of the work which he has hewn out of one of Africa's most jungled forests. . . .

At 7.30 the bell rang for breakfast, and we came out into the strange world which darkness had covered, as we came into it the night before. And what a world! Those who know French and German houses and farmyards will get the picture. . . . Under the house and around it, is a veritable menagerie: chickens, geese, turkeys, cats, dogs, goats, antelope, birds, etc. A pelican is a faithful devotee and, although Mrs. Schweitzer insists on its going off to sleep, still it comes back daily to mingle with the congregation of birds and beasts which have gathered around Dr. Schweitzer. . . . He is truly another St. Francis of Assisi. . . . Nights, as he writes on his philosophy, a yellow and white cat which he saved as a kitten, curls up around his lamp. As he talked to us of Karl Barth and other philosophers, he would occasionally stroke the cat's head tenderly and speak to it or of it. His tenderness and his great love of fun were a part of his character which I had not known. At meal time he kept the whole table laughing at joke after joke which he told.

The Hospital is not exactly a New York hospital. Dr. Schweitzer believes in keeping things, as much as possible, on a level with the culture of the people. Yet with all its crudeness it has a wonderful record both for quantity and quality of work. Africans and Europeans alike swear by it and flock to it for hundreds of miles around. . . . There are scores of Africans with all sorts of maladies. I went down among them with the Doctor one day. It was lovely to see his tenderness, his concern, his closeness to them in spirit.

In the summer of 1947, Dr. Charles R. Joy and Mr. Melvin Arnold flew to Africa to interview Schweitzer and to take pictures of the Hospital for a forthcoming book, part of a publishing project undertaken by The Beacon Press and other publishers on both sides of the Atlantic to make Dr. Schweitzer and his work better known in America. These men were no mere visitors; they were taken into the Hospital family and "permitted to share the problems, the anxieties, the hopes, the plans, the dreams of this extraordinary jungle Doctor." They tell how anxious he is to be able to finish the third volume of his *Philosophy of Civilization*:

Late at night, under the flickering light of a kerosene lamp, the Doctor labors at the writing table in his tiny study-office-bedroom. . . . As he finishes chapters, he piles them on the top shelf above his head. Chapters on which he is still working are hung by strings to nails behind him—"the way a hunter hangs up his pheasants," he laughs.

In his first interview on world affairs in more than a decade, Dr. Schweitzer told us: "We must substitute the power of understanding the truth that is really true, for propaganda; [we must substitute] a noble kind of patriotism which aims at ends that are worthy of the whole of mankind, for the patriotism current today; [we must substitute] a humanity with a common civilization, for idolized nationalisms, [we must substitute] a restored faith in the civilized state, for a society which lacks true idealism . . . a faith in the possibility of progress, for a mentality stripped of all true spirituality. These are our tasks."[1]

Albert Schweitzer remained at Lambaréné without vacation for nearly ten years. Mme. Martin reported that when he returned to Günsbach in November, 1948, his friends were much concerned over his extreme weariness. It must be, however, that with some rest at Königsfeld in the mountains of the Black Forest and in Switzerland, where he saw his four grandchildren for the first time, that his strength is coming back to him. He has written that he expects to visit the United States in the summer of 1949.

Schweitzer has had, through the years, many invitations to come to America. To mention just a few of these: Harvard asked him to deliver the Lowell Lectures and later to take part in the Tercentenary Celebration; The Institute of Advanced Studies at Princeton, to come there and complete his "Third Volume"; and many other academic, ecclesiastical and musical bodies, to give lectures and concerts. He has finally accepted an invitation to deliver the memorial address at the celebration of the two hundredth anniversary of Goethe's birth, which will be held in this country at Aspen, Colorado.